J. DAN ROTHWELL
WESTERN WASHINGTON UNIVERSITY

TELLING IT LIKE IT ISN'T

LANGUAGE MISUSE & MALPRACTICE / WHAT WE CAN DO ABOUT IT

A SPECTRUM BOOK

Prentice-Hall, Inc., Englewood Cliffs, New Jersey 07632

Library of Congress Cataloging in Publication Data

Rothwell, J. Dan.
    Telling it like it isn't.

    "A Spectrum Book"
    Bibliography: p.
    Includes index.
    1. Language and languages.   2. General semantics.
I. Title.
P106.R676   415   81-19897
                   AACR2

ISBN 0-13-903161-8

ISBN 0-13-903153-7 {PBK.}

This Spectrum Book can be made available to businesses and organizations at a special discount when ordered in large quantities. For more information, contact: Prentice-Hall, Inc.; General Publishing Division, Special Sales; Englewood Cliffs, New Jersey 07632.

To Karen, Pumpkin, and Cally,
who taught me how to love,
and taught me how to cry!

10 9 8 7 6 5 4 3 2 1

Editorial/production supervision
and interior design by Eric Newman
Manufacturing buyer: Cathie Lenard

PRENTICE-HALL INTERNATIONAL, INC., *London*
PRENTICE-HALL OF AUSTRALIA PTY. LIMITED, *Sydney*
PRENTICE-HALL OF CANADA, LTD., *Toronto*
PRENTICE-HALL OF INDIA PRIVATE LIMITED, *New Delhi*
PRENTICE-HALL OF JAPAN, INC., *Tokyo*
PRENTICE-HALL OF SOUTHEAST ASIA PTE. LTD., *Singapore*
WHITEHALL BOOKS LIMITED, *Wellington, New Zealand*

CONTENTS

PREFACE

When people ask me, "What's your book about?" I'm somewhat uncertain how I should answer. I'm uncertain not because I don't know what it's about, but because it doesn't package neatly into a one- or two-sentence description.

For instance, I've tried responding to the inquiry with "Oh, it's about language misuse and malpractice," which inevitably receives a polite "Oh really?" At that point the subject usually changes to more interesting topics like the weather, or what you had for lunch.

I've tried the grapeshot, rapid-fire approach where I unload a barrage of topics covered in my book, hoping to create excitement. That usually works but the topic chosen most frequently is "verbal taboos." Before I know it my book has been boiled down into a treatise on "dirty words."

Other times I've responded, "Well, it's about how we use language irresponsibly and carelessly and the serious consequences that result from such misuse." This usually produces an editorial on how we are debauching our language by violating grammatical rules. We need to crack down and make people use their language the way it was meant to be used, and so forth.

There is no quick and easy way to describe this book, but let me sketch some of its features for you.

This is a book about how language affects our perception and behavior. It is a book that tries to instill an appreciation for the enormous power of language to shape our world views and influence our actions. It is a book that focuses on numerous sources of language misuse and malpractice and the terribly serious consequences of irresponsible language behavior. And it is a book that examines in some detail what we need to do in order to clean up our language act and begin using language conscientiously.

This is not a book on grammar, although grammar is discussed. It is not a book about linguistics or sociolinguistics, although research and insights from both these fields of inquiry are used. This is also not a book on general semantics, an area of academic pursuit most interested in the influence of language on perception and behavior. I do, however, rely heavily on general semantics' principles of language analysis. General semantics provides the basic approach to language taken in this work.

In essence, this book defies easy description because I have tried to accomplish many things under one cover. First, and probably foremost, I have written this book to appeal to those readers who are bored to tears (as I often am) by ponderous recitations of scientific research with little effort made to spark interest and enthusiasm for the subject matter.

Second, I have included substantial scientific research in this work, nevertheless, because I feel that such research does not have to be dull, and because it is time to go beyond the anecdotal approach of most works written from the general semantics perspective. To these ends, I have tried to blend interesting and relevant research with anecdotes and examples that ignite interest, invite laughter, encourage an appreciation of the subject matter, and arouse anger and a sense of horror at the insensitivity and sheer wrongheadedness of so many charter members of humankind who misuse language.

Third, I have concentrated considerable energy on bringing the general semantics perspective, scientific research, and anecdotal illustrations to bear on significant areas of human concern. This is not a textbook on what language is, but rather it is an interesting (I hope) and exciting work that explores the social consequences of language misuse and malpractice, misuse and malpractice that emanate from an ignorance of how we might use this powerful instrument of communication and human survival, our language, in more constructive and productive ways.

One final note concerning the title of this book: Although it is meant to be "catchy" (some have said "cutesy"), it was chosen primarily for another reason. "Telling it like it isn't" is an underlying theme of this work. What needs to be understood fundamentally is that our perception of the world as reflected and influenced by our language is *not* the way the world *is*, only the way we selectively *perceive* it. The significance of this and the title of this book should become clear when you've finished reading what lies ahead.

Acknowledgments

I would like to thank the many people who helped me complete this book. To Glen Hiemstra, Ron Bergeson, Jack Robert, Darrell Beck, Pete Peterson, Jim Costigan, Dominic La Russo, Karen Patterson, and my anonymous reviewers, I say thank you for all your constructive criticisms. Some of you saved me from embarrassment. Lynne Lumsden, my editor at Spectrum Books, deserves a special tribute for sticking with me even after a bad false start. To my typists, Margaret Patoine and Ellen Faith, and all those lovely folks at the Bureau for Faculty Research at Western Washington University, I say thank you for performing a thankless task with such great efficiency and good humor. You preserved my sense of humor. To family, friends, and colleagues who were so supportive during this very lengthy project, I offer a special thanks.

Excerpts from "Perrier water is in good taste, but does it taste good?" *The Herald,* August 19, 1980, p. 8A, used by permission of *The Herald* (Bellingham, Washington).

Quotation from B.L. Whorf from *Language, Thought and Reality* by Benjamin Lee Whorf, edited by John B. Carroll (MIT Press, copyright 1956 by the Massachusetts Institute of Technology), reprinted by permission of the MIT Press.

Quotation by Edward Sapir from D.G. Mandelbaum (ed.), *Selected Writings of Edward Sapir,* used by permission of University of California Press, 1949, p. 162.

Quotation from C. Kluckholn, *Mirror for Man,* 1949, pp. 154–155, used by permission of McGraw-Hill Publishing Co.

Quotation from Jean-Paul Sartre, *Being and Nothingness* (New York: Philosophical Library, 1956), used by permission of the Philosophical Library, Inc. © Editions Gallimard 1943.

Excerpt from [the Canadian] *Criminal Law Quarterly.* Pomerantz, H., and Breslin, S., "Judicial Humour—Construction of a Statute." *Criminal Law Quarterly,* 1965, *8,* 137–139. Used by permission of Canadian Law Book Co. Ltd.

Quotation by E. Goffman from *Stigma: Notes on the Management of Spoiled Identity,* 1963, p. 5. Used by permission of Prentice-Hall, Inc.

Quotation from Charles E. Silberman, *Crisis in the Classroom: The Remaking of American Education,* 1970, used by permission of Random House, Inc.

Quotations from James A. Michener, *Kent State: What Happened and Why,* 1971, used by permission of Random House, Inc.

Quotation from C.M. Turnbull, "Some Observations Regarding the Experiences and Behavior of BaMbuti Pygmies," *American Journal of Psychology,* 1961, *74,* 305, used by permission of the *American Journal of Psychology.*

Quotation from L. Hobbs, *Love and Liberation,* 1970, p. 56, used by permission of McGraw-Hill Publishing Co.

Excerpt from James Herriot. *All Things Bright and Beautiful,* 1973, pp. 261–262 (Bantam edition), used by permission of St. Martin's Press, Inc.

Excerpt from "The New Permanence," *Eugene* [Oregon] *Register-Guard,* August 30, 1975, p. 8A, used by permission of the *Eugene Register-Guard.*

Quotation from Wendell Johnson, *People in Quandaries,* 1946, used by permission of Harper & Row.

Excerpt from N. Postman et al. (eds.), *Language in America,* © 1969, p. 110, used by permission of Bobbs-Merrill.

Quotations by S. Freud, *Totem and Taboo* (J. Strachey, ed. and trans.), 1950, pp. 18 and 32, used by permission of Norton Publishing Co. and Routledge and Kegan Paul Ltd.

Quotation from O. Jesperson, *Language: Its Nature, Development and Origin,* 1922, p. 246, used by permission of Holt, Rinehart & Winston.

Excerpts from "FCC Allowed to Ban Words," *Eugene* [Oregon] *Register-Guard,* July 3, 1978, p. 1A, used by permission of the *Eugene Register-Guard.*

Excerpt from A. Montagu, *The Anatomy of Swearing.* Quoted by Wayland Young in *Eros Denied,* Grove Press, New York, 1964, and used by his permission.

Quotation from D. Walker, *Rights in Conflict,* 1968, p. ix, used by permission from New American Library.

Quotation from D. Wells, *The War Myth,* © 1967, p. 125, used by permission of Bobbs-Merrill.

Quotation from R.J. Lifton, "Existensial Evil." In N. Sanford et al. (eds.), *Sanctions for Evil: Sources of Social Destructiveness,* 1971, p. 42, used by permission of Beacon Press.

Quotation by Richard Goodwin from J.A. Donovan, *Militarism, U.S.A.,* 1970, p. 174, used by permission of Charles Scribner's Sons.

Quotation by Franz Six from H. Bosmajian, *The Language of Oppression,* 1974, p. 21, used by permission of Public Affairs Press.

Quotations by R. Grunberger, *A Social History of the Third Reich,* 1971, p. 330, used by permission of Weidenfeld and Nicholson Publishing Co. and A.D. Peters and Co. Ltd.

Quotation by J. Frank, *Sanity and Survival: Psychological Aspects of War and Peace,* 1967, p. 185, used by permission of Jerome D. Frank.

Quotation from T. Merton from "War and the Crisis of Language" in R. Ginsberg (ed.). *The Critique of War,* 1969, p. 112, used by permission of Regnery Gateway.

Quotation from R. Clarke, *The Science of War and Peace,* 1975, p. 145, used by permission of McGraw-Hill Publishing Co.

Quotation from D.L. Rosenhan, "On Being Sane in Insane Places," *Science,* 1973, *179,* p. 253, used by permission of the American Association for the Advancement of Science and D.L. Rosenhan. © 1973 by the American Association for the Advancement of Science.

Adapted version of Triangle of Meaning from original, which appears in C.K. Ogden and I.A. Richards, *The Meaning of Meaning,* 1923, p. 11, used by permission of Harcourt Brace Jovanovich and Routledge & Kegan Paul Ltd.

Excerpts from A. Montagu, *The Anatomy of Swearing,* 1967, used by permission of Macmillan Publishing Co., Inc., and André Deutsch. Copyright © 1967 by Ashley Montagu.

CHAPTER 1

THE SIGNIFICANCE OF LANGUAGE

Dr. C. Scott Johnson of the Naval Underseas Center once told a conference of shark experts that the standard shark "repellent" issued to the armed services for twenty-five years never really worked, but it gave people a false sense of security because they didn't know it didn't work. ("Antishark," 1976, p. A10). This so-called "repellent" not only didn't repel, it was sometimes eaten by the sharks.

Two English professors in Chicago discovered that most teachers give higher marks to inflated rhetoric than to straightforward, direct language. Three out of four high school teachers and two out of three college professors from a total sample of ninety-nine teachers graded a paper higher when it was loaded with verbosity and pedantic terminology than a paper conveying the same content but written in simple, clear language (Bricklin, 1977, p. 85).

R. H. Bruskin Associates asked people whether they thought various advertising claims were completely true, partly true, or not true at all. Their findings showed that 35 percent thought the vacuous slogan for Coca-Cola, "It's the Real Thing," was completely true, and 29 percent thought it was partly true. Alcoa's hollow slogan, "Today, Aluminum Is Something Else," was deemed completely true by 47 percent of those surveyed and 36 percent thought it was partly true (cited in Preston, 1975, p. 28).

Dr. Hiroshi Shimizu ("Children Labeled," 1978, p. 13C), Director of the Speech and Hearing Clinic at Johns Hopkins Hospital, estimated that as many as one-third of the 5000 institutionalized people in Maryland labeled *retarded, brain damaged,* or *schizophrenic* may simply be deaf instead.

Examples such as these of sloppy and indifferent use of language are noteworthy, not because of their infrequency, but because of their prevalence in our daily verbal discourse.

We have grown complacent about our language usage. We treat language as a passive vehicle of communication, a commonplace means of transmitting the raw material of dialogue, rather than as a dynamic tool necessary to our human survival. Consequently, we assume a nonchalant attitude about our use of language which encourages its misuse.

The facility for language is not the privilege of a few people. We are all born with the potential for language acquisition and unless something quite unusual develops, we all learn language. Its ubiquity, however, makes it ripe for abuse. The uncaring and the irresponsible are capable and free to communicate with words just as those who will use language responsibly and conscientiously are likewise free to do so. As we all suffer the consequences of air and water pollution, so do we all share in the consequences of an overabundance of semantic effluent.

The magnitude of the consequences of sloppy language usage is the subject of this book. I will endeavor to demonstrate that irresponsible and careless use of language can and does produce sometimes humorous, oftentimes terribly serious consequences, not merely to the careless but to the caring as well.

A better understanding of these effects of faulty language practices and some of the sources of this misuse and malpractice can be gained by first exploring why language is significant to human beings, the primary focus of this chapter.

LANGUAGE, PERCEPTION, AND BEHAVIOR
Signal Reaction: Our Verbal Salute

Human beings are symbol-making creatures. Like Dr. Frankenstein, however, whose supercharged creation did a bit of unscheduled meandering and mayhem, we are often victimized by our unthinking, knee-jerk responses to symbols of our own invention. This automatic, unreflective, and usually inappropriate response to symbols is called a *signal reaction.* Pledges, oaths, slogans, ritualized greetings, chants, and buzz words in politics and advertising are a few examples of signal reactions at work. What is called for in each of these instances is not careful analysis and inquiry but rather a hair-trigger response, a Pavlovian conditioned reaction to a verbal stimulus.

Responding to symbols in a signal way is one manifestation of the power of words (symbols) to influence and shape our perception and behavior. A few specific examples of signal reactions to words amplify this point.

Edmund Carpenter (1972) relates an appropriate instance from a *New York Post* news story. On November 30, 1971, five heavily armed thieves robbed a New York bank in broad daylight. Two of the robbers shattered the glass doors of the bank entrance with shotguns. Once inside, the bandits unleashed a fusillade of bullets from automatic weapons, wounding twelve people. One of the bank tellers, Fannie Pandiella, escaped to an upstairs ladies' restroom. She related afterwards that one of the thieves chased her up the stairs, but when she bolted into the ladies' room, he stopped and insisted that she come out. When she refused, he went away.

The reflex response of the holdup man to the word *ladies* on a door was ludicrous but illustrative. He could shoot innocent people, but he could not bring himself to violate that sacred taboo that we learn with toilet training. His behavior was determined by that single word *ladies.*

A vintage segment of the television program "Candid Camera" offers a similar example of signal reactions to words. Two pay telephone booths were placed against a wall, side by side, in a long hallway of a building. A sign was hung on the outside of each phone booth, one reading *Men* and the other *Women.* Even the most casual observer probably would have considered it at least a bit odd if not downright ridiculous that pay phones should be segregated by sex. What could one possibly do in a public phone booth that would necessitate such separation? Nevertheless, in this segment that lasted about five minutes, *no one* violated the sign's implicit instructions. Men always used the "men's" phone booth and women faithfully used only the "women's" pay phone. It became so silly that at one point a man in a long overcoat, apparently in a great hurry, stood in front of a perfectly empty "women's" phone booth despite his evident need to make a phone call. After experiencing considerable frustration, he finally decided to take the plunge and use the "women's" pay phone. Collecting his courage, he surreptitiously crept into the empty but taboo booth. No sooner had he deposited his coin and begun dialing than, as luck would have it, a woman walked up and peered into the phone booth; whereupon the man hit the coin return, opened the door, profusely apologized for his indiscretion, and with great embarrassment ushered the woman into the "women's" phone booth.

Silly? Nonsensical? Ridiculous? Yes, it is, but such behavior is not unlike the way all of us react to words at some time or other, and in far more significant circumstances. In 1967, George Romney was an undeclared candidate for President of the United States. He was, in fact, the leading Republican contender in all the polls for almost a year. Yet in September of that year he responded to a question on his change of heart concerning our involvement in Vietnam with the statement "When I came back from Vietnam, I had just had the greatest brainwashing that anybody can get when you go over to Vietnam." Romney's incautious use of the term *brainwashing* created a firestorm of controversy. Overnight his ratings in national polls dropped precipitously. From front-runner for almost a year he fell to fourth place behind

Rockefeller, Nixon, and Reagan. The Harris Poll showed a loss of 12 percentage points immediately following the "brainwashing" statement. Yet Romney, with some justification, defended himself by asserting that the offending word "woke up the country [caused a signal reaction]. Nobody was paying any attention when I only used words like *snow jobs* ["The Bell Tolls . . ." 1967, p. 27]."

Candidate Jimmy Carter's colossal linguistic blooper, his use of the term *ethnic purity* when attempting to explain his policy on open-housing laws during the 1976 presidential campaign, is another example of signal reactions to words. It did not cost him the presidency, but he spent several mistake-filled days looking for a way out of the suspicion that he was really a closet racist. His clumsy attempts to explain what he meant by *ethnic purity* included such phrases as "the intrusion of alien groups" and "black intrusion," which certainly did not help his cause any. It was not his policy on open housing that created the furor, because that was a fairly common position shared by many liberal Democrats. It was his choice of language used to partly explain the policy, in conjunction with worries that maybe Carter, a Southerner, was only pretending to be antiracist, and the *ethnic purity* slip merely showed his true colors despite months of campaigning and numerous policy statements to the contrary.

A simple little study published in the Bellingham, Washington, newspaper *The Herald* under the headline "Perrier water is in good taste, but does it taste good?" is yet another example of signal reactions to words. A small sample of newspaper editors and reporters, most of them sparkling-mineral-water drinkers, were asked to sample seven brands of mineral water without knowing which brand they were tasting. They were asked to rate each water for taste, then rate each of the brand names according to degree of comfort when ordering each brand in public. The results were startling. Perrier was the top "prestige" choice receiving an average score of 1.5 on a scale from 1 (high score) to 4 (low score). Yet it ranked fifth on the blind taste test. One subject, a self-proclaimed fancier of Perrier, wrote prior to the test, "I get a natural high on Perrier with a dash of lime—adding Scotch seems superfluous [p. 8A]." She then rated Perrier a 4 on flavor and aftertaste and wrote a disdainful "Yucch" and "Salty, like Alka-Seltzer" across her questionnaire. The word (label) alters our perception of the thing (product). If it's *Perrier* it must taste good. It is an automatic reaction to a symbol of our own invention.

While signal reactions to words are usually inappropriate, there are a very few instances where a signal reaction is an appropriate response to a verbal stimulus. When you are about to have your head caved in by a low-lying tree branch, the warning "Duck!" merits instantaneous reaction, not casual reflection. Such instances, however, represent the exception not the rule. More often than not we would profit from a more reflective, less automatic reaction to verbal stimuli.

The several examples cited thus far of signal reactions to words merely illustrate the point that language is significant because it influences our perception and behavior. The enormous power of language will become more obvious as we explore in subsequent chapters specific effects of language used carelessly and irresponsibly.

Sapir-Whorf Hypothesis: Semantic Incarceration

Edward Sapir, an anthropologist, and his student Benjamin Whorf created quite a stir in the first half of this century when they asserted that we are largely the prisoners of our own language. This became known as the Sapir-Whorf hypothesis. In 1929, Sapir stated it in this fashion:

> Human beings do not live in the objective world alone, nor alone in the world of social activity as ordinarily understood, but are very much at the mercy of the particular language which has become the medium of expression for their society. . . . No two languages are ever sufficiently similar to be considered as representing the same social reality. . . . We see and hear and otherwise experience very largely as we do because the language habits of our community predispose certain choices of interpretation [quoted in Mandelbaum, 1949, p. 162].

A bit later, Sapir (1931) argued that meanings are "not so much discovered in experience as imposed upon it, because of the tyrannical hold that linguistic form has upon our orientation in the world [p. 572]."

It was Whorf, however, who refined the hypothesis principally through his study of American Indians. Whorf (1956) concluded that the linguistic system (that is, the grammar) of each language "is itself the shaper of ideas, the program and guide for the individual's mental activity, for his analysis of impressions, for his synthesis of his mental stock in trade [p. 5]."

Evidence to support the Sapir-Whorf hypothesis typically falls into two categories: differences in number of lexical (vocabulary) items and differences in grammar of various languages. The first deals with cultural differences in classifying knowledge and experience.

Cultures vary widely in what they choose to name and in the number of fine distinctions they identify for a specific item or phenomenon. The Eskimo language has no single term for snow but numerous distinct terms for different kinds of snow. The Masai of Africa have seventeen terms for cattle, the Hanunoo of the Philippines distinguish ninety-two kinds of rice. Trobriand Islanders have dozens of terms for yams. Arabic has more than 6000 words for what to most of us in America is your basic hump-backed camel, its parts and equipment, and here in the United States we have dozens of words to distinguish makes and models of automobiles.

While such anecdotal evidence of lexical differences between languages is interesting, it does not prove that speakers of one culture are unable to perceive objects, ideas, or relationships identified by a language in another culture. What it does demonstrate is that camels are important in Arabia, rice is important to the Hanunoo of the Philippines, snow is significant to Eskimos, cattle are significant to the Masai, yams are important to Trobriand Islanders, and automobiles are important to Americans. A speaker of one culture can see numerous distinctions made by speakers of other languages and cultures once they are pointed out.

In fact, the availability of a lexicon can serve as an aid to the recognition and retention of various phenomena. Brown and Lenneberg (1954), Lenneberg (1953, 1957), Lantz and Stefflre (1966), and others have experimentally demonstrated that colors are more unhesitatingly named, recognized, and remembered when a language has readily available labels to designate such colors than are colors which have no such convenient labels available.

Thus, the availability of certain lexical terms that create distinctions enables members of a culture to perceive and remember phenomena more easily than if such linguistic codes did not exist. Identifying a certain configuration of stars as the *Big Dipper* helps us recognize it and remember it for future reference. Absence of such a code would make that group of stars less readily noticeable. The availability of labels to classify knowledge and observations can aid the learning process by assisting us to see what might remain hidden from view because the relationship (classification) had not been pointed out to us by means of a linguistic code.

Some languages allow us to recognize, remember, and communicate more easily certain things because their system of classification is more flexible or suitable for particular purposes. Farb (1973) asserts that German is a more efficient language than French for creating new terms for the human anatomy because it is easier to compound words in German than in French. Several tribes in New Guinea have only two basic color terms, which roughly translate into our *black* and *white*. You obviously would not utilize such a restricted language in discussing what color to paint your kitchen.

Nevertheless, a speech community has available precisely those terms that describe the phenomena of concern to it. Fashion designers, artists, manufacturers of housepaints, and members of the cosmetic industry have a color terminology far more complex than that which is readily available to ordinary speakers of English. The requirements of their trade or profession necessitate a more detailed linguistic code, so one is invented. Likewise, if tribes in New Guinea required a more elaborate color code beyond *black* and *white*, they would create one.

The number of lexical terms for a given phenomenon merely reflects the degree of interest a particular speech community has for that phenomenon. Although the availability of labels can help us perceive and remember such phenomena, the absence of such labels does not prevent us from seeing such things. It merely makes it more difficult to perceive when language labels are not readily available to the speech community.

A second form of proof for the Sapir-Whorf hypothesis concerns differences in grammatical structure of languages. Edmund Glenn (Fishman, 1960), for instance, observed that in English the adjective precedes the noun, whereas in French it comes after the noun. What is *the red wine* in English becomes *le vin rouge* in French. Glenn argues that such a difference reflects differences in the thought pattern of the two cultures. The English use primarily an inductive thought pattern (begin with particulars [that is, adjectives] and build to the more general [that is, nouns]) whereas the French are more deductive (start with the general and from that deduce the specific). Glenn notes that the English legal system is principally inductive, establishing a series of precedents and case law that produces general principles, whereas the French legal system begins with general principles and deduces specific cases.

Whorf's study of Hopi language and culture revealed that the Hopi language possesses no tenses such as European languages do that divide time into past, present, and future. Cultures that employ European languages are traditionally time oriented as reflected by their concern for proper tenses in verbal expression. Time is said to be wasted, saved, lost, gained, even bought and sold. The Hopi culture thinks in terms of events. Plant a seed and the concern is not how long it takes for the seed to become a tree; rather the Hopi concern is that the event of growth follows the event of planting. The order of events, not the time it takes, is important to the Hopi.

Kluckholn (1949) notes that you cannot say, "answer me yes or no" in Chinese because there are no words for yes and no. Chinese is oriented toward *how* and nonexclusive categories; European languages are concerned with *what* and exclusive categories.

Nootka, spoken by inhabitants of Vancouver Island, is very process oriented. Categories of things and events do not exist, so in Nootka one says "a house occurs" or "it houses."

These and many other differences in the grammatical structure of human languages reflect differences in cultures. They do not, however, prove that such differences in language *cause* differences in culture and contrary ways of perceiving the world. As Dale (1972) puts it, "Differences in language prove only that languages differ [p.

207]." The proverbial chicken–egg argument comes to the forefront. Which came first, the grammar or the perception? Does lack of tenses cause disinterest in time or does disinterest in time cause lack of tenses in the language of that culture? Efforts to resolve this issue have revealed little support for the former view (see Dale, 1972). The language of a culture is not the great molder of thought and perception from which there is no escape. We are not prisoners of our language except when we allow our language to do our thinking for us by unreflective, careless, and naïve language practices.

Failure to prove the Sapir-Whorf hypothesis, however, does not compel us to view language in a neutral light. While the lexicon and grammar of a language do not imprison our vision of the cosmos, language can and does have a powerful influence on our perception and behavior. To argue that language has little or no effect on perception and behavior would mean that Hitler's ravings did not move a nation, that propaganda has no influence on attitudes and behavior, that the rhetoric of great orators such as Martin Luther King stirs no emotions and produces no persuasion, that inaccurate labels have no social consequences, and that dehumanizing and racist language is inconsequential.

Language reflects our perception of reality, and in so doing it acts as a conceptual blueprint for organizing our thoughts. These conceptual blueprints that emerge from our description of reality may be muddled, misleading, or inaccurate. As a result, carelessly formulated language blueprints can produce serious social consequences.

Language also influences and shapes our reactions to events, ideas, and people because words woven together to form the fabric of a language carry an emotional baggage as well as a conceptual content, and such affective meanings for words can be subjective and private.

It is too soon to elaborate on these points. Let me simply reiterate that we are not the helpless victims of our language, but we need to become more aware of the ways our language can condition us to see the world when little attention is paid to using language more carefully and precisely. Language can dramatically distort perception and influence behavior, sometimes even when we are cautious and reflective, frequently when we are the opposite.

LANGUAGE AND HUMAN SURVIVAL

Language is significant in a second respect. It is a primary tool of human survival. The human species is rather weak and puny when compared to many other animals. We must survive by our wits. The ability to share understanding of symbols significantly assists us in such an endeavor. A comparison of human language and animal communication, especially with our closest animal relatives, the apes, can provide us a better understanding regarding how language can help or even hinder (if used unwisely) our efforts to survive.

Humans are principally symbol users, although we also use signs, whereas animals are primarily sign users. There are several distinctions between signs and symbols, but there are two that warrant explanation for our purposes. First, both signs and symbols convey meaning and information, but signs have a natural connection to things signified whereas symbols have an arbitrary connection to their referents. Thunder is a sign of rain and the two are naturally related because there is a physical connection between the movement of clouds of water vapor and the consequent thunder. Fever is a sign of illness and the fever also produces a sick feeling in the victim. Fingerprints are a sign of human presence and are used as physical evidence of such in court trials.

This intrinsic relationship between sign and thing signified does not exist between symbol and referent. The bald eagle is our national symbol, yet the choice was arbitrary. Meaning was invested by our Founding Fathers in this magnificent bird, but the Pilgrims did not see the bald eagle for the first time and exclaim, "So that's what this country is." There is not a natural, fixed, and intrinsic relationship between the bald eagle and America. We provide the meaning. After all, the wild turkey roamed America at the time a national symbol was selected. In fact, Ben Franklin preferred the wild turkey to the bald eagle. Considering our near extermination of our national symbol, perhaps Franklin's choice would have been more appropriate (in a symbolic sense, of course).

The cross is a symbol of Christianity—not a natural sign, but the residents of Eugene, Oregon, spent a decade arguing the point in court. A 51-foot cement cross sits atop a hill—called Skinner's Butte—overlooking this picturesque city. In the late 1960s an enormous controversy developed regarding the religious meaning of the cross. Some argued it violated separation of church and state and was insulting to those who were not Christians (presumably, Jews, atheists, and agnostics, although atheists and agnostics were hardly every mentioned). It went all the way to the Oregon Supreme Court, which ruled that the cross must come down. Then the plot thickened. An initiative petition led to a city-wide referendum aimed at declaring the cross a *war memorial*. It passed (better a war memorial than no cross at all). The local American Legion affixed a plaque to the cross designating to the world that this was indeed a war memorial rather than a symbol of Christianity. It worked. The Oregon Supreme Court reversed itself in December 1976. The citizens of Eugene, Oregon, clearly demonstrated that a symbol has no inherent relationship to its referent. The cross can in fact be declared a war memorial, a religious symbol, or simply a rather ugly-looking chunk of cement sitting nakedly upon a hill, conveying no special meaning to anyone.

Language symbols are likewise arbitrarily related to their referents. If they were naturally related to their referents, *white* would not be printed in black type, nor would the word *big* contain fewer letters than the word *small*. *Invisible* would be impossible to read, *oral* could not be written, and *right* could never precede any other words. Condon (1975) points out just how arbitrary the relationship between symbols and referents is when he poses the questions "Where does your *lap* go when you stand up?" and "What happens to your *fist* when you open your hand?" In these instances the referent simply disappears.

Words are not naturally related to their referents anymore than the cross on Skinner's Butte naturally denotes Christianity. The cross controversy does, however, exemplify a second distinction between signs and symbols. Signs are in a one-to-one relationship with their referents while symbols have flexibility of meaning. When a dog wanders into the territory of a cat, the cat will emit a sign of warning in the form of a hiss or snarl (along with appropriate arched back, bared claws, and hair standing out like a bristle brush). The message is unambiguous. No negotiation takes place. It is a straightforward one-to-one message, namely, "Come one step closer and I'll rip your face off." The dog's response is equally unambiguous. The dog can fight or take flight.

When the cross was erroneously treated as a *sign* it was argued that only a single meaning could be attached to it—Christianity. Yet the final outcome showed that a symbol, unlike a sign, can have many meanings and referents.

Language is a symbol system and thus provides us with great flexibility in both message content and potential reactions to a single message. The 500 most frequently used words in the English language have more than 14,000 meanings assigned to them. The linguist Richard Ohmann (1969), with the help of a computer, estimated that it would take 10 trillion years to articulate all the possible combinations of sentences in English using exactly twenty words. Consequently, any twenty-word sentence you utter in your lifetime, unless memorized for some reason, is likely to be unique and spoken for the first time.

Yet this flexibility is a mixed blessing. The flexibility of our language provides us with a rich, creative means of expression, but with flexibility comes ambiguity. A newspaper headline reading "Thief Gets 6 Months in Guitar Case" requires some interpretation on the part of readers.

One word doesn't have simply one meaning. We must, in some cases, choose from dozens of possible meanings. Shades of meaning (connotations) sometimes enter in to confuse the picture, and unintended reactions to words can occur.

One way of eliminating these ambiguities is to treat symbols as signs. This is what has already been termed *signal reactions* to words and several examples were provided. *Ethnic purity* meant that Carter was a racist. It is a simple-minded one-to-one relationship allowing for no alternatives.

When we treat our language symbols as signs, we exhibit behavior that is inappropriate, limiting, and even dangerous. We understand and utilize symbols at a much higher level than any other animal. It is not an advantage about which to gloat and feel superior. It is an advantage that should be exploited for all its potential worth to the human species.

The extent to which we exercise an advantage in symbol comprehension over other life forms can be ascertained by briefly surveying research with primates, especially chimpanzees and gorillas. Chimps and gorillas are generally considered to be intelligent creatures, our closest animal relatives, and the first nonhuman creatures to demonstrate substantial linguistic potential.

In June of 1966, Allen and Beatrice Gardner, psychologists at the University of Nevada, began an intensive program to train a chimpanzee named Washoe to communicate with symbols. Since previous research attempting to teach chimps to speak words had failed rather totally, the Gardners chose the American sign language, a code of arbitrary symbols devised for the deaf. In the first seven months Washoe acquired four reliable signs,* *come-gimme, more, up,* and *sweet.* Within four years Washoe commanded a 160-sign vocabulary (Gardner and Gardner, 1969). In addition, she used as many as twenty-nine signs per day combined in simple phrases and demonstrated an ability to generalize and differentiate. For instance, she used the sign *more* for continued play and additional food and the sign *open* for opening a soda bottle, a door, or a stuck zipper.

Success with Washoe spurred a great interest in chimp research. Soon several chimps were taught methods of communicating with symbols. For instance, David Premack and his associates taught a chimp named Sarah to communicate by constructing sentences with colored chips of plastic placed on a magnetic board, each chip representing some word symbol. Sarah soon began comprehending and constructing simple sentences such as "Sarah insert banana pail" and "Mary give apple Sarah." Further work with Sarah revealed that she also understood relational concepts such as *on* and *under.* Sarah's crowning achievement, however, was the day she set up a series of incomplete sentences and gave her astonished trainer a multiple-choice sentence-completion examination (Premack, 1969, 1970).

Lana, a chimp trained to use a specialized typewriter attached to a computer at the Yerkes Primate Research Center in Georgia, has also manifested surprising linguistic ability. She has learned seventy-five

---

*The term *sign* in this context refers to a precise finger gesture, and although it is called a sign it is closer to a symbol than a sign. These signs are arbitrary inventions of humans. Signs created by humans typically assume symbol functions.

word symbols which appear as geometric configurations on the keyboard, can distinguish between correct and incorrect grammatical sentences, actively requests that her trainers name objects that interest her, performs simple problem-solving by conversing with her trainer, and uses words in novel ways (Rumbough and others, 1973; Fleming, 1974; and Bourne, 1977).

In the meantime, one of the Gardners' graduate students, Roger Fouts, continued Washoe's linguistic development in Oklahoma. Under his tutelage, Washoe made additional advances, specifically in originating novel word combinations for objects (Fleming, 1974). She invented the combination *water bird* for ducks. Since her capture in the first year of her life Washoe had seen another chimp only once, so when she encountered other chimps in her new environment she called them *bugs*. Fouts then taught Washoe the sign for *monkey*, which she used in reference to squirrel monkeys and siamangs, but she concocted another name for a rhesus macaque who threatened her. She called him a "dirty monkey." Prior to this incident with the rhesus macaque, Washoe had used *dirty* to refer only to soiled objects or excrement. Since this encounter, however, she applied it not only to the bellicose macaque, but also to various teachers when they did not comply with her wishes.

Even more astonishing results have been recorded by Francine Patterson (1978) during her lengthy training and study of a gorilla named Koko. Ignoring some previous views among researchers that gorillas are intellectually inferior to chimpanzees, Patterson began teaching Koko American sign language in July 1972 when Koko was barely one year old. After three years of training, Koko was using 184 signs, each one used spontaneously and at least once a day, fifteen days out of a month. By age seven, Koko had a working vocabulary—signs she used regularly and correctly—of 375 signs and had used at some time or other 645 different signs.

Koko also displayed a wide array of linguistic functions. She asked and answered questions. She assigned names to objects, events, and people; for example, she called a young biologist she likes *Foot* and referred to a zebra as a *white tiger,* a Pinocchio doll as *elephant baby,* and a mask as *eye hat.* She also responds to symbols whose referents are not immediately present (Koko had never seen a real alligator but knew the sign for this creature and was petrified by toothy stuffed or rubber facsimiles of alligators) and appeared to know how to lie—an exercise that requires a fairly sophisticated grasp of language abstraction.

An example of apparently telling a lie occurred when Koko was caught chewing on a red crayon. Confronted with the question "You're not eating that crayon, are you?" (which, of course, she was), Koko signed *lip,* and began moving the crayon across her lips as if applying lipstick.

In addition, Koko possesses an impressive lexicon of insults she hurls at those who displease her. Her worst insult is "You dirty bad toilet." She also called her trainer a "toilet dirty devil" during a fit of anger.

More recently, Koko made reference to past and future time sequence. While her trainer poured her a glass of milk, Koko signed, "First pour that. Later Koko drink." Koko has even conversed with her trainer about death, a very abstract, future event. When asked what it means to be dead, Koko replied, "finished" (Hillinger, 1979, p. 11c).

Koko can define objects (an orange is *food, drink*), perceive right and wrong, and understand hundreds of spoken words. In fact, a specially designed keyboard–computer linkup permits Koko to "talk" through a speech synthesizer by pressing buttons that represent words. She can hear a female voice reproducing her messages in vocal form. Thus far, she commands a forty-six-word "spoken" vocabulary. It seems reasonable to assume that Koko, who is an adolescent at this writing, will expand this "spoken" vocabulary and probably demonstrate additional linguistic ability once thought to be an exclusive characteristic of human beings.

Are apes, then, our linguistic equals? Not really. There are still several important differences between human language and simian antics with semantics.

First, humans have a predisposition for language acquisition. Children learn language because it comes to them naturally as a part of the maturation process. Chimps and gorillas have been force-fed a diet of artificial symbols by human trainers. It is only through human intervention that apes have exhibited their surprising linguistic abilities. Allowed to fend for themselves, it is doubtful that apes would develop their own language system. For one thing, they have not exhibited a language in their natural habitat, and for another, they probably have no pressing need to develop a language. So although they may have the capacity for understanding at least a rudimentary language, they have no apparent need to learn one.

Second, there is a quantitative difference between the demonstrated lexicon of apes and humans. Washoe's 160-sign vocabulary (the largest of any of the chimps'), learned in a four-year period of intensive training, and Koko's working vocabulary of 375 signs and total lexicon of 645 different signs, learned in a six-year period, is hardly comparable to the linguistic development of human children. Lenneberg (1969) notes that the average child begins with an initial vocabulary of two to three words at the age of one, but within *two* years commands about a 1000-word vocabulary. Wood (1976) further notes that a four-year-old may use well over 2000 different words and probably understands many additional words as well. By the time preschoolers are ready to enter the formal educational system the quantity and diversity of their vocabulary is often quite astonishing.

Third, there appears to be a qualitative difference between human language and linguistic abilities of apes. Neither chimps nor gorillas have yet demonstrated an understanding and an ability to generate metaphors, a creative use of language that is fairly abstract. For instance, there is a real difference between drawing a picture, drawing attention, drawing up a contract, drawing a breath of fresh air, and drawing for an inside straight. In addition, the clever apes have not exhibited an ability to use puns, a very sophisticated language exercise, although their appreciation of a joke (usually their own) and their impish sense of humor is well demonstrated. Nor have they exhibited an appreciation and understanding of irony.

In all fairness, however, we can no longer rule out the possibility that such abilities may exist among apes simply because we have not observed them. We once confidently asserted that humans were the only life form capable of using language. Where once certainty existed, doubt now prevails. It may only be a matter of time before differences in linguistic abilities of humans and apes are shown to be a matter of degree rather than kind.

Finally, there is a self-reflexive aspect to human language. We use words to refer to objects, events, and relations in the world, but we also use words about words. De Vito (1970) argues that unless language can make reference to itself via metalanguage—language used for talking about and analyzing language—it is not really language but simply a medium of communication. Self-reflexiveness means we use language to discuss language.

In essence, that is what this book does. Our language also permits us to discuss and evaluate the communication system of other living creatures as I have just done. Chimps and gorillas have not yet manifested self-reflexive use of words by questioning such things as the appropriateness of grammatical rules and syntax or evaluating the symbol system imposed on them by human trainers.

Comparisons like these between human language and animal linguistic abilities provide a sharper picture regarding what language is and what it allows us to do. In this light, De Vito (1970) defines human language as "a potentially self-reflexive, structured system of symbols that catalog the objects, events, and relations in the world [p. 7]." Its self-reflexive nature allows us to correct problems in the language system and learn to use it flexibly. It is a *structured system* of symbols that permits a sharing of messages, rather than a random conglomeration of words. Words gain meaning and become useful tools of communication because we agree to their meaning. This does not contradict a previous statement, however, that symbols are arbitrary. Word origin (that is, what we initially choose to call something) is arbitrary because there is no inherent connection between symbol and referent, but word usage is conventional (that is, agreed to and shared by others). Once conventionality has been established concerning the association of a word and its referent, it has utility only if that understanding continues to be shared. Gibberish is composed of words strung together in an *unconventional,* random fashion which prevents the sharing of meaning with others. And lastly, the fact that we can catalog objects, events, and relations in the world allows us to generalize, to abstract at very high levels. This cataloguing process can influence our perceptions of the world as well as reflect world views.

The limits of our imagination are the limits of language. Without language we would learn at the rudimentary level of most other animals, and while some may be content to operate at the level of your garden variety slug, the fact of the matter is that our species has survived, progressed, and grown to unparalleled stature because of our ability to communicate with language. In the words of Alfred Korzybski, language allows us to time-bind. Humans can draw upon their past experiences and apply them to the present to make ready for the future. We can share the ideas, inventions, theories, wisdom, and folly of previous generations. We can build upon the accumulated wisdom of centuries of human endeavor to meet present needs and prepare for future necessities. Rather than being doomed to repeat previous mistakes (a not altogether uncommon human failing), we can create superior alternatives. Language used prudently insures our survival and development more certainly than the strongest pair of arms, the sharpest set of teeth, the swiftest pair of legs, the keenest pair of eyes, or the most sensitive set of ears. Language is the key that unlocks the wonders of our minds for all to share.

Conversely, language used imprudently can threaten our very existence. We are probably the only animal on earth that will sometimes fight and even kill each other for the sake of symbols, oftentimes symbols that have no clear referent. When was the last time, for instance, you witnessed your pet dog attack another animal to make his backyard safe for "democracy"? When have you ever seen two cats try to kill each other on "principle" or to demonstrate their "patriotism"? And given their sexual proclivities, what rooster would ever defend the "honor" and "virtue" of any hen? Virtually all other animals kill out of necessity, whereas we frequently kill out of allegiance to ill-defined symbols and call it necessity. History is strewn with the carcasses of fallen "heroes" who killed for often intangible ideologies, beliefs, and religious convictions—in essence, symbols.

At the same time, we can fear phantoms, vampires, bogey men, and monsters, and ignore very palpable threats to survival such as overpopulation, world famine, and the nuclear arms race. Our capacity for foolishness is unsurpassed when language becomes our own worst enemy.

SUMMARY

Language does affect our perception and behavior. Used carelessly and cavalierly it will distort our perceptions and influence behavior in a multitude of ways. The remainder of this book will demonstrate just how significant the problem of language misuse and malpractice really is.

Language also serves as a primary tool of survival. When we respond signally to words, we mimic the monkeys and other animals who rely principally upon signs for their communication and survival. Our capacity for language is a precious gift. It is our birthright, but understanding how to use language intelligently is not developed in the womb. We must work at it diligently. It is a challenge worth pursuing.

C H A P T E R 2

REIFICATION:
Eating the Menu,
Savoring the Feast

We live essentially in two worlds—a verbal world of words and a nonverbal world of objects, events, observable phenomena, and so forth. Words are used to represent (symbolize) the nonverbal world of things, but the words are not the things symbolized. Since words are symbols, not signs, there is no natural, intrinsic connection between a word and its referent. Alfred Korzybski (1933) calls this the nonidentity principle of language.

Korzybski provides a useful analogy to clarify this nonidentity principle. A word is to a thing as a map is to a territory. A map of San Francisco is not the city of San Francisco, but only a representation. A word is similarly only a representation of its referent, not the referent itself.

Mental patients sometimes exhibit difficulty in distinguishing words from things. Some have been known to write words such as *meat* or *potatoes* on slips of paper and proceed to eat them for dinner. Would that it were so simple to concoct duck a l'orange or chocolate mousse. The work of Jean Piaget with the language and thought of children also reveals a confusion of words and things. Young children often assume that objects have certain "correct" names. The *moon* cannot be called the *sun*, for example, because everyone knows the sun rises in the morning and the moon appears at night. A fireplace is called a *fireplace* simply "because it's a fireplace." Some so-called "primitives" manifest a belief that the name of a person is part of that person. Thus, a child is customarily given two names at birth—one known only to the parents, and one for public use. To know their "real name" is to exert power over them.

While we might wish to relegate such foolish confusion of words and things to children, "primitives," and the insane, we cannot. It would seem trite to emphasize such an obvious difference between words and things if it were not for the fact that despite our linguistic sophistication much of our language usage reveals a striking ignorance of this fundamental characteristic of language.

Violations of the nonidentity principle, commonly referred to as *reifications*, are conspicuous by their frequency. A closer examination of reification is warranted, not simply because it occurs often, but also because the consequences of such primitive language usage are serious and should be cause for concern.

Two aspects of our language produce reifications. They are problems associated with the meaning of words and the "is of identity" problem. Each of these will be discussed in turn, followed by an explanation of the consequences of reification.

SOURCES OF REIFICATION
Problems of Meaning

Ogden and Richards (1923) were among the first to diagram the process of meaning. They created a "triangle of meaning," which is similar to the figure shown opposite.

The figure depicts three essential parts to meaning. These parts are the thought process of a person that links the thing symbolized with the symbol. The dotted line between symbol and referent indicates that there is no inherent connection between the two as noted in the last chapter. It is the *person* who connects the symbol with the referent, not Mother Nature. Words have no meaning until we provide it. Meaning is harbored in the minds of people, not anchored in the words themselves.

A friend of mine related a story that aptly illustrates this point. He once worked in a lumber mill while at the same time working on his Master's thesis in journalism at the University of Oregon. One Monday morning my friend was asked by a fellow millworker, who had a limited education, what he had done over the weekend. My friend replied, "I xeroxed my thesis," which elicited the immediate question from the startled millworker, "Geez, did it hurt?" It seems that the millworker, not knowing what a *thesis* was nor familiar with *xeroxing,* thought my friend's comment was a fancy way of saying that he had accidentally castrated himself over the weekend. The meaning of a word resides in a person's head, not in the word itself.

Since symbols and referents are not intrinsically connected, words gain objective meaning when a person determines how the word is used in a specific context. The word *fire* may produce images of flames and a raging inferno, but not if the same word is used as a stern command at an execution—"Fire!" Consider the word *wind.* At first blush you probably thought of a movement of air, perhaps at substantial velocity, yet how inappropriate this obviously becomes when placed

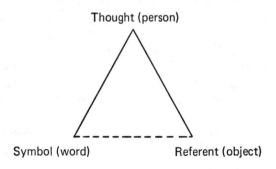

Thought (person)

Symbol (word)   Referent (object)

in the sentence "Wind your watch." *Fire* and *wind* are acts of nature until placed in another context. Then, although they appear to be the same words, the context reveals that they are actually different words with different meanings that are spelled the same. It is the context that allows us to sort out the meaning of a sentence such as "He felt a tear in his eye and a tear in his pants."

When we consult a dictionary, it may seem that meaning is severed from any context, yet a closer inspection reveals that dictionary definitions are compiled by examining the extensive usages (contexts) of each word and providing definitions that reflect such usages. Conflicts regarding the "correct" meaning of a word are often "resolved" by consulting the dictionary. Yet a dictionary is not a sacred document that prescribes "good" usage and decrees the "true" meaning of a word. It is a historical reference book that *describes* the commonly understood meanings for words in a specific language community. A dictionary reports how a word has been used, *not* what meaning a word should have.

The Ogden and Richards triangle of meaning is a useful depiction of basic elements of meaning, but it is not a complete picture. One limitation is that it includes denotative meaning but ignores connotative meaning. Denotative meaning is shared meaning ascribed to a word as a matter of convention that directs our attention to some object, event, condition, or process. Denotations are more clinical and objective than connotations. Connotative meaning is private meaning, subjective in nature, possessing both cognitive and affective components that are influenced by personal experiences, associations, and so forth. Comparing the two, the word *home* denotes the place where one resides but may connote safety, comfort, and privacy (cognitive or thought component) and joy (affective or emotional component).

Berko's (1958) study presents several notable examples of the cognitive component of connotative meaning that clearly shows its private, subjective nature when compared to denotative meaning. When young children were asked to explain the etymology of certain compound words, some of them replied as follows:

"An airplane is called an *'airplane'* because it's a plain thing that goes in the air."

"Breakfast is called '*breakfast*' because you have to eat it fast when you rush to school."

"Friday is a day when you have fried fish."

"A handkerchief is a thing you hold in your hand and you go 'kerchoo' [p. 170]."

Thus, a word acquires a myriad of personal meanings (connotations) in addition to its objective meaning (denotation).

Both kinds of meaning produce problems. Denotative meaning is more objective than connotative meaning, but the referent is not always easily grasped. This happens because the meaning is derived from common agreement and requires similarity of experience in order to be understood since the meaning is not found in nature but rather in people. Take the instance of a nun teaching third grade in a parochial school who attempted to drill the answer to the question "Who is God?" into the heads of her students. She kept repeating "God is a Supreme Being." Finally, she decided to test the fruits of her patient labor and called upon one of the boys in the class. When asked "Who is God?" he promptly and proudly replied, "God is a string bean." The concept of a *supreme being* is so remote from a child's sense experience (an adult's too, for that matter), so abstract, that it has no referent. But since even a child's mind resists a vacuum it makes sense where none exists. When no referent for a word comes to mind despite an objective definition, words are meaningless noises, as a foreign language is to a person who is monolingual.

Cross-cultural communication is also made more difficult because the same word may denote different referents in other cultures speaking the same language. Our *private school* is Britain's *public school;* our *first floor* is their *second floor. Boot* to us is a type of shoe, but to the English it is also the trunk of a car. Likewise, the statement "Keep your pecker up" might shock the fainthearted in America, but in England it merely means the equivalent of our oft-stated expression "Keep your chin up." It is no wonder that George Bernard Shaw reputedly remarked, "Great Britain and America are two countries separated by the same language."

Although the words used by our two cultures are the same, the meaning is often different. That, of course, would not be the case if the words themselves, isolated from their context, had inherent meaning. If problems exist between two similar cultures, it is not difficult to see the dimensions of the problem of translating languages of dissimilar cultures. Linguists have catalogued almost 3000 distinct languages in the world. Trying to translate messages from one language into another, one runs into problems of denotative meaning. Those of us who have labored through a foreign language class in college appreciate the futility of simply looking up each word in a foreign language dictionary. Such translations often produce nonsense or different messages entirely because the meaning of the words resides in the experience of those using the language of their culture, not in the words themselves. Kluckholn (1949) cites two examples of tortured translations probably produced in just such a fashion:

> I asked a Japanese with a fair knowledge of English to translate back from the Japanese that phrase in the new Japanese Constitution that represents our "life, liberty, and the pursuit of happiness." He rendered "license to commit lustful pleasure." English to Russian and Russian back to English transmuted a cablegram "Genevieve suspended for prank" into "Genevieve hanged for juvenile delinquency [pp. 154–155]."

Words, foreign or domestic, gain meaning from their context. Dictionary definitions, although listing meanings based on conventional usage, cannot supply a "correct" meaning for a foreign word, phrase, or sentence separated from its actual usage. It can merely supply a list of possibilities. The interpreter, whose knowledge of the culture may be limited or comprehensive, must choose which meaning is probably intended. Obviously, the less one knows about the culture and its people, the greater will be the difficulties of accurate translation. As Ray Gordon (in Brembeck and Howell, 1976), a sociologist and an expert on Latin America, puts it: "If you know the language but not the culture in a country you visit, you will be able to make a fluent fool of yourself [p. 205]."

In some cases, problems of denotative meaning produced by translations from one language into another may result in far more serious consequences than merely making a fool out of oneself. William

Coughlin (1953) speculates on the basis of some historical evidence that the mistranslation of one Japanese word, *mokusatsu,* may have been at least partly responsible for one of history's most terrifying events. The literal translation of *mokusatsu* is "to kill with silence." Denotatively, this can mean two things to a Japanese: (1) to ignore or (2) to withhold from comment. When Premier Suzuki confronted the press on July 28, 1945, in response to the Potsdam Declaration of the Allies, which demanded the unconditional surrender of the Japanese armed forces at the end of World War II, he announced that the Japanese cabinet was holding to a policy of *mokusatsu.* Testimony after the war from Japanese cabinet officials indicated that Suzuki's intended meaning was "to withhold from comment" until the Allies' ultimatum was communicated to the Japanese government through official channels. To do otherwise would have meant acting upon unofficial, perhaps erroneous information that was transmitted over radio. Japanese translators at the Domei News Agency, however, chose the "ignore" meaning. Thus, the Allies received the message, "The Japanese government *ignores* the demand to surrender." Not only was the denotative meaning erroneous, but the connotations associated with being "ignored" are usually quite negative. The atom bomb was dropped a week later on Hiroshima, killing approximately 70,000 people. Is it not plausible that a signal reaction to this mistranslation played a part in the final decision to unleash history's most awesome weapon?

While problems with denotative meaning are significant, the problems with connotative meanings are far more numerous, and often severe. The word *mother* denotes a female parent but may connote warmth, admiration, loathing, hostility, neutrality, fear, compassion—the list could go on and on depending upon what associations come to mind when the word is heard. Such connotations are largely responsible for signal reactions to words. Osgood, Suci, and Tannenbaum (1957) shed some light on why this is the case. Their research reveals three basic affective elements of meaning. The first is *evaluation.* Evaluation involves a good—bad, valuable–worthless, pleasant–unpleasant, or similar response to words. The second element is *potency.* This includes continuums like strong–weak and hard–soft. The third element is *activity,* which is the response to words on such dimensions as fast–slow and active–passive.

These three elements of meaning and the dimensions they represent correspond to the affective component of connotative meaning. For instance, the denotative meaning of the word *drug* would be a narcotic substance or a substance that is used in medicines that produces physiological alterations. The connotations, however, might be very negative (evaluative dimension), intense (potency dimension), and fast-acting (activity dimension). Such connotations often obscure denotative meanings. When we obscure denotations we experience signal reactions to words (a form of reification) because we turn into our private connotations. Thus, if we hear alcohol called a *drug* we may experience a signal reaction—a response to individual connotative meanings. Likewise, George Romney's *brainwashing* faux pas evoked passionate reaction to connotative meaning and contributed to his political demise.

These affective reactions on the evaluative, potency, and activity dimensions can obscure denotative meaning to the point that the message received is not the message intended. Jimmy Carter's *ethnic purity* gaffe is a case in point. Intended to reassure ethnic communities that his support of open-housing laws to achieve racial integration did not mean wholesale destruction of Polish, Italian, and other strongly ethnic neighborhoods, Carter unintentionally created a furor by his ill-conceived choice of language. He aroused connotations of racism, hatred, revulsion, and the like. He evoked visions of Southern bigotry and Hitlerian genocide in the minds of many voters. The message he intended was not the message received because the connotations were overpowering. Carter's efforts to stipulate what he meant by the phrase *ethnic purity* failed to convince those who would not accept the fact that the poorly chosen phrase did not have an intrinsically racist meaning.

This brief explanation of some of the problems associated with word meaning hardly scratches the surface of a very complex subject. Entire books such as Ogden and Richards's (1923) *The Meaning of Meaning* have been written about it, yet as De Vito (1970) notes, "Meaning . . . is so complex and so little of a substantial nature is known about it that linguists, until recently have all but abandoned its study [p. 11]."

It is not relevant to this work, however, to become heavily involved in the complexities of meaning. Such a discussion can be more fruitfully undertaken elsewhere. Our focus is not on what meaning is but rather what problems associated with denotative and connotative meanings of words arise and what bearing this has upon the nonidentity principle.

In this respect, reification, the confusion of words with things, can result from a failure to appreciate that the denotative meaning of a word is not always shared cross-culturally nor even intraculturally in some instances. Unless we become aware that people determine the meaning of words, and denotations are the product of cultural influences, shared experiences, conventional usages, and the like (that is, their contextual environment), we will fall prey to the illusion that meaning is intrinsic to the word itself and assume meaning is immutable.

Likewise, connotative meaning is too often presumed to be shared meaning when in fact it is private meaning produced by each person's unique experiences and associations with the word. The affective meaning of a word depends upon each person's experience with that which the word represents. While we can "share" our private connotations with others in the sense of telling others what they are, this "sharing" loses in the translation because the personal experiences that call forth the affective reaction are unique to each person and cannot be fully experienced by another. Consequently, a word gains connotative personal meaning based on individual associations attached to the word.

Such connotations, which may be anticipated by others or may produce real surprises (not always happy ones) can cloud denotative meaning, confuse messages, and ignite signal reactions to words. It is yet another affirmation that language is not a neutral medium of communication.

"Is of Identity":
The "Telling It Like It Is" Fallacy

According to Korzybski, the copula *is* as contained in the English language contributes mightily to reification. He calls it the "is of identity" problem.

Whenever we say something *is* such and such we create the illusion that we have identified reality rather than merely described our *perception* of reality. Language should reflect a *close approximation* of reality but it can never be the reality itself.

This "is of identity" problem is more clearly explained in a story of three baseball umpires discussing their profession. The first umpire says, "Some are balls and some are strikes, and I call them as they are." The second replies, "Some's balls and some's strikes, and I call 'em as I see 'em." The third thinks about it, then says, "Some's balls and some's strikes, but they ain't nothing 'till I calls 'em!"

The first umpire is guilty of the "is of identity" problem. *Balls* and *strikes* assume an identity simply by declaring them to be such. The label is assumed to be an *identification* of reality. The second umpire espouses the principle of nonidentity. What the umpire calls *balls* and *strikes* is not reality, but rather one person's *perception* of reality. Words are not the things themselves. The third umpire, however, manifests the social consequences of treating words as things. Those who put labels on the things exercise power because language labels are not inconsequential.

A paradox of language is contained in Korzybski's oft-quoted dictum "Whatever you say it is, it is not." Whenever you label, classify, and describe, you distort. A study by Carmichael, Hogan, and Walter (1932), later replicated by Herman, Lawless, and Marshall (1957), demonstrated this very point that whatever we label it, it is not. Ambiguous figures, such as

were presented to subjects who were instructed that they would have to reproduce them as accurately as possible at a later time. One group was given the description "curtains in a window" for the figure above; another group "diamond in a rectangle." Subjects tended to distort the original figure upon reproduction to conform more closely to the verbal label. For instance, "curtains in a window" often became

and "diamond in a rectangle" became .

The verbal description distorted the reality and influenced the perception of the figure.

A study by Kelley (1950) at the Massachusetts Institute of Technology similarly demonstrates that labeling does not identify essences. Students in economics classes were told that their regular instructor was out of town and a different instructor, one the department faculty were allegedly interested in hiring, would teach the class. A description of the instructor was passed out to the students giving his background in brief. Half the class received this with the following statement included: "People who know him consider him to be a rather cold person, industrious, critical, practical and determined." The other half of the class received exactly the same description except the above sentence had the word *warm* substituted for *cold*. At the end of the instructor's lecture students were asked to rate him on several dimensions. The group receiving the *warm* description tended to rate the instructor as considerate of others, informal, sociable, popular, and humorous. Those receiving the *cold* description, in marked contrast, perceived the instructor as self-centered, formal, unsociable, unpopular, and humorless. In addition, a significantly greater number of students from the *warm* group participated in class discussion than did those from the *cold* group. Every student observed exactly the same lecture but the inclusion of only one word, *warm* or *cold* in the pre-lecture description, significantly altered perceptions of the instructor and even affected behavior.

Korzybski, then, was correct when he said, "Whatever we say it is, it is not" and "Whenever we describe, we distort." When we classify by placing a person, event, phenomenon, and so forth, into a category, we have not identified the substance of reality. Classifications reveal our view of the world, our perception of what reality seems to be, not what exists in nature.

Since the meaning of a word doesn't reside in nature but in us we are free to invent words that have no tangible nor apparent referents. In such a case, the word assumes an existence of its own. It is the ultimate reification. The word becomes a thing unto itself. Consider some examples.

During the Middle Ages, victims of disease were bled because physicians believed bleeding released evil "humors" from the body, thus effecting a cure. The practice persisted for some time despite rather conclusive evidence that this "cure" assisted many to their grave. Evil "humors" correspond to nothing in nature yet it was an article of faith (believed to be fact) that humors existed. The word was reified. A symbol was invented to represent something that did not exist except in the minds of some people. It was a verbal map that represented an illusion, not a territory.

Jean-Paul Sartre (1956), existentialist philosopher, wrote a book entitled *Being and Nothingness*. In it he speaks of "nothingness" as if it were a real entity while at the same time recognizing that it is not. Consider several statements by Sartre. He states that "it is from being that nothingness derives concretely its efficacy [p. 16]." He further explains, "It is in nothingness alone that being can be surpassed [p. 18]." He continues, "We see nothingness making the world iridescent, casting a shimmer over things [p. 23]." Finally, we see Sartre strangled by his own reification of *nothingness*.

> The Being by which Nothingness arrives in the world must nihilate Nothingness in its Being, and even so it still runs the risk of establishing Nothingness as a transcendent in the very heart of immanence unless it nihilates Nothingness in its being in connection with its own being [p. 23].

Sartre becomes entangled in his own rhetoric because he has reified the word *nothingness*. He has created what amounts to a mirage for his verbal map. Whatever Sartre says nothingness is, it is not.

The "is of identity" problem, along with problems of meaning, fosters reification, treating words as things. The social consequences of reification are ubiquitous and oftentimes alarming. In the ensuing section of this chapter some of the most significant general consequences of reification will be isolated and briefly explained. Later chapters will amplify these consequences, painting a picture which I will merely sketch at this juncture.

CONSEQUENCES OF REIFICATION
Mislabeling: Our Inaccurate Verbal Maps

To "natural food" enthusiasts and increasingly to the general public, the word *organic* assumes a special meaning. It denotes a type of food that is not subjected to pesticides, chemical or synthetic fertilizers, and preservatives. What often passes as "organic," however, would make "health food" lovers choke on their granola. *Consumer Reports,* in an article entitled "Organic Foods: Merchandising Health" (1980), reveals some startling evidence that food labeled "organic" often has levels of pesticide residue equal to or in excess of food not so labeled. Agriscience Laboratories analyzed twenty-eight samples of "organic" fruits and vegetables from health-food stores and fourteen "nonorganic" samples from supermarkets. Tests revealed no difference overall in the level of pesticides present in the supermarket and "organic" produce. Moreover, only two of the total forty-two samples tested were free of pesticide residue and one of these was from a supermarket. In other laboratory tests, "organic" lettuce was found to have pesticide residues, in some cases in higher concentrations than supermarket lettuce, and some "organic" foods tested in Florida were contaminated with PCB's, a dangerous class of chemicals.

A 1978 study by the House Subcommittee on Oversight and Investigations notes that some pesticides registered for agricultural use in the U.S. have been linked to cancer, birth defects, genetic mutations, and reproductive disorders. Many other pesticides have not been adequately tested for safety. Increasingly, the American consumer is worried about the possible deleterious effects from pesticides and chemicals. More and more people are purchasing "organic" foods, sometimes paying double the price of "nonorganic" foods. Yet if the label *organic* communicates a message that is in reality a sham, then we are misled by a verbal map that purports to represent a territory which it does not.

Our classifications, our labels, provide maps that guide our thinking and behavior. Much as a map of New York City will lead us astray in San Francisco, so also will a verbal map applied to the wrong territory lead our thinking astray. If our verbal maps are inaccurately applied to territories that do not correspond to our maps we produce confusion, misunderstanding, or in some cases far more serious social consequences.

In our system of jurisprudence, our verbal maps are meticulously drawn and are meant to be applied precisely. If the verbal map *murder,* for instance, were applied to a person who does not fit the precise meaning society ascribes by law to such a verbal map, it would be an outrageous injustice. A trial is an elaborate method for accurately labeling an individual accused of antisocial behavior. Safeguards are built in to protect the individual from mislabeling and the consequences that result.

We are not nearly so careful in our nonjudicial labeling practices. A prime example is the almost casual attribution of *senility* to older people who manifest a variety of symptoms commonly believed to result from a declining brain function brought about by old age. *Senility*, however, is a garbage label, not a medical diagnosis. Tenenbaum (1979) observes that what is usually called senility is now more accurately termed *pseudosenility*. The reason is most people mistakenly believe symptoms of memory loss and forgetfulness, difficulty in attention and concentration, and decline in general intellectual acuity is part of an irreversible organic brain disease called senile dementia. In actuality, much if not most of what physicians and laypeople alike call *senility* is caused by *reversible* viral infections, reactions to medication, depression, malnutrition, anemia, or dehydration, among other things (Galton, 1979).

Thus, there is accurate and inaccurate labeling, but it is important to note that such accuracy or inaccuracy is not derived from nature. It is derived instead from social convention. Search as you may, nowhere in nature will you find the answer to the question "Is bombing civilians in wartime an act of murder?" Nor will you be able to determine from nature the right answer to the question "Does the act of rape include husbands and wives?"

Verbal maps used accurately are those labels which reflect social agreement. If we agree that the word *murder* refers only to *illegal* killing, then acts of war are not appropriate territories for such a classification. When we argue that bombing civilians in war *is* "murder" we are reifying, falling victim to the "is of identity" problem. Such an act is not "murder" until we agree to label it so. "Murder" is not inherent in the act itself; it is socially defined. If we as a society wish to expand the territory covered by the verbal map *murder* by outlawing such acts of war as bombing civilians, we are free to do so and no one can logically claim, "It can't be called murder."

The same is true of the classification *rape*. In most states a husband cannot be legally guilty of raping his wife. The marriage contract serves as a legal consent form for the husband to have sex with his wife, even if she does not desire it. Arguing that husbands who force their wives to have sexual intercourse with them is "really" an act of rape reifies the word. It is not *really* rape. We as a society can and I think should agree to include such an act as part of the territory reflected in the verbal map *rape*, but such a social agreement is not inherent in the word, nor mandated by nature.

In some cases we won't agree which verbal map should be used to represent a territory. Is a person who terrorizes women and children and commits acts of sabotage a *terrorist* or a *freedom fighter*? It depends on which side of the conflict you happen to favor. Those who are victimized will call such a person a *terrorist* and those who see it as a means of gaining freedom from an oppressor will label the person a *freedom fighter*. Who is right cannot be determined by examining the act. Once the world community agrees that anyone who intentionally spreads mayhem and suffering by indiscriminate acts of violence no matter what the ends shall be labeled a *terrorist*, then the term will have objective meaning and can be applied with accuracy. Without such international agreement, however, *terrorist* and *freedom fighter* will be verbal maps that incite signal reactions and confuse rather than illuminate our vision.

Ultimately, verbal maps that provide no consistent picture of what they represent will distort, mislead, confuse, and can lead to suffering and even death. Such fields as law, medicine, education, even government are realizing the importance of accurate labeling practices and the seriousness of mislabeling. Words used as labels and classifications can mean whatever we decide they will mean, but once social agreement has been reached concerning a word's meaning, applying the word to a new territory will confuse and distort until the new meaning is agreed upon.

A satirical piece by Pomerantz and Breslin (1965) that appeared in the *Canadian Criminal Law Quarterly* shows in an amusing way the difficulties that can befall us when we begin straying from agreed upon meanings for classifications. It also demonstrates via tongue-in-cheek that what we choose to call something is a matter of convention, in this case legal convention.

Judicial Humor—Construction of a Statute
(IN THE SUPREME COURT)
REGINA v. OJIBWAY

Blue, J.   August, 1965

Blue, J.:—This is an appeal by the Crown by way of a stated case from a decision of the magistrate acquitting the accused of a charge under the Small Birds Act, R.S.O., 1960, C. 724, s. 2. The facts are not in dispute. Fred Ojibway, an Indian, was riding his pony through Queen's Park on January 2, 1965. Being impoverished, and having been forced to pledge his saddle, he substituted a downy pillow in lieu of the said saddle. On this particular day the accused's misfortune was further heightened by the circumstance of his pony breaking its right foreleg. In accord with Indian custom, the accused then shot the pony to relieve it of its awkwardness.

The accused was then charged with having breached the Small Birds Act, s. 2 of which states:

> 2. Anyone maiming, injuring or killing small birds is
> guilty of an offence and subject to a fine not in excess
> of two hundred dollars.

The learned magistrate acquitted the accused holding, in fact, that he had killed his horse and not a small bird. With respect, I cannot agree.

In light of the definition section my course is quite clear. Section 1 defines "bird" as a "two-legged animal covered with feathers." There can be no doubt that this case is covered by this section.

Counsel for the accused made several ingenious arguments to which, in fairness, I must address myself. He submitted that the evidence of the expert clearly concluded that the animal in question was a pony and not a bird, but this is not the issue. We are not interested in whether the animal in question is a bird or not in fact, but whether it is one in law. Statutory interpretation has forced many a horse to eat birdseed for the rest of its life.

Counsel also contended that the neighing noise emitted by the animal could not possibly be produced by a bird. With respect, the sounds emitted by an animal are irrelevant to its nature, for a bird is no less a bird because it is silent.

Counsel for the accused also argued that since there was evidence to show accused had ridden the animal, this pointed to the fact that it could not be a bird but was actually a pony. Obviously, this avoids the issue. The issue is not whether the animal was ridden or not, but whether it was shot or not, for to ride a pony or a bird is of no offence at all. I believe counsel now sees his mistake.

Counsel contends that the iron shoes found on the animal decisively disqualify it from being a bird. I must inform counsel, however, that how an animal dresses is of no concern to this court.

Counsel relied on the decision in *Re Chicadee*, where he contends that in similar circumstances the accused was acquitted. However, this is a horse of a different colour. A close reading of that case indicates that the animal in question there was not a small bird, but, in fact, a midget of a much larger species. Therefore, that case is inapplicable to our facts.

Counsel finally submits that the word "small" in the title Small Birds Act refers not to "Birds" but to "Act," making it The Small Act relating to Birds. With respect, counsel did not do his homework very well, for the Large Birds Act, R.S.O. 1960, c. 725, is just as small. If pressed, I need only refer to the Small Loans Act R.S.O. 1960, c. 727 which is twice as large as the Large Birds Act.

It remains then to state my reason for judgment which, simply, is as follows: Different things may take on the same meaning for different purposes. For the purpose of the Small Birds Act, all two-legged, feather-covered animals are birds. This, of course, does not imply that only two-legged animals qualify, for the legislative intent is to make two legs merely the minimum requirement. The statute therefore contemplated multi-legged animals with feathers as well. Counsel submits that having regard to the purpose of the statute only small animals "naturally covered" with feathers could have been contemplated. However, had this been the intention of the legislature, I am certain that the phrase "naturally covered" would have been expressly inserted just as 'Long' was inserted in the Longshoreman's Act.

Therefore, a horse with feathers on its back must be deemed for the purposes of this Act to be a bird, and *a fortiori*, a pony with feathers on its back is a small bird.

Counsel posed the following rhetorical question: If the pillow had been removed prior to the shooting, would the animal still be a bird? To this let me answer rhetorically: Is a bird any less of a bird without its feathers?

[pp. 137–39].

Appeal allowed

When the meanings we attach to classifications become less and less precise, incorporating an increasingly broad territory, distinctions become fuzzy and so does our thinking. As Postman (1976) aptly observes, the word *racist* has been applied to such diverse and disparate groups and individuals that its once narrow meaning has been largely lost. Its meaning has become imprecise because it is a map that points us in many directions at once. It is a term that invites a signal reaction, yet it suggests a broad territory with vague boundaries.

Stigma: Semantic Dehumanization

One of the most serious consequences of reification is the dehumanizing negative evaluations we attach to people when they have been plastered with a damning label. Because we have slapped a label on them, we assume we have identified the essence of this person semantically branded. A prime example is the label *criminal* or *felon*. Steffensmeier and Kramer (1980) show that convicted felons are stigmatized for their criminal behavior. Moreover, this stigma may remain long after formal sanctions have ceased, making exit from a criminal status difficult to achieve. Once labeled a criminal, an individual may be victimized by society's frozen evaluation. The stigma remains despite payment of dues to society because, in the minds of many, once a criminal always a criminal. The label hangs like a millstone around the necks of those trying for a fresh start.

My primary interest, however, is not centered on those who invite stigmatization by their antisocial behavior, although we should be quite concerned that our labeling practices accurately reflect changes individuals make in their attitudes and behavior. My principal concern is stigma that results from libelous labeling practices and prejudice against nonstandard language variations.

I use the phrase *libelous labeling* in a nonlegal sense. The language malpractice I refer to here rarely allows its victims legal recourse. The labels are libelous, however, because they are undeserved, inaccurately applied (note the close connection to mislabeling), yet invite contempt, public ridicule, and an unswerving belief that those wrongfully stigmatized are inferior beings. As Goffman (1963) observes:

> By definition, of course, we believe the person with a stigma is not quite human. On this assumption we exercise varieties of discrimination, through which we effectively, if often unthinkingly, reduce his life chances. We construct a stigma-theory, an ideology to explain his inferiority and account for the danger he represents, sometimes rationalizing an animosity based on other differences, such as those of social class [p. 5].

A study by Swartz and Skolnick (1962) demonstrates one way the stigmatizing label *criminal* can "reduce life chances." Four employment folders were prepared, identical in all respects except for the criminal record of the bogus applicant. One folder showed no criminal record, the second revealed an acquittal on an assault charge with a letter from the judge certifying a "not guilty" verdict and reaffirming the legal presumption of innocence, the third indicated arrest on an assault charge but an innocent verdict in court, and the fourth showed a conviction for assault.

A law student posing as an employment agent presented each folder to twenty-five different employers. Nine employers expressed interest in the applicant who had no criminal record, six gave positive responses to the applicant found innocent of assault who also had an accompanying letter from the judge, only three wanted a closer look at the applicant found innocent of assault with no letter from the judge, and only one employer showed interest in the applicant convicted of assault.

The difference in employment opportunity is quite substantial when comparing the applicant with no criminal record and the applicant with a felony conviction. Perhaps more disturbing, however, is the apparent failure of employers to make much distinction between a convicted felon and a person merely accused of a felony but later acquitted. To be stigmatized for an act you never committed is not only a serious injustice, it is also an apt example of the potency of misapplied labels. It is one thing to be stigmatized for something you did do, quite another to suffer the same fate for merely being accused. While our libelous labeling practices stigmatize undeserving individuals, prejudice against nonstandard language variations also produces significant stigma. As cultures establish norms for appropriate behavior in general, so also do cultures generally create norms for "proper" linguistic behavior. Deviance from cultural norms results in stigma to the person stepping out of bounds. When a person speaks a nonstandard variety of the prevailing language of the culture, that individual will more than likely be stigmatized for speaking "incorrectly."

According to Wolfram and Fasold (1974), Standard American English, the yardstick used to judge "correctness" of language behavior, is the spoken language of the educated middle class. Nonstandard English includes those language variations that are uniformly rejected (stigmatized) by educated speakers in all parts of the country.

Languages and language dialects vary in three ways: (1) in grammar, (2) in sounds, and (3) in vocabulary. Variations in all three are primary sources of stigma.

For generations, English teachers and parents who have been willing accomplices have tyrannized students with their rules of linguistic etiquette. All school children have had certain rules of "correct" grammar and pronunciation drilled into their heads. The guardians of the mother tongue by the sheer power of incessant, mind-numbing repetition and punitive reinforcement have managed to convince most of us that a grammatical construction such as "It ain't nothing" instead of "It isn't anything," and the pronunciation of "these, them, and those" as "dese, dem, and dose," among other examples, debauches the English language. In addition, we are instructed that some words should be stricken from our vocabulary because they are taboo. Deviation from the rules of linguistic etiquette marks you as a misfit, an ignorant boob, a second-class citizen.

Do I exaggerate? Perhaps. Yet there are many people who believe that nonstandard language varieties are inferior to the standard language of a culture. Prescriptive language etiquette is taught to students so they might communicate more intelligently and precisely. Prescriptive rules of standard English, however, assert status, not communicative efficiency and clarity.

Grammar, for instance, is a *description* of the structure of a language as it is actually used. Prescriptive rules for "correct" grammatical constructions are not derived from any inherent qualities of the language. Admonitions against splitting infinitives or ending a sentence with a preposition result from an attempt to impose arbitrary standards of social acceptability. Such rules do not describe how the language actually works. In some cases, rules of "correct" grammar are blatantly absurd. The statement "I ain't got no beer," for example, sends a shudder through the ranks of grammatical purists. The malefactor who utters the offending construction will more than likely be stigmatized as an "illiterate," a "boor," or some equally uncomplimentary attribution. Yet the denotative meaning of this sentence is clear and intelligible. Even purists, clutching their book of rules, cannot fail to understand that, despite the oft-stated rationale that two negatives make a positive, "I ain't got no beer" and "I haven't any beer" denote the same thing. Prescriptive "meanings" that ignore how words are used invest meaning in the words themselves, not in the people using the words. Language does not follow algebraic formulas. Two negatives do not make a positive in language. If you think I am wrong, try insisting that your host bring out the beer forthwith when he says "I ain't got no beer." Don't be surprised if you end up with your face rearranged.

Prescriptive grammar and pronunciation is pretentious nonsense. It reveals an antideluvian mentality, a desire to preserve what once was, not what is. "*Whom* did you call?" may be considered grammatically "correct," but *who* did you ever hear using such a pretentious construction?

Oddly enough, many of these grammatical dinosaurs are skeletons of earlier language corruptions. *Lesser, nearer,* and *more* are corruptions from an earlier time. They are equivalent to saying *gooder* instead of *better*. Even some pronunciations are corruptions that have survived. *Murder* used to be pronounced murther, *burden* was once pronounced burthen, and so on. Even many of our taboo words were once part of standard English vocabulary.

The title of this book, *Telling It Like It Isn't*, violates a rule of prescriptive grammar. *Like* should be *as*. Nevertheless, as far back as the sixteenth century some people used *like* and some used *as*. Around the middle of the nineteenth century, someone decided the use of *as* in such constructions was the mark of a superior person. The tide, however, is clearly turning in favor of *like* rather than *as* (thanks in part to Howard Cosell). No amount of cajoling, berating, and pontificating will stem the flow. Descriptive grammar will merely "tell it like it is," not *as* it *should* be.

The great error which the linguistic Emily Posts of this world make is a belief that those who do not conform to the arbitrary rules of "correct" language speak an inferior language variety. Nonstandard language varieties are not inherently inferior communication codes. As Wolfram and Fasold (1974) explain:

> All language varieties are equally capable of use in reasoning, abstracting, and hypothesizing. Middle-class dialects are no more or less inherently equipped to deal with abstract or logically complex reasoning processes than are lower-class dialects. . . . The social acceptability of a particular language variety is totally unrelated to its adequacy as a communicative code [p. 7].

Whether I say, "Go introduce yourself" or "Go swap howdies" reveals my social class and level of education. Both examples, however, communicate a clear message. Some might even argue that the latter example is remarkably to the point.

It is not unusual for the dominant group in a culture to brand the language of a subordinate group as "inferior." A circular reasoning process is then set in motion. The subordinate group is "inferior" and they use an "inferior language" which in turn is another sign of their intrinsic inferiority to the dominant group. The belief that a subordinate group's language is inferior, however, is linguistic ethnocentrism. The "inferiority" does not reside in the language dialect itself (nonidentity principle). It resides in the minds of those who perceive nonstandard language as not simply different, but rather deficient.

The Black English dialect was for a long time considered a deficient, impoverished version of Standard American English. A black child could say "He sick" or "He be sick" and be ridiculed and reproached for speaking incorrectly. It "proved" that blacks really are "inferior" because obviously they couldn't even master simple English. What most people failed to understand is that the black child spoke a different dialect, one that possessed its own grammar and contained subtle differences in meaning not always easily expressed in Standard English. "He sick" means "He is sick *today*," while "He be sick" describes a continuing or permanent condition. A child using Standard English would only say the less descriptive and imprecise "He is sick."

Consider another difference. A Black English speaker says "Dey ain't like dat," which most Standard English speakers assume means "They aren't like that." Wrong! It actually means "They didn't like that." Black English, Appalachian English, or any other nonstandard dialect is not deficient but merely different.

Does this, then, mean we should adopt a permissive attitude? Should we no longer teach grammar and pronunciation in school? Do we abandon all concern for standard rules and encourage everyone to "do their own thing" so no one is stigmatized because of their choice of language?

First, it isn't a matter of permitting anything. It is a matter of recognizing the inevitability of linguistic diversity. Linguists and English teachers do not control speech in America. Speech is controlled by the masses. One's immediate group exerts primary control over an individual's language choice. The language we speak, whether nonstandard or standard, gives us a group identity. We risk rejection by the group when we speak a "foreign" language. A black man who speaks impeccable Standard American English when visiting with Nonstandard Black English speakers in the ghetto will be seen as an outsider despite the similarity of skin color or appearance. For a child, the schoolyard is a more powerful learning environment than the schoolroom. One thunderous sneer from a peer group will do more to "correct" language varieties that do not conform to the norms of one's group than all the harping and homework the teacher can muster.

Language diversity is not only inevitable, it is desirable. If language is to be an effective tool of communication, it must be used flexibly. When we insist that Standard English must be learned at the expense of Nonstandard English, we seek to limit our ability to adapt our own language to the audience and occasion. A truly skilled speaker of any language knows both standard and nonstandard varieties of the culture's language. This allows the speaker, for example, the freedom to meet the necessities of a formal presentation that require conformity to an expectation that standard grammar, pronunciation, and vocabulary be used, while allowing a shift to a more informal, nonstandard language often appropriate in casual social engagements with friends.

No one is a single-style speaker. We all shift styles according to the purpose, occasion, and audience. Some people, however, are capable of more pronounced style-shifting than others. Some individuals so mindlessly and repetitively punctuate their language with verbal obscenities that they become like a twitching muscle—annoying and obtrusive. Other people so steadfastly adhere to impeccably "correct" speech that they make everyone around them uncomfortable because they cannot "relax" their speech and mingle with the "peons."

While nonstandard language is inevitable and desirable, a speaker of Nonstandard English can profit from learning the standard language of the dominant culture. For language to function effectively as a communication code, that code must be *shared*. Unless an individual plans on never leaving the warmth and security of the nest, never venturing outside one's immediate group, understanding and being able to utilize the standard language of the larger culture increases one's choices. It allows greater flexibility in communicating with diverse groups. It improves one's ability to adapt to changing and varied situations in a complex society. It can open up opportunities that might otherwise be closed because the stigma attached to nonstandard speech, whether deserved or not, can markedly influence people's perceptions of a nonstandard speaker.

English teachers cannot stamp out nonstandard speech, and they perform a great disservice when they inaccurately brand nonstandard speech as "inferior." English teachers can perform an important service, however, by helping students appreciate when certain language varieties are appropriate or inappropriate given a specific audience, purpose, and occasion. This would include a discussion of when *Nonstandard* English might be more appropriate than Standard English. They can help students learn Standard English without denigrating nonstandard speech. They can encourage students to broaden their linguistic horizons and they can provide the guidance for such an endeavor.

This stigmatizing effect of language will be considered in greater detail later. What is worth noting here is that choices we make concerning our language style and the judgmental labels we employ are not inconsequential decisions. People can be dehumanized, discriminated against, degraded and humiliated by the way they use language and the connotations we concoct regarding how others use their language. In each case discussed here, the violation of the nonidentity principle which several pages back probably appeared trivial and self-evident, is the source of the stigma. Some stigma is an outgrowth of behavior that deserves our contempt, but violation of the nonidentity principle provides no such comforting excuse for stigmatizing others. It reveals linguistic naïveté that produces punitive results.

Self-Fulfilling Prophecy: Believing Is Perceiving

Thomas Merton (1948) coined the term "self-fulfilling prophecy" which has become the focus of numerous studies. In essence, a self-fulfilling prophecy is a behavior that is produced by an expectation or prediction of that behavior's occurrence. Silberman (1970) describes self-fulfilling prophecy in action with the following vignette:

> Three children are in a special class—children with perceptual problems. The teacher insists on talking with the visitor about the children in their presence, as though congenital deafness were part of this difficulty. "Now, watch, I'm giving them papers to see if they can spot the ovals, but you'll see that this one"—he nods in the direction of a little boy—"isn't going to be able to do it." A few seconds later, he says triumphantly, "See, I told you he couldn't. Now, I'll put something on the overhead projector, and this one"—this time, a nod toward a little girl—"won't stay with it for more than a line." Five seconds later, with evident disappointment: "Well, that's the first time she ever did that. But keep watching. By the next line, she'll have flubbed it." The child gets the next one right, too, and the teacher's disappointment mounts. "This is unusual, but just stick around . . ." Sure enough, the child goofs at line five. "See, I told you so [pp. 139–40]."

Prediction of failure created a climate conducive to the actualizing of the prophecy of failure.

The classic study on self-fulfilling prophecy by Rosenthal and Jacobsen (1968) reveals the influence of language labels in contributing to this process. In the spring of 1964, children in the lower grades of Oak School on the West Coast were given a test which purported to predict academic "spurters" or intellectual growth. Actually it was simply a new I.Q. test unfamiliar to the teachers at the school. The experimenters randomly chose 20 percent of the children, some who scored high on the I.Q. test and some who scored low. Teachers at the school were told that the results of the test revealed that these random 20 percent were the "spurters" and could be expected to make unusual intellectual gains in the coming year.

The label *spurter* assumed a life of its own when applied to the random group of children so designated. This 20 percent actually did spurt intellectually; in some cases dramatic increases of 25 I.Q. points were noted. Teachers evaluated these "spurters" very favorably, considering them happier, more curious, and more interesting than the other 80 percent of the children.

Teachers treated children labeled as *spurters* differently from those not so labeled. They did not spend more time with the achievers but subtle communication cues apparently indicated an expectation of achievement. Facial expressions, gestures, posture, and amount of praise, probably contributed to the results. Ultimately, a fictitious label was treated as fact and the prophecy consequently became a reality.

Such an effect may seem beneficial to those students who were not really high achievers but became such because of teacher expectations. The flip side paints a less rosy picture. Those who were not included in the preferred group did not manifest intellectual gains equivalent to those accorded higher expectations.

Although Rosenthal and Jacobsen's study has been criticized on methodological grounds (Thorndike, 1968), subsequent studies have presented convincing evidence of the power and scope of the self-fulfilling prophecy. Brophy and Good (1970) found that teachers demanded better performance from those children viewed as high achievers and were more likely to praise performance commensurate with the expectation. Conversely, they tended to accept poor performance from students for whom expectations were low and infrequently praised good performance from this group. Additional research reveals a self-fulfilling prophecy produced by labeling in many areas. Haskett (1969) found such an effect produced by teachers' expectations of achievement potential among 267 educable "mentally retarded" adolescent students. Rosenhan (1973) noted a self-fulfilling prophecy resulting from mental illness labels. Friedmann and others (1980) found similar results. Gold and Williams (1969) and Gold (1970) also discovered a similar effect in relation to *delinquency* labels and recidivism.

Labels do not identify essences, but they can produce behavior that seems to suggest real intimacy between word and thing. Not all labels produce self-fulfilling prophecies. When connotations associated with certain labels are highly evaluative, potent, and active in the minds of people, however, a self-fulfilling prophecy can occur. Saying something is so can bring it about, not because words are magic, but because we sometimes treat words with almost mystic reverence. We should respect the power and potency of language, not worship labels of our own creation. When language labels create behavior that did not previously exist, the potential for good and ill is enormous. The probability that good will triumph over its opposite, however, seems fairly haphazard.

Affects Self-Esteem

A close relative of the self-fulfilling prophecy and stigma effects of language is the effect of labels on self-esteem. Stigmatizing labels can produce low self-concepts while labels with positive connotations can bolster a person's self-esteem. Studies by Edgerton (1967) and Jones (1970, 1972) reveal low self-concept among individuals labeled *mentally retarded.* Perhaps the most revealing experiment on this subject, however, was conducted by a third-grade school teacher, Jane Elliott, in Riceville, Iowa (Zimbardo and Ruch, [1977], pp. 13A–13D). In an attempt to sensitize her students of this all-white, rural community to the devastating consequences of discrimination and prejudice, she abruptly announced to her class one day that brown-eyed people were more intelligent and better people than blue-eyed people. Blue-eyed children were labeled *inferior* and brown-eyed children were accorded the privileges of the "ruling class" befitting their label. Almost immediately blue-eyed children (who were in the majority) lost self-esteem. Words they chose to describe themselves (after taking a spelling test and selecting the most appropriate) were: *sad, bad, stupid, dull, awful, hard,* and *mean.* Brown-eyed children used terms such as *happy, good, sweet,* and *nice.* Individual responses are quite revealing. The *inferior* group said things such as, "You don't want to even try to do anything," and "I felt like a dog on a leash," or "I felt like you were jailed in a prison and they threw the key away." The *superior* group made statements such as, "I felt like a king" and "I ruled them like I was better than them, I was happier." Power is a heady brew.

The following day, the teacher reversed the process to show the arbitrariness of prejudice. Blue-eyed children were designated *superior* and brown-eyed children were labeled *inferior. Kings* and *queens* were dethroned and *white trash* were crowned. The self-esteem of the two groups coincided once again with the labels.

Incidentally, a self-fulfilling prophecy was also created. *Inferior* students exhibited depressed academic performance during the course of the experiment and *superior* students exhibited enhanced academic performance. Behavior of students reflected a *superior* or *inferior* self-concept.

Elliott still conducts this experiment in her third-grade classes with similar results. She has also exposed adult groups to the same experiment with comparable findings.

The power of labels to stigmatize, create self-fulfilling prophecies and reduce or enhance self-images is awesome.

SUMMARY

When we treat words as things, it is tantamount to eating the menu rather than the food. Words are not naturally related to their referents anymore than "filet mignon" is intrinsically connected to the piece of dead steer meat lying lifeless on your plate. The violation of this nonidentity principle produces language maps that are inaccurate representations of the territory. In some cases, our labels have no apparent referents at all, but are merely connotations floating around in our heads.

When we violate the nonidentity principle several serious consequences can result. We can mislabel, stigmatize people, create self-fulfilling prophecies, and negatively affect an individual's self-esteem. To use language responsibly, we must seek to base our language labels on an empirically verifiable foundation wherever possible. Until we learn to appreciate the power of language and the importance of using it responsibly, we will continue to produce negative social consequences for those victimized by dangerous language habits.

THE ABSTRACTING PROCESS: Climbing the Tower of Babble

All words are symbols, but all words do not reflect the same level of abstraction. Some are more general and remote from verifiable referents than others. Abstracting is the process of selective perception whereby we ignore a great amount of the characteristics of any stimuli, focusing on only a limited number of such characteristics, which are in turn arranged or ordered into recognizable patterns we call classifications. Such classifications depend upon which characteristics we happen to notice.

When we classify we pay attention to similarities and ignore differences. This book has many differences from other books. The differences might include size, color, typeface, paperback versus hardback, thickness, weight, words on the cover and inside, and so forth, yet it is still classified as a *book* that emphasizes characteristics in common with other objects so identified such as printed pages, a cover, and binding of some sort. When a book is put to different uses, it may be reclassified as a paperweight, a doorstop, a weapon, or an article of trash.

The illustration on the next page depicts a diagram of this selectivity or abstracting process, which is an adaptation of Korzybski's (1933) Structural Differential. The parabola represents the world we live in, the territory. It is an infinitely complex world of rapid and perpetual change with no two things ever exact duplicates. The circles in the parabola depict the characteristics of our world and the dotted line indicates the infinite variety, complexity, and change. Molecules, atoms, electrons, and other phenomena probably undiscovered by science compose our world. We perceive only a small fraction of this vast array of goings on.

The second component of the diagram, sense experience, is depicted by a circle. The progression from the territory to sense experience is the first step of abstracting. It is our contact with our world perceived through our senses. Our sight, hearing, taste, touch, and smell allow us to experience our cosmic territory, but the characteristics we perceive are restricted in number and limited by finite perceptual capacities.

This "reality" we experience is but a glimpse of what lies hidden from us. Sophisticated scientific apparatus like the electron microscope help us see portions of our world normally camouflaged from view by the limited capacity of our senses. This "reality," however, is subjective not objective because even with the aid of science each individual senses the world through a unique filtering system.

For instance, science claims that heat is generated by rapidly-moving molecules and cold is the result of slow-moving molecules. The sensations of hot and cold, however, do not exist in the territory itself. There is no hot and cold until we abstract such sensations by bringing our nervous system in contact with either fast-moving or slow-moving molecules. It is a subjective experience. Arctic water is "freezing" to us but not to the fish who inhabit this undersea world. The attribute of hot and cold does not exist in nature but in our sense experience with nature. If you doubt this, try an experiment suggested as early as 1690 by John Locke. Put your left hand in a bowl of "hot" water, and your

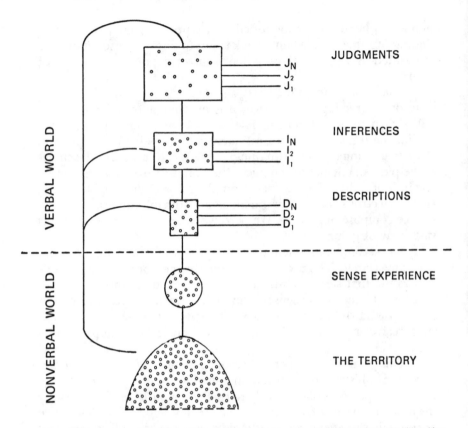

VERBAL WORLD

NONVERBAL WORLD

JUDGMENTS

J_N
J_2
J_1

INFERENCES

I_N
I_2
I_1

DESCRIPTIONS

D_N
D_2
D_1

SENSE EXPERIENCE

THE TERRITORY

This diagram is a modification of Alfred Korzybski's Structural Differential (1933). (Used by permission of the Alfred Korzybski Estate.)

right hand in a bowl of "cold" water for a few minutes. Now put them both in a third bowl filled with "lukewarm" water. If you trust the accuracy of your senses and believe that hot or cold resides in the water itself, then you'll have to explain the paradox of a single bowl of water being both hot and cold at the same time.

While we all have the same senses, assuming nothing dramatic has occurred to rob us of one or more of our perceptual apparatus, we do not all have identical sense experiences. Commonality (similarity of sense experience) exists for sure, otherwise we'd all be colliding into one another. But differences also exist, some so subtle they go un-noticed and some so stark that they cause consternation, incredulity or even ridicule.

The process of selectivity, of sensing certain characteristics of the territory, is influenced by our cultural and personal experiences, our expectations, interests, values, beliefs, emotions, and motives in addition to the quality of our sensory receptors. Consider some examples.

The "picture" you see on a television screen isn't really a picture at all. An illusion of moving figures on a screen is created by the phosphorescent flicker of 300,000 tiny dots. Only some of the dots are lit simultaneously. Those that are on produce the "picture." Our brains collect the sensations and organize them into recognizable patterns. This translation of light energy into images in the brain occurs about ten times per second while the sequential lighting of these tiny dots occurs at thirty times per second. Thus, we aren't "seeing it like it is." The territory is a series of tiny dots of light. Our sense experience tells us there is a "picture" out there.

Similarly, a photograph in a magazine or newspaper is composed of an organized pattern of tiny dots which when magnified become recognizable as dots, but when seen more abstractly are grouped into representations of people or objects. When members of less literate cultures have been shown photographs of themselves, they have not recognized the likeness because they are not accustomed to organizing their sense experience in a way we take for granted. Adults who have been blind all their lives but have suddenly regained vision through cataract surgery or some other means, have enormous difficulty in organizing what they see into recognizable patterns (London, 1960). Even the faces of friends, relatives, and other persons significant to them remain those of strangers for months, sometimes much longer. Senden (1932) cites one example of an exceptionally intelligent patient who could identify only four or five faces by sight two years after an operation restored the patient's vision.

Environment strongly influences our perception of events and objects. An anecdote related by an anthropologist, Colin Turnbull (1961), demonstrates such an effect. A certain tribe of Pygmies live in tropical forests so dense that the natives can rarely see for more than a few yards in any direction. Perceptual judgments are based largely on sound rather than visual cues of distance or depth discrimination. When a Pygmy named Kenge traveled with Turnbull to an unobstructed plain, some interesting perceptual problems developed. Turnbull reports:

> Kenge looked over the plains and down to where a herd of about one hundred buffalo were grazing some miles away. He asked me what kind of *insects* they were, and I told him they were buffalo, twice as big as the forest buffalo known to him. He laughed loudly and told me not to tell such stupid stories, and asked me again what kind of insects they were. He then talked to himself, for want of more intelligent company, and tried to liken the buffalo to the various ants and beetles with which he was familiar.
>
> He was still doing this when we got into the car and drove down to where the animals were grazing. He watched them getting larger and larger, and though he was as courageous as any Pygmy, he moved over and sat close to me and muttered that it was witchcraft. . . . Finally, when he realized that they were real buffalo, he was no longer afraid, but what puzzled him still was why they had been so small, and whether they really had been small and had so suddenly grown larger, or whether it had been some kind of trickery [p. 305].

Kenge saw what he had been trained to see by virtue of his personal experience and interaction with his environment.

In analogous ways we are conditioned to seeing our environment in certain set ways. We learn to expect our environment to look a particular way because our past experience has conditioned us to see in a certain manner. Witkin (1954) performed a group of experiments demonstrating this perceptual set. Subjects were seated in chairs in a room whose walls could be tilted. The perceptual set (expectation) of subjects was that objects and people can move in a room but not the walls themselves, so when they remained stationary and the room tilted the people perceived themselves and other vertical objects as tilted and the tilted walls as unchanged and vertical.

A fun little demonstration that reveals the perceptual set phenomenon can be tried on your friends. Have them spell the word *shop* to themselves. Now ask them to respond immediately to the question "What do you do when you come to a green light?" The vast majority will respond, "*Stop.*" Spelling the word *shop* creates an expectation in our minds. We do not perceive the territory as given but only as expected. Another version of this same demonstration asks the person to spell *joke* and then respond to the question, "What do you call the white of an egg?" You may be surprised at the number who will answer "yolk" even after the first version has victimized them.

The power of perceptual set is dramatically evidenced by experiments testing the "effects" of placebos (for example, sugar pills) on patients when they are led to believe they are taking powerful "drugs." In a study by Brodeur (1965) forty-five pharmacy students took a capsule. Fifteen were told the capsule contained a "stimulant," fifteen that it was a "tranquilizer," and the last group of fifteen were informed the capsule was cornstarch (which all of the capsules were in reality). Generally, 60 percent of the subjects reported feeling the "drug" effects. Even pulse rates were noticeably altered in the appropriate direction.

Beecher (1959) found about one-third of all patients treated with placebos, even for severe pain associated with cancer, experienced positive results. Belief in the efficacy of the doctor's "medicine" alters the perception of pain and suffering. The perceptual set is that doctors don't prescribe inert remedies. For serious diseases and severe pain the doctor prescribes potent drugs. Placebo-treated patients have even complained of side effects such as nausea, headaches, sleepiness, and decreased concentration.

Thus, the first step in the abstracting process operates at the nonverbal level of sense experience. Reality is in the eyes, ears, nose, skin, and tongue of the observer. While there is usually substantial agreement among people, especially of the same culture and similar background, concerning what the territory looks like, there are also significant differences frequently ignored or overlooked. When differences become so dramatic and similarities so minimal in the absence of other plausible explanations such as cultural experiences, differences in environment, and the like, we claim that a person is hallucinating. Even under normal circumstances, different people abstract different characteristics of the territory because of each person's unique physiological and psychological construction.

The sense experience stage of abstraction is where we live our lives. Without language these experiences would remain essentially private experiences. With language we are able to share sense experience, perceptions of our world, with others.

The second stage of abstraction, then, is our description of our sense experience. Here again, however, it must be noted that these descriptions are the result of what our senses perceive. Kenge, the Pygmy native, saw "insects" not buffalo because of environmental conditioning. His description was a reflection of his view of the world. He classified what he saw on the basis of the similarities between that and other phenomena he had experienced. Consequently buffaloes were described as "insects" and these in turn were likened to "beetles" and "ants."

These several classifications by Kenge of one item in his environment additionally demonstrate that descriptions of sense experience do not all operate at the same level of abstraction. The degree to which a word selects and includes details about its referent, or limits and excludes details reveals the level of abstraction of each description. *Insects* excludes many details and is vague in comparison to the more specific and detailed *ants* or *beetles*. Levels of abstraction can be determined by the specificity of the words in relation to referents and the subsequent degree of guessing required to form a mutually understood picture of the phenomenon described. If I say, for example, "I participate in sports," I have revealed very little to you. You might solicit greater detail by asking, "What type of sports?" If I respond, "contact sports," I have provided further detail and consequently eliminated many alternatives such as swimming, track and field, and hang gliding. If I simply said at the start, however, "I participate in football and ice hockey," I would save everyone a lot of tedious questions by being very specific and thus eliminating the guesswork.

The lower levels of description provide a more accurate verbal map of the territory since there is less ambiguity and greater detail. As our verbal descriptions of our nonverbal world become more abstract, characteristics perceived at the sense experience stage are progressively reduced in number. The verbal map *sports* encompasses a wide range of activities but is vague, specifying only similarities among a diversity of athletic endeavors. *Contact sports* is a descriptive map that limits the range of activities that can be included but provides sharper detail, and so on.

The next stage of abstraction is the inferential stage. Inferences are statements about the unknown based on the known. They are guesses, educated or otherwise. Some inferences are more educated than others because their probability of accuracy is higher. One can infer that a neighbor is not home because newspapers have accumulated on the front porch and the mailbox is bulging. This is a relatively safe inference since a simple phone call or inquiries of other neighbors increase the probability that your inference is correct.

On the other hand, the inference based upon the same observations that your neighbor is away on vacation is a greater guess, less easily verified, and more likely erroneous than the first inference because a greater range of possibilities exists to explain the newspapers and mail. Your neighbor may be away on business, visiting relatives, attending a funeral, searching for a new house, or in fact enjoying a vacation. A simple phone call to the house will not verify such an inference.

Knowledge is produced by forming inferences and testing them against experience, observation, or laboratory scrutiny. Science depends on inferences (hypotheses), and theories are derived from a series of inferences that lead us into progressively higher levels of abstraction. We draw hundreds of inferences every day. If we didn't, an act as basic as going to the store would be troublesome. Without making inferences we wouldn't be sure our car was still in the garage where we left it yesterday, or that the store didn't burn down overnight, or that it is open during posted business hours, or if open whether it has shelves stocked with goods, or if stocked whether we can purchase them, and so on. Life's daily script is a series of inferences.

The *quality* of the inferences we make should be our primary concern, not whether to infer or not to infer. Inferences predicated on careful observations by competent individuals provide relatively reliable inferences. Careless observations by uninformed individuals produce unreliable inferences.

For example, let's assume you need your car repaired and you have only two establishments from which to choose. The first is a broken-down garage behind a goat farm called "Norm's Natural Car

Cures" (Slogan: "One man's tragedy is another man's gold mine"), and its claim to fame results from pioneer work on the use of acupuncture for automotive repair (balancing the car's electrical energy with its cosmic energy, don't you see?). The second choice is a brand-new, well-equipped car-care center with licensed mechanics. Local opinion based upon actual car repairs reveals that the car-care center does quality work, but Norm's is a flaky outfit that cheats customers. The inference concerning which establishment will perform the higher quality work should be obvious. While the examples are admittedly a bit exaggerated, they should clarify what constitutes a reliable inference from an unreliable one. Quantity of information, quality of observation, reliability of your sources providing information, and, where appropriate, the qualifications of "experts" performing services or offering advice are essential ingredients of reliable inferences. Inferences based on less will put you in the clutches of the Norms of this world.

From inferences we often leap higher still into abstraction by interjecting our personal values in the form of statements of judgment. This is selective perception working overtime. A man in love may consider the woman of his fancy beautiful beyond comparison. A pregnant woman who eats peanut butter on dill pickles may find it a delectable combination. And a child who sees a "Creature Feature" such as "Godzilla Meets the Smog Monster" may consider it vastly superior to such movies as "Gone With the Wind" or "Love Story." These all reflect personal values and perceptions of the person making such judgments. You can't objectively determine whether peanut butter on dill pickles tastes good or bad. It depends on the subjective sense experience of each person.

Judgments reveal our internal evaluations once we have interacted with some aspect of our world. Internal evaluations by others to the same stimuli may agree with our own but this does not validate the truth of the judgment. It simply reflects similarity of values. Reading this book, carefully scrutinizing its contents, and maybe comparing it to other books on the subject of language will not reveal whether this book is a good book. Your personal values and tastes in reading materials will produce a judgment concerning its worth and quality. This, however, is clearly subjective, as are all book, art, and movie reviews.

Questions such as "Does God exist?" "Is premarital sex immoral?" "Is homosexuality disgusting?" are unanswerable because no objective criteria based on observations can be constructed to reveal conclusively the correct answer to any of these questions. Yet these questions can produce very heated arguments given the appropriate combination of kinetic energy and dogmatic intolerance of contrary views of the world. A recent news story exemplifies the depth of feeling sometimes associated with personal judgments. Two friends were engaged in a lively dialogue concerning an interpretation of a particular passage in the Bible. A major disagreement over the "correct" interpretation slowly developed over several hours of impassioned exhortations by the two men. The conflict of values apparently ran deep because the argument became ugly. Finally, in the true Christian spirit of brotherhood, one of the combatants whipped out a gun from a dresser drawer and resolved the issue by killing his friend.

Conflict of values can produce ugly incidents such as this, yet arguments over personal judgments are conflicts over symbols. For instance, cruelty does not exist in nature. It resides in our subjective perception of events influenced by cultural conditioning. The NBC docudrama "Holocaust," reenacting the extermination of the Jews by the Germans during World War II, dramatized the extent to which some people can be pushed and rationalized into accepting as humane and even noble acts that invite revulsion and outrage from the great majority of people who share common values.

The reactions to the Vietnam War manifested a conflict of values. Some Americans considered the war moral and just and others argued the exact opposite. So who was right? It can never be determined. Morality and justice do not exist in nature. They are human inventions, symbols perhaps necessary to establish order, but nevertheless human creations.* General agreement among members of a society concerning what constitutes justice and morality demonstrates human convention not natural law. When we make judgments, even ones supported by a great number of people, we reveal more about ourselves than the

---

*The issue of whether morality is God's handiwork and therefore a divine creation makes for an interesting philosophical discussion, but it is itself an unresolvable question and therefore it will be avoided in order not to stray from the central topic—judgment as an order of abstraction.

thing evaluated. We do not "tell it like it is." Rather, we tell it as it selectively appears to us. No one is cruel because I label them such. What I perceive as cruel another observer may perceive as necessary discipline or even an act of humanity. The problem lies not so much in the fact that we make judgments, but rather that we believe unalterably in the essential rightness of these judgments. Such an attitude breeds intolerance and closed-mindedness.

Like descriptions and inferences, judgments also exist at different levels of abstraction. One judgment can lead to another and yet another and so on, each one in turn becoming more remote from the event or original stimuli that produced the initial judgment. For example, you may observe your neighbor spanking his son. From this observation, you may logically draw the inference that the son has done something to anger his father. You may also form a judgment, however, that the spanking is a cruel act because it was done in full view of the neighbors and would cause embarrassment to the son. This judgment of cruelty based on inference may lead to yet another broader judgment—that your neighbor is a bad parent. This in turn may produce still further evaluation—that your neighbor is a cruel person. In each case, the judgment is broader, first linking your neighbor's act with other acts you deem cruel, then generalizing beyond the single act by associating your neighbor with parents you view as bad parents, and finally linking your neighbor with cruel people in general, which could include anyone from Attila the Hun and Hitler to your boss.

The process of abstracting, then, consists of stages with each stage becoming progressively more remote from sense experience and fewer and fewer details of the original territory included. Compare the following three statements:

1. The woman sitting behind the table is wearing a white blouse.
2. The woman sitting behind the table is angry.
3. The woman sitting behind the table is unkind.

All three statements begin the same, yet the first is a description of fact, the second is an inference, and the third is a judgment. Descriptions are observations capable of verification. Inferences are interpretations of observations, guesses about the unknown on the basis of the known. We infer the woman is angry (unknown) from facial expressions, actions, and so forth (known). Judgments express preferences. They are evaluations. They go beyond simple observations or interpretations of observations. They express a value.

Descriptions may lead to inferences, which in turn may produce judgments. The process is analogous to taking off in an airplane. When the plane taxis down the runway there is high definition of limited territory (description). We cannot see very much beyond the airport, but what we see is detailed and specific. Once we leave the ground the territory we see increases in size, but many details fade away, replaced by a less precise impression of what once was a clear view of the terrain (inference). When we reach 30,000 feet the world stretches far beyond what we were capable of seeing on the ground, yet the detail is lost (judgment). Mountains, awesome when looking at them from ground level, may appear puny, little more than hills dotting the surface below. People are no longer visible, even buildings are difficult to discern.

Similarly, our verbal maps become larger, encompassing greater territory but providing fewer details as we move up the stages of abstraction. Descriptions provide detail but incorporate a relatively limited territory. Inferences encompass far greater territory and details are no longer as sharp and distinct. Judgments include a very broad territory but very few details, and these details, such as they are, include only the gross characteristics of the territory. Stating what the woman behind the table is wearing specifies characteristics of the territory but does not generalize beyond this. Saying she is angry specifies limited detail in the absence of description (for example, red-faced or shouting) but broadens the territory to include a generalization about the behavior that likens it to similar behavior of other people. Stating she is unkind lumps her into a category that includes a great number of people similarly perceived, yet in the absence of description, an individual hearing this assessment is left to guess what the judgment is predicated upon.

The degree of specificity and detail and the amount of guesswork required are indicators of how high we have traveled up the stages of abstraction. Sometimes we become so removed from the territory, so ambiguous and vague, that we completely lose sight of what precipitated the original inference or judgment. The arrows in the illustration on page 52 represent the link that should exist between symbols and referents, words and things, the verbal world of description, inference, and judgment and the nonverbal world. If there is nothing to point to, if there is not even an indirect connection with our sense experience, if we are merely mouthing words about words, then we have reached dizzying heights of abstraction and we are literally speaking "nonsense."

Abstracting is thus the process of selectivity whereby we sense a finite number of characteristics of our nonverbal world and verbalize with language what it is that we experience. Since words are not the things themselves, the fit between our language and our experience is always imperfect. To complicate the process even further, recent research on what has been termed *brain lateralization* has revealed that our perception of reality and our ability to verbalize this perception are influenced dramatically by how the two hemispheres of our brain have been conditioned to respond to stimuli.

Our brain is divided into two halves, the right and left hemispheres. These two hemispheres appear to be physically symmetrical, and it was assumed that they were also functionally symmetrical as well until the early 1960s, when Roger Sperry of the California Institute of Technology began testing split-brain patients. These were individuals who had undergone radical surgery that severed the connecting bundle of nerve fibers called the *corpus callosum* that allows the two hemispheres to communicate with each other. While the surgery controlled life-threatening epileptic fits for these patients, it produced some startling new evidence of the specialization of each brain hemisphere.

Rather than two functionally symmetrical hemispheres, each sharing the same tasks, our brain is divided into two brains in one package. The differences between our right and left brains is remarkable. Based on split-brain research and experiments with patients who have damaged one hemisphere of their brain by stroke or accident, several differences have emerged.

For most people, the left brain controls language and mathematical abilities, the ability to reason logically, to think sequentially and analytically. Our right brain, on the other hand, controls nonverbal images, is intuitive, governs emotions, and thinks holistically and synthetically.

Some practical results of this brain lateralization (left–right separation of function) are exhibited by patients who have received electric shock treatments. When shock is administered to only one hemisphere, that hemisphere is temporarily reduced to a state of stupor.

When the left-brain is shocked, the person briefly becomes a "right-brain person," and shocking the right-brain produces a "left-brain person." Blakeslee (1980) reports the results. "Left-brain persons" become very verbal, yet their voices sound monotonous, dull, and lifeless and acquire a nasal twang or something like a barking sound. They are unable to decipher anger, enthusiasm, or playfulness from tone of voice. They can't sing or recognize familiar tunes. They may deduce that it is winter because it is January, but snowdrifts and trees brown and leafless offer no clues to a left-brain patient. Typically, such persons will manifest optimism and cheerfulness even when their circumstances do not warrant it.

"Right-brain persons" assume a negative emotional outlook. They become largely nonverbal in their communication, preferring mime and gestures to words when answering questions. What speech there is does not include abstract concepts. Their recognition of voice intonations is enhanced. They recognize music immediately and can identify the season of the year from looking out the window even though they do not know the date. Right-brain patients have trouble remembering names of objects but can show how these objects are used.

Although brain lateralization is well established by research, it should be understood that there are certain exceptions to the pattern. Although more than 99 percent of right-handed people (the right side of the body is controlled by the left hemisphere of the brain, and vice versa) use their left hemisphere for language and their right hemisphere for nonverbal spatial functions, a few right-handers are reversed and some share various brain functions in both hemispheres.

Left-handers are the most apparent exception of all. Language should be in the right hemisphere for left-handers (the opposite of right-handers), yet it is reversed about 44 percent of the time (Restak,

1979). A reliable means, however, of determining hemisphere dominance was discovered by Dr. Jerre Levy. Both right- and left-handers who invert their hand when writing have cerebral specialization that is opposite the norm, whereas those whose writing position is noninverted follow the norm of brain lateralization.

The implications of brain lateralization research on our discussion of abstracting and perception are significant. First, it brings into focus the power of language to *restrict* and limit our view of the world if we become too dependent on language to do our thinking. As Restak (1979), Blakeslee (1980), and many others warn, left-brain dominance (language) has been emphasized in our educational system to the detriment of "right-brain intelligence." As some have wise-cracked, we may be developing a nation of half-wits, skilled in reading, writing, and arithmetic (primarily left-brain operations) and unskilled in creativity, intuition, emotional expression, and other aspects of the nonverbal human potential.

You don't have to sever the corpus callosum or receive electric shock treatments, however, to cause poor communication between the two brain hemispheres. Take just one example. Dr. Betty Edwards ("Drawing Better," 1978) has experimented with students who have difficulty drawing (a right-brain activity). She has discovered that a primary impediment for most students is their left-brain dominance when trying to perform this right-brain task. In other words, their language restricts their ability to draw because they "see" not in images, but in labels ("that's a 'nose,' 'eyes'," etc.). What she has her students do is take the picture being reproduced and turn it upside down so that it is unrecognizable and can't be named so easily. The student must draw the images rather than the words. The right brain is activated and the left-brain is rested. Students' drawings have improved remarkably as a result.

Similarly, Marcel Kinsbourne (in Restak, 1979) found that our vision of the world is profoundly affected by brain lateralization. Kinsbourne discovered that our attention is inherently biased toward the right (left-brain activation) when viewing objects and the world around us whenever we try thinking in words.

Dr. Levy (in Restak, 1979) further discovered that when viewing pictures, the right hemisphere is selectively activated, biasing our attention toward the left visual field. Levy speculated that pictures with more important content or greater heaviness on the right side are considered more esthetically pleasing. Such was the case in studies Levy performed. Right-handers overwhelmingly preferred pictures in which the important content was on the right side of the picture.

Therefore, what we are likely to perceive is highly selective not only because of the finite capacity of our vision but also because our perceptions are biased by brain lateralization that can determine what we are likely to see as well as what we may unconsciously ignore. This in turn can affect what we consider beautiful, pleasurable, and so forth.

The crux of this research on brain lateralization is summed up by Restak (1979, p. 213). He observes that our ability to perceive "reality" seems contingent on the mental set triggered at any given moment. Merely saying to people, "I want to ask you a question" activates the left-hemisphere, biasing their perception of objects to their right visual field. How can we answer questions such as "What is reality?" or "What is truth?" when the very act of asking the question biases us to perceive certain aspects of our environment while screening out others?

The process of translating our nonverbal experience into a verbal representation capable of communicating an approximation of that experience to others is thus a complicated one. This abstracting process poses problems for us when we are not vigilant in our language use. Four such problems will be discussed here. They are confusing stages of abstracting, dead-level abstracting, stereotyping, and semantic camouflaging.

PROBLEMS OF ABSTRACTING
Confusing the Stages of Abstracting

A vintage story is told of two American women, a matronly grand-mother and her comely granddaughter, and a Romanian officer and a Nazi officer seated in a railroad compartment. As the train passes through a dark tunnel, the sound of a loud kiss and a vigorous slap shatters the silence. As the train emerges from the tunnel no words are spoken but a noticeable welt forming on the face of the Nazi officer is observed by all. The grandmother muses to herself, "What a fine granddaughter I have raised. I have no need to worry. She can handle herself admirably." The granddaughter thinks to herself, "Grandmother packs a powerful wallop for a woman of her years. She sure is a spunky lady." The Nazi officer, none too pleased by the course of events, ruminates to himself, "How clever this Romanian is. He steals a kiss and gets me slapped in the process." The Romanian chuckles to himself, "I am indeed clever. I kissed my hand and slapped a Nazi."

This story presents in a rather amusing way a common difficulty associated with the abstraction process. Inferences and judgments are mistaken for descriptions of facts. The facts reported are that there was a kiss followed by a slap when the train traveled through a tunnel. A fairly reliable inference upon observing the welt on the Nazi's face would be that he was the victim of the slap. A not so reliable inference was made by each person, however, regarding who kissed whom and which party responded to the kiss with a slap. The grandmother inferred it was her attractive granddaughter who was kissed by the Nazi and had retaliated with a slap. The granddaughter assumed it was her grandmother, and the Nazi inferred that the Romanian did the kissing but got the Nazi slapped. Only the Romanian knows the truth.

In each case a judgment followed close on the heels of the inference. The grandmother was proud of her "fine granddaughter." The granddaughter marvels at her "spunky" grandmother and the Nazi grudgingly concedes that the Romanian is "clever." A value accompanies the erroneous inferences. The inferences and judgments are perceived as facts in the minds of the two women and the Nazi officer. It is a common mistake made by people who fail to recognize the leaps in abstracting from descriptions of fact to formulation of inferences followed by judgments or evaluations.

Confusing stages of abstracting is a rather common and often unnoticed language problem. In the previous chapter I discussed grammar in the context of stigmatizing individuals who use nonstandard language varieties. The distinction I drew between prescriptive and descriptive grammar serves to illustrate the confusing stages of abstracting problem as well.

Bostain (1981) perceptively explains that grammatical rules are usually presented to schoolchildren as factual statements when they are actually "wish statements." When grammarians state that *like* is a preposition and *as* is usually a conjunction, they are not describing what is but rather what *ought to be* from their point of view.

To insist that *like* is not a conjunction ignores what our own ears tell us is true. As Bostain observes, we hear such statements as "nobody can do it like McDonald's can," "looks like it's gonna rain," "like I was saying," "don't do like I do, do like I say," and of course "tell it like it is" every day of the week. Insisting that *like* is not a conjunction when in fact it is quite often used as a conjunction confuses the descriptive and judgmental stages of abstracting.

Judgment concerning what ought to be is inaccurately presented as a description of what is. A conjunction is commonly defined as a word that joins other words and groups of words. When the word *like* is used in such a fashion is it not then a conjunction? The great mass of speakers of Standard American English frequently use *like* as a conjunction. How, then, can we say with a straight face that "like is a preposition, not a conjunction" is anything more than wishful thinking?

While such wishful thinking passed off as factual statement may cause people to feel self-conscious about their "poor English," or produce a cadre of insufferable little elitists running around dogmatically correcting people's grammar, the consequences of confusing stages of abstracting can be far more serious than this.

During the Vietnam War, a helicopter crew returning to home base spotted a group of soldiers sitting around a campfire in an open field. One of the crew suggested that they drop in on the little cookout and grab a bite to eat. The crew agreed and the helicopter descended. They had accepted the inference that enemy soldiers would not appear in the open with a helicopter gunship approaching. They were tragically mistaken. The enemy soldiers opened fire and one crew member was killed, another critically injured because an inference was misconstrued as fact.

Lisa Hobbs (1970) cites a similar instance:

> [In New York City] a Spanish woman entered a bar to get telephone change. Nobody understood her, she became excited,

somebody called the police, she became terrified, the police took her to a hospital, nobody understanding a word, and there she was forcibly held for five days, now in a state of total madness. Only on the fifth day did a social worker visit her tenement home and find her two babies dead from thirst in their cots. That was what she had been trying to say. She was listed on the hospital records as a female hysteric [p. 56].

Inferences were drawn, but never verified. A judgment of the woman's emotional stability was made (and treated as factual) without benefit of so much as an interpreter to translate her desperate pleas into English. There is also an element of self-fulfilling prophecy. She was assumed to be "unstable" and did in fact become so for very good reason.

A study by Harris, Teske, and Ginns (cited in Gaylin, 1976) demonstrates how prevalent the problem of confusion of stages of abstraction apparently is. A mock jury trial was conducted to test the ability of jury members to distinguish between statements of fact (descriptions) and statements of inference. Jurors assumed inferences were facts in over 70 percent of the statements presented. Justice hangs on a very thin thread if jurors in real courtroom trials assume their inferences are facts and judge defendants accordingly.

"Unloaded" pistols become lethal weapons because inferences are mistaken for facts. Automobile accidents occur when two drivers both infer the right-of-way simultaneously. The "facts" are frequently just assumptions we've made in our heads. The consequences may be more serious than an unwarranted slap in the face.

Another aspect of the problem of confusing stages of abstraction is the two-valued orientation, or seeing the world in blacks and whites. It's a division of the world into good and bad, success and failure, rich and poor, ugly and beautiful, etc. There are no gray areas.

Politicians are plagued by two-valued questions. Are you a liberal or a conservative? Do you favor law and order or permissiveness? Do you advocate higher taxes or reduced government spending? To limit choices to only two alternatives narrows our vision to the point where we do not see other, perhaps obvious possibilities and solutions. For instance, we can be both conservative and liberal depending on the issue, but a person with a two-valued orientation sees this as a contradiction because a single act (low order abstraction) is confused with general political philosophy (higher order abstraction).

Or consider the abortion controversy. The battle lines have been tightly drawn between the "Right to Lifers" and the "Pro-choice" advocates. Yet even here there is a shade of gray that escapes many caught in the web of passionate belief. Those who advocate the "Pro-choice" position are not necessarily pro-abortion. They may be against abortion *personally* but in favor of all people's having the freedom to choose for themselves whether to have an abortion.

Both sides of this controversy frequently confuse two stages of abstracting. "Abortion is murder," the position of the Right to Life group, is not a statement of fact. It is a statement of value, a belief, a judgment. Right to Life advocates, apparently without always realizing it, are saying that abortion *ought to be* viewed as murder. Likewise, the Pro-choice position that abortion is not murder is a statement of what ought to be, not what is.

The abortion issue is not as unambiguous as Pro-choice and Right to Life proponents often characterize it. There is an honest, genuine disagreement on this question of value. When does human life begin? Is the fetus a human being, or must it exist outside of the womb in order to be considered such? Science can help us formulate our own opinions on this subject, but it cannot give us *the* answer.

Consider another example. Can parents both love and hate their children? Aristotelian logic would classify this as a contradiction, and yet, it is of course possible to exhibit hatred and still love a person for whom the hatred is targeted. Contradictions are often confusions of different stages of abstraction. A parent can tell a child, "I love you," then later beat and curse the child. Does it follow that the parent no longer loves the child? The two exist at different stages of abstraction. The act of beating and cursing exists at the sense experience stage or the descriptive stage if reported as an observation. "I love you," however, is an inference or even a judgment depending on the context. A consistent pattern of beatings and cursing might produce a valid inference that the parent does not love the child, but the single incident does not make for a reliable inference, nor is it contradictory by itself since it exists at a lower order of abstracting. Other behaviors might exhibit love.

Granted, there are some things that fall fairly readily into the either-or framework. It is quite difficult to be sort of pregnant or an "experienced virgin." Dichotomies, however, are often thought to exist where none need be.

Confusing stages of abstraction can thus pose serious problems. Misunderstanding and perceptual distortion are products of such confusion. The consequences of such confusion can even be life-threatening.

Dead-level Abstracting:
Spinning Our Verbal Wheels

Wendell Johnson (1946) has coined the phrase *dead-level abstracting* in reference to the practice of freezing on one level of abstraction. Perhaps the most common form of dead-level abstracting occurs at the higher levels. James Herriot (1974), a veterinarian in Yorkshire, England, and author of several autobiographical books on his experiences tending to the afflictions of various animals in his rural community, relates an amusing instance of dead-level abstracting:

> And sometimes it isn't easy to get a clear picture over the telephone
> . . .
>
> "This is Bob Fryer."
>
> "Good morning, Herriot here."
>
> "Now then, one of me sows is bad."
>
> "Oh, right, what's the trouble?"
>
> A throaty chuckle. "Ah, that's what ah want YOU to tell ME!"
>
> "Oh I see. . . ."
>
> The fact that I had heard this joke about two thousand times interfered with my full participation in the merriment, but I managed a cracked laugh in return.
>
> "That's perfectly true, Mr. Fryer. Well, why have you rung me?"
>
> "Damn, I've told ye—to find out what the trouble is."

"Yes, I understand that, but I'd like some detail. What do you mean when you say she's bad?"

"Well, she's just a bit off it."

"Quite, but could you tell me a little more?"

A pause. "She's dowly, like."

"Anything else?"

"No . . . no . . . she's a right poorly pig, though."

I spent a few moments in thought. "Is she doing anything funny?"

"Funny? Funny? Nay, there's nowt funny about t'job, I'll tell that! It's no laughin' matter."

"Well . . . er . . . let me put it this way. Why are you calling me out?"

"I'm calling ye out because you're a vet. That's your job isn't it?"

I tried again. "It would help if I knew what to bring with me. What are her symptoms?"

"Symptoms? Well, she's just off color, like."

"Yes, but what is she doing?"

"She's doin' nowt. That's what bothers me."

"Let's see." I scratched my head. "Is she very ill?"

"I reckon she's in bad fettle."

"But would you say it was an urgent matter?"

Another long pause. "Well, she's nobbut middlin'. She's not framin' at all."

"Yes . . . yes . . . and how long has she been like this?"

"Oh, for a bit."

"But how long exactly?"

"For a good bit."

"But Mr. Fryer, I want to know when she started these symptoms. How long has she been affected?"

"Oh . . . ever since we got 'er."

"Ah, and when was that?"

"Well, she came wi' the others . . . [pp. 261–262]."

Inability to drop down into the lower descriptive levels of abstraction prevented Herriot from learning the nature of the animal's illness by simply conversing with its owner. Dead-level abstracting, however, can be more serious than this anecdote reveals.

Stuart Chase (1954) conducted a survey of one hundred people in 1937. He asked each person to describe what *fascism* meant to them. They all shared a common revulsion of fascists, but no two people could agree upon what it meant. Chase also reports another study conducted by the *Capitol Times* in Madison, Wisconsin, in 1953. Almost two hundred persons on the street were asked the question "What is a Communist?" Not only was there no agreement, but 123 of the 197 persons interviewed confessed they did not know how to define *Communist*. This study occurred during the peak of the so-called McCarthy era when many innocent individuals were blacklisted and many lives were ruined because people were branded Communists for having liberal political attitudes or disagreeing with the practices and tactics of the "witch hunters."

A number of studies have been conducted over the years concerning civil liberties. Respondents in such studies typically support our constitutionally guaranteed rights in principle, but often object to the exercise of our civil liberties in specific cases (Zellman, 1975). Blumenthal and others (1972) refer to several such studies. In 1953, only 19 percent of a national sample supported the right of members of the Communist Party to speak on the radio. In 1965, only 59 percent of a sample agreed with the statement, "People have the right to conduct peaceful demonstrations against the war in Vietnam," a not very impressive endorsement of First Amendment guarantees given the specific qualification "peaceful" demonstrations. In 1969, another study revealed that only 38 percent of Americans felt that "students have a right to make their protest." The Blumenthal study (1972) also discovered that 50 percent of American men surveyed agreed with the statement, "People who make speeches stirring people up should be put in prison before they cause serious trouble [p. 173]."

These findings are not too surprising when considering a national study in 1970 undertaken by CBS revealing that a majority of Americans were against at least five of the ten amendments which constitute the Bill of Rights (they were not identified as the Bill of

Rights but merely paraphrased). Generally, respondents were opposed to such things as "extreme" groups demonstrating and the right of individuals or the press to criticize the government when such criticism might jeopardize the "national interest." Notice the reliance on vague abstractions such as *extreme* and *national interest.* These are most elusive terms.

We wax eloquent about *freedom* and *democracy* and we fear and hate the *Communists, Fascists,* and others without having any clear denotative meaning for such terms. We become lost in the upper levels of abstraction. Freedom of speech sounds great as an abstraction and we're all for it until groups seeking gay rights or self-proclaimed Neo-Nazis want to speak their mind. Then our passionate espousal of liberty becomes suddenly muted. High-level abstractions separated from clear referents make it difficult to know what it is that arouses such passion. Connotations, those private meanings swimming around in our heads, are presumed to be shared meaning, and we blithely assume agreement exists among "right-thinking" people. When someone challenges us, however, to make sense by dropping down into lower abstraction levels we find ourselves in deep trouble.

"Define your terms" is a common phrase expressing a desire for greater message clarity, a request for low-level specifics. Yet standard definitions for abstract terms are usually just synonyms that remain at high levels of abstraction. Unfortunately, definitions usually afford only the illusion of increased clarity and understanding.

Consider, for instance, definitions found in dictionaries. Look up the word *joyful* and you will likely find it defined as "happy." Look up *happy* and sure enough it means "joyful." Consult a dictionary for a definition of *naughty* and it will say "disobedient or guilty of misbehavior." Ask a child to define *naughty,* however, and you'll likely get a definition such as, "It's when you punch your little brother in the face and make him cry." A dictionary defines *fun* as "amusement." Ask that same child to define *fun* and you're liable to get, "Punching my little brother in the face and making him cry."

The child's definitions are specific and low-level abstractions whereas the dictionary remains at the high levels of abstraction. A dictionary, of course, could not list all the possible contexts for each word, so it provides a broad, abstract definition of words. Although dictionaries have their place and function, the ability to move easily from high levels of abstraction to lower levels when using language is a desirable goal, one not found in most dictionaries.

Inability to come out of the clouds and down to earth can produce what George Orwell, author of the apocalyptic book *1984,* called *double-think* or the holding of two contradictory beliefs simultaneously and accepting them both. An example is the term *free world* to refer to any country not under communist control. The contradiction lies in the fact that many countries under dictatorships are included as part of this free world. As a vague abstraction the contradiction tends to be believed.

The *Eugene* [Oregon] *Register-Guard* cites a lovely example of doublethink in an editorial dated August 30, 1975, entitled "The New Permanence":

> The 10-cent rate for mailing a first class letter, which had been temporary, will be permanent by Christmas. In the new-speak of government, that means that by Christmas the temporary rate will be 13 cents and the permanent rate won't be permanent at all. The rules are that once the Postal Rate Commission has established a permanent rate, the Postal Service can establish a temporary rate that is 33 percent higher than the permanent rate [p. 8A].

Need I add that the situation has long since deteriorated even further? When one becomes submerged in high-level abstraction, almost anything appears to make sense, even blatant contradiction.

The person who persists in using only the lower levels of abstraction is no better off than the individual who refuses to come out of the stratosphere and chooses instead to remain immersed in high-level obscurity. Johnson (1946) explains this form of dead-level abstracting:

> Probably all of us know certain people who seem able to talk on and on without ever drawing any very general conclusions. For example, there is the back-fence chatter that is made up of he said and then I said and then she said and I said and then he said, far into the afternoon, ending with, "Well, that's *just* what I told him!" Letters describing vacation trips frequently illustrate this sort of language, detailing places seen, times of arrival and departure, the

foods eaten and the prices paid, whether the beds were hard or soft, and so forth [p. 270].

Trivia is dead-level abstracting at the lower levels. An encyclopedic mind may make one a hit at parties and a veritable titan at trivia games, but information isolated from a larger context, not generalized beyond the simple facts, is useless minutia.

The teacher who is concerned solely with principles and theories but ignores their practical application does little to advance the wisdom of students. Conversely, what often passes for education is little more than the game of trivia. Moran (1969) argues that "most of what is called education today is concerned more with forgettable facts than with consequential learning [p. 110]." Requiring students to memorize long lists of facts with little or no attempt to create understanding concerning the significance and application of these facts is dead-level abstracting disguised as "education." See Moran for copious examples.

Consider, for instance, the following two questions:

1. "Give me liberty or give me death" was a famous statement made by (a) George Washington, (b) Nathan Hale, (c) Patrick Henry, (d) Paul Revere.
2. "Ungawa Timba Macumba" was a famous statement made by (a) Tonto, (b) King Kong, (c) Tarzan, (d) Jungle Jim.

If asked to decide which of these two questions is more legitimate for inclusion on a history exam, you probably would say number one. Yet on the face of it both are equally trivial. Facts in isolation, set adrift from any larger framework, are trivia. How do we determine which facts are worth committing to memory unless they fit into a higher level of understanding and application? Why is it important for me to know the answer to the first question but not the second? Until you can answer *this* question, you remain frozen at lower levels of abstraction!

Ultimately, efficient language usage results from a constant interplay among the various levels and stages of abstraction. Political leaders, for instance, should attempt to achieve both high-level goals (freedom, justice, civil rights) and lower-level goals (prison reform, higher wages for coal miners, equal employment opportunities for women).

Language is a flexible tool of communication. We should exploit this flexibility by moving freely and gracefully in an orderly fashion from low levels of abstraction to higher levels and back down again. In this way we remain grounded in reality while we are free to explore the vast frontiers of abstract thought so necessary to our survival.

Stereotyping: Homogenizing People

We all carry around images of what members of particular groups are like. For instance, what image is conjured in your mind for a dope smoker, New York cab driver, black athlete, college professor, construction worker? These images are often shared by others. Typically, they stress similarities and ignore differences among members of a group. These images, then, become stereotypes—the attribution of certain characteristics to a group often without the benefit of first-hand knowledge.

Stereotypes are judgments (high level abstractions) of individuals not on the basis of direct interaction with those individuals specifically (the territory) but based instead on preconceived images for the category they belong to. Stereotypes, however, are not inherently evil. Some stereotypes, when predicated upon personal experience and empirical data, can be valid generalizations about a group.

There are several potential problems with stereotypes, however. First, these preconceived images of groups may produce a frame of reference, a perceptual set in our minds concerning the group as a whole. Then when faced with an individual from the group, the preconceived image is applied indiscriminately, screening out individual differences. Individuals become mere abstractions devoid of unique qualities, pigeonholed and submerged in the crowd, a crowd that is thought to be homogeneous.

Indiscriminate application of stereotypes is particularly troublesome because stereotypes are not necessarily grounded on evidence or even direct experience. The classic study of stereotyping by Katz and Braly (1933) clearly revealed that stereotypes are often formulated in ignorance. They reflect attitudes toward labels, racial, ethnic, and others, frequently without benefit of actual contact with members of the group stereotyped. Student subjects held Turks in low esteem, yet most had never interacted with any member of this group.

A second problem with stereotypes is what general semanticists term *allness*. This is the tendency to characterize an individual or an entire group in terms of only one attribute or quality. This one characteristic becomes all that is necessary to know about a person. Once you realize that the person is a woman, or a Jew, or a Southerner, no more information is sought. This unidimensional view of a person is nothing more than a simplistic conception of an individual. You may be a Jew but also a brother, son, brilliant lawyer, charming compassionate individual, devoted father, loving husband, and so forth. Allness sacrifices complexity and substitutes superficiality. Racial and ethnic characteristics do not lend themselves to change, yet racial or ethnic labels may be the prepotent characteristic that supersedes all others. In fact, allness orientation may produce exaggerated perception of group characteristics. Secord et al. (1956) showed "prejudiced" and "unprejudiced" subjects several pictures of blacks and whites. The prejudiced observers exaggerated the physical characteristics of blacks such as thickness of lips and width of nose. Racial labels accentuated the stereotyped differences between "races" for prejudiced (allness oriented) subjects.

A final problem associated with stereotyping is that it can produce frozen evaluations. Juvenile delinquents or adult felons may never shed their stigmatizing label despite "going straight." Zimbardo and Ruch (1977) summarize studies conducted at Princeton University over several decades regarding stereotypes by Princeton students of various ethnic groups. While the stereotypes did change, they tended to do so relatively slowly. In 1933, blacks were deemed superstitious by 84 percent of Princeton students, 41 percent in 1951 and 13 percent in 1967. Thirty-four years is a very long time for people to acquire an accurate image of blacks on this one item.

Stereotypes are thus troublesome because they are often indiscriminate, exhibit an allness orientation, and can produce frozen evaluations. Considering the pervasivenes of stereotyping in our society, one should not take it lightly. When we stereotype we define a person and this definition, superficial at best, can be quite powerful.

To stereotype is to define and to define is to control, especially if the definition is widely accepted regardless of its accuracy. In a male dominated society women may be stereotyped as empty-headed and illogical. The fact that the stereotype has persisted for years manifests the control men have over women, control that excludes women from executive positions and relegates them to mindless housekeeping duties. Women's liberation is fundamentally the struggle to define, to reject male stereotypes of females.

Stereotypes are sometimes seductive, however. When women are told repeatedly that they are stupid, they may begin believing it. A self-fulfilling prophecy may develop. Low self-esteem produced from male definitions of women as unintelligent can lead to poor performance and the consequent belief that the stereotype has merit. The stereotype is thus nurtured and perpetuated. Stereotyping can thus control, insidiously imprisoning its victims in constraining roles.

So while stereotyping isn't intrinsically evil, most stereotypes lack empirical foundations and are assertions of power and dominance over less powerful groups. Reduced to an abstraction, victims of stereotyping must struggle to define themselves or be content to accept roles others have carved out for them. It is little wonder our society has been experiencing turmoil.

Semantic Camouflage:
Fog × Fog = Fog²

Language can promote clear thinking or it can obfuscate, confuse, and conceal, making clear thinking and understanding messages a matter of blowing away the semantic fog so a little light can penetrate our minds. I call this use of language to obfuscate, confuse, and conceal semantic camouflage.

There are three primary types of semantic camouflage. They are jargon, euphemism, and gobbledygook. Before I discuss each of these in turn, let me note that while this section appears in Chapter Three, elements of Chapter Two are also applicable as we shall see. Since, however, this section does not warrant a separate chapter, at least not in this book, its present location seems to be the most appropriate spot.

Jargon: The Language of Mystification.   Law, medicine, education, government, business, theology, and professions in general have their own specialized terminologies or jargons. These jargons serve several purposes.

First, jargon is a kind of verbal shorthand that makes lengthy explanation unnecessary to those familiar with the technical code. Bross, Shapiro, and Anderson (1972), for instance, did a study of medical jargon and concluded that the technical terminology of surgeons facilitated the communication of factual information with brevity and clarity, at least among surgeons.

Second, jargon is a badge of group identification. Doctors, lawyers, professors, bureaucrats, etc. speak a specialized lexicon partly because it says, "I am one of you. Know me by the language I speak." Those who do not speak the lexicon of the group typically are excluded from membership in the group. Jargon is in this sense a code of conformity to group norms.

Third, jargon lends an air of authority, prestige, and profundity to messages and speakers. This professional shoptalk may simply glaze over lightweight ideas with heavyweight words, but to the uninitiated and sometimes to the initiated it may sound profound and insightful.

The First International Symposium on Humor held at the University of Wales in 1976 ("Killing Laughter," 1976) shows jargon serving the purposes I've just listed. Titles of symposium presentations were heavily weighted with jargon, not merely to be concise and precise, although this was undoubtedly one of the intentions, but also to establish identification with the group by speaking its language, and to impress fellow colleagues. Simple, straightforward, nontechnical language may leave the impression that one's ideas are simple-minded and unworthy of careful consideration. So symposium presentations were burdened with such uninspiring titles as: "Humor *in situ:* The Role of Humor in Small Group Cultures," "Ethnic Humor as a Function of Social-Normative Incongruity on the Basis of Multiple Dependent Variables," "Degrees of Hostility in Squelches Featuring Retaliatory Equity as a Factor in Humor Appreciation," and "Phylogenetic and Ontogenetic Considerations for a Theory of the Origins of Humor." While such titles may be precise and accurate in their identification of the content of the presentations, a more dreadfully sterile, lifeless depiction of an ordinarily interesting subject matter would be difficult to devise.

Actual presentations during the conference also revealed a penchant for jargon. Contributors at the conference on humor proposed establishing "designed, unifunctional anxiety-release centers in a community situation" (chuckle centers), they discussed "arousal fluctuations," "stimulus discrepancies," "glee rates," and whether some people are "inherently teaseworthy." "A very meaningful humor-making session" was enjoyed by participants who listened to a nightclub comedian deliver pathetic one-liners guaranteed to pickle your funny-bone. One can only guess what the "snooze rate" was during the conference.

The principal problem with jargon, however, is not that the terminology is sterile and sometimes laughable. The far more serious consequence of using jargon is that it mystifies those unfamiliar with the terminology. The message becomes an exclusive one, understandable to only a select few. Oftentimes, however, messages ladened with jargon have a wider audience. Many become bewildered by the jungle of jargon that camouflages the message.

A study by the National Education Association (cited in Farb, 1973) disclosed that in many classrooms, half of the words used by teachers mystify students.

Legalese used on insurance forms, legal contracts, etc. mystify the lay public. We hire lawyers to demystify the jargon so we might understand the law. Medicalese such as *bilateral perorbital hematoma* (black eye), *agrypnia* (insomnia), *cephalalgia* (headache), *deglutition* (swallowing), and *emesis* (vomiting) are symbols without referents to most people unfamiliar with this medical lexicon.

Dr. Lois De Bakey ("Cutting Words," 1966) argues that much of this medicalese unnecessarily mystifies patients and even physicians from other regions. A survey by *Physician's Management* (cited in "Patients' Rights," 1978) revealed that medical jargon was a primary complaint of patients regarding their doctors. A study by Korsch and Negrete (1972) found that medical jargon used by physicians mystified patients and jeopardized effective treatment of ailments. Bross (1964) linked the thalidomide tragedy of the early 1960s, which resulted in deformed babies, to the camouflage created in part by the technical jargon used to debate the potential hazards posed by this drug.

Examples from other fields could be cited that would demonstrate how jargon often mystifies those who need to understand the message the most. The point, however, seems clear. When we speak a jargon that is incomprehensible to the lay public or to individuals outside the group using the specialized terminology, we are using verbal maps that conceal the territory. The jargon becomes the message; the word becomes the thing. The terminology lends prestige or legitimacy to its users without communicating anything intelligible to nonusers. The message is mystified when it should be clarified, concealed when it should be revealed.

Euphemism: Linguistic Novocaine.   Euphemism is a kind of linguistic novocaine which numbs us to the unpleasant or offensive. Euphemisms are not intrinsically evil. Referring to mentally retarded or brain-damaged children as *exceptional children* disguises what is for many an ugly reality, yet it shows a sensitivity to the stigmatizing effects of language labels. It also points to a different reality, one often unnoticed, namely, that such children are not subhuman and are truly out of the ordinary in ways that are quite human. Their typical openness, trust, expressions of affection, and appreciation of simple beauty and simple pleasures make them quite exceptional and very human.

Likewise referring to institutions for the insane as *mental hospitals* rather than the previous *lunatic asylums* numbs us to an ugly reality, but also steers our thinking in a socially constructive direction. *Lunatic asylum* creates a vision of dangerously irrational people who should be imprisoned, whereas *mental hospital* suggests illness and cure. Each label, of course, reflects our values, attitudes, and sometimes our ignorance as a society.

Using euphemisms becomes a dangerous and undesirable linguistic cover-up when it blinds us to an unpleasant reality without broadening our perception to a new "truth," a new vision. In other words, a euphemism that simply lies to us by keeping us as far removed from the territory as possible is an example of language misuse and malpractice.

One of the truly noteworthy instances of this kind of euphemizing was the Watergate conspirators' attempt to tidy up their criminal activities. Burglars were called *plumbers,* burglary was *surreptitious entry,* illegally obtained and illegally used money was *laundered* (cleansing the filthy lucre), criminal conduct in general was termed *White House horrors* (giving it a sense of unreality—ghostly rather than ghastly), criminal conspiracy was a *game plan* (as in a sporting event), spying became *visual surveillance,* illegal wiretap was *electronic surveillance,* and what most of us ordinary folks call *casing the joint* was concealed as *a vulnerability and feasibility study.* Nowhere is criminality even suggested. Quite the contrary. The euphemisms lie to us. They suggest a reality which isn't there, a vision which is blind to the facts.

Such verbal novocaine was clearly intended to dull our sense of outrage and horror at discovering such monstrous criminality rampant in the Nixon White House. The verbal maps were constructed to remove the territory from our purview. The attempted cover-up was semantic as well as criminal.

Not all euphemisms that lie to us are as dangerous and as significant as the Watergate example. Nevertheless, Watergate should alert us to the potential consequences of such euphemizing.

Gobbledygook: Semantic Smog.   Texas Congressman Maury Maverick coined the term *gobbledygook* a number of years ago to refer to the word salads contained in reports and communications from bureaucrats. It has since come to mean verbosity and circumlocution that buries a message in an avalanche of verbal rubble.

Watergate is once again a prime example of the dangers of semantic camouflage, this time in the form of gobbledygook. Ron Ziegler, Nixon's press secretary, was asked by a reporter whether John Dean, the President's personal counsel, had called L. Patrick Gray, nominee for Director of the F.B.I., and requested that Gray change his testimony before a Senate Committee. Ziegler spoke the following gobbledygook as his answer:

> The statement that Mr. Dean called Mr. Gray is absolutely correct.
> And I supposed I would do the same thing if it was suggested—
> that—well, I suppose any individual would make a phone call such
> as that if it had been indicated that the individual, as the exchange
> stated, probably lied for the purpose of making sure that those who
> were involved in that discussion, a discussion which resulted, of

course, in extensive reports of that—and I am not being critical of that—said that Mr. Dean probably lied [in King, 1979, p. 222].

Clear?

John Ehrlichman produced an equally convoluted answer to a question concerning Jeb Magruder and the Watergate cover-up:

> There came a time when there was a feeling that, at least on my part, based on what Mr. Dean was telling me about the unraveling of this thing, that Mr. Magruder may have had some involvement, and that culminated in a meeting with the Attorney General (Mitchell) at the end of July, on the 31st of July, where Magruder was specifically discussed. But just where in there I acquired the information, I can't tell you. [Gambino, 1974, p. 23].

Here we have inflated babble to avoid answering a direct question with a direct answer.

The Watergate hearings were swamped by such gobbledygook. From John Dean's "I was trying to test the chronology of my knowledge" to Ehrlichman's "we gathered together to compare ignorances," the American people were subjected to a barrage of blather from Watergate conspirators and their mouthpieces.

We have perhaps become accustomed to gobbledygook in government and politics, but Watergate developed it to an art form. The Watergaters rarely touched down from the clouds of circumlocution. High-level abstraction became their shield against criminal charges. It was Ron Ziegler, however, who manifested just how divorced from reality the language of semantic camouflage can become when he said straight-faced and with apparent sincerity that "all previous White House statements about the Watergate case are inoperative."

SUMMARY

Abstraction is the process of selective perception. Incapable of attending to or sensing the world in all its complexity, we sense only a minute segment of the world. We share these perceptions of the world with others via language. But words are not things, so we can drift away from sense experience into progressively higher stages of abstraction, remote from our sense experience. Abstraction can produce serious problems when poorly understood or ineptly used. We can confuse the stages of abstraction, be guilty of dead-level abstracting, stereotype groups of people, and semantically camouflage realities. All four produce confusion, misunderstanding, inaccurate language maps, or worse. Using language flexibly, grounding our vague abstractions in lower levels of abstraction, and verifying our inferences will produce greater accuracy, increased understanding, and more intelligent communication—worthy goals to be sure. Recognizing differences between descriptions, inferences, and judgments, and avoiding stereotyping where possible, or basing unavoidable stereotypes on empirical evidence, and clarifying not concealing the meaning of our messages will also help us to achieve those goals.

C H A P T E R   4

VERBAL TABOOS:
The Semantics of
the "Gutter"
and the "Toidee"

Verbal taboos of one kind or another have existed among every human culture and probably originated with the development of language. The history of English-speaking peoples, especially the more recent chronicles, attests to the prevalence of and attention paid by such cultures to verbal taboos. Lexicographer Noah Webster in 1833, offended by the coarse phrasing of the Bible, proceeded to "cleanse" it of its offensive terminology, thereby improving the divine rhetoric. He replaced *teat* with *breast* (a word soon to fall into disrepute), *to give suck* with *nourish, to go awhoring* with *to go astray, whoredom* with *carnal connection,* and references to the male genitals with *secrets* (certainly the world's most poorly kept).

Victorian prudery produced what must seem to many present day observers supremely silly verbal taboos. One's lower extremities were not called *legs* but rather *limbs*. Children were not *born* but *sent* and never *breast-fed* but rather *nursed*. If you look at Victorian language as an accurate reflection of life as it was lived, then sex and elimination did not exist as human functions.

World War I temporarily diminished the strict Victorian taboos regarding verbal propriety. In the 1930s, however, Hollywood stepped into the breach. American moviemakers, under threats of censorship, issued a list of banned words never to be uttered in any motion picture. Some of the culprits included *virgin, harlot, slut, tart, whore, son-of-a-bitch, sex, asexual, virtuous,* and *bum*.

Although such censorship of words can be easily mocked as the foolish prudery of previous generations, the significance of verbal taboos in our culture has real currency. Virtually all states have laws that restrict certain language from being used in public places. The United States Criminal Code forbids "obscene, indecent, or profane language" on the radio. Radio, television, print media, and the movie industry all have established codes dealing with taboo language, although these codes are vaguely worded and not always followed.

Verbal obscenity became an issue of no small consequence during the political and social protests of the 1960s and '70s. Ultimately the U.S. Supreme Court was drawn into the controversy and issued numerous decisions dealing with the use of offensive language. Richard Nixon, doomed to resign as President, created a national incident when his private language was found to be more preoccupied with the sexual and excretory side of life than many would have imagined.

Despite this long history of linguistic trepidation, verbal taboos are gradually eroding. Cameron (1969) determined that several tabooed terms are among the seventy-five most frequently used words in the English language. Many people pay lip service to the verbal taboos but privately ignore sanctions placed on language. Restrictions on printing offensive language have loosened considerably in the last decade or so.

Nevertheless, as the restrictions on taboo language usage erode, pressures to revive and preserve such taboos on language seem to increase. The National Council of Teachers of English (NCTE) conducted a "censorship survey" in 1966 and 1977 (Burress, 1979). It found that there was a greater reported incidence of attempts to censor educational materials in secondary schools in the 1977 survey compared with the 1966 survey. The most common objection noted by the teachers answering the survey was to the language in the books in question. While the more explicit "obscenities" and "profanities" were cause for objection, some dictionaries that do not include such terms came under fire (Jenkinson, 1979). *The American Heritage Dictionary, Webster's New World Dictionary of the American Language,* and the *Random House College Dictionary* were some of the works singled out by members of various American communities both large and small, rural and urban. These dictionaries carried such words as *bed, fag, horny, hot, knock, queer, rubber, shack,* and *slut* with their appropriate sexual definitions.

Increasing attempts to censor materials containing language deemed objectionable (even "bad grammar" is a target of censorship attempts) comes from a variety of sources. Concerned parents, nervous librarians, school board members, administrators, the clergy, and perhaps most publicized, the efforts of Mel and Norma Gabler, founders of the Educational Research Analysts, Inc., in Longview, Texas, are the principal sources of such censorship pressure.

Interestingly, 75 percent of the objections from such groups reported in the NCTE 1977 survey concern language and sex (which often overlap) but only 4 percent concern violence as the grounds of complaint (Burress, 1979). Clearly, taboo language remains a highly charged issue of no small consequence.

Some guardians of the public morals herald the maintenance of verbal taboos as a sign of an advanced civilization, while at the same time decrying the erosion of these taboos as a sign of moral and social decay. Such a view equates words with things. No word is intrinsically dirty, however. Obscenity is in the mind of the beholder. Words become tabooed by social convention largely divorced from logic. A friend related a story to me a few years ago that illustrates this point. His two-year-old daughter was playing in their backyard with a neighbor's son who was about the same age. Apparently the little boy did something quite irksome to this usually even-tempered, cheerful little girl. She expressed her anger by turning to the little boy and proclaiming, "I'm going to shit on your head." She was immediately admonished by her mother, "Janie, we don't talk like that," whereupon Janie turned to the little boy and said: "I'm going to shit on your arm." The "logic" of arbitrary social convention that brands a word taboo must be learned. Relegating a few words to the dirty linen closet where they are scrubbed clean and transformed into euphemisms, circumlocutions, or babytalk hardly stands as one of humankind's crowning achievements.

To carry this a bit further, consider the two terms *sexual intercourse* and *fuck*. Both terms can denote copulation or sexual connection between two people, yet the connotations attached to the latter are often so powerful that only obscenity is perceived.

I have queried students concerning the difference between these two terms. Common answers include: *fuck* is more aggressive, harsher, more shocking, and it's dirty. Once I posed this question to a group of more than 200 students in a large lecture hall. When I asked what the difference was between *fuck* and *sexual intercourse,* a male voice from the back of the room echoed forth, "Technique!"

Some words are designated obscene, coarse, or vulgar, not because of their denotative meanings, but primarily because of the associations, experiences, and conditioning that produce such connotations as the ones above. Of the three elements of connotative meaning isolated by Osgood, Suci, and Tannebaum (1957), a word such as *fuck* might conjure very negative evaluations inside our heads, generate great intensity on the potency dimension, and summon an image of fierce activity. Thus, the connotative meaning of the word *fuck* would be negative, strong, and active. When such connotations come to mind, denotations are obscured and we signally react to the word. (Have you already demonstrated such a signal reaction to my inclusion of "obscenities" in the last few paragraphs?)

Muriel Schultz (1975) points out the illogic produced by such signal reactions. She observes that the word *rape* is an acceptable "four-letter word," yet it denotes a vicious, violent act that many would label *obscene*. The word *fuck,* however, can denote sexual intercourse, a universal human act proscribed only in certain instances. It can also have a nonsexual referent, as in "I'm all fucked up," which, of course, does not mean "I'm all sexual intercoursed up." Yet *fuck* is taboo no matter how it is used. Obviously it is not the act nor the way in which the word is used that brands certain words taboo. This brings to mind a statement attributed to D.H. Lawrence, "Tell me what's wrong with words or with you, that the thing is all right but the word is taboo."

Verbal taboos are not hallmarks of a civilized society but rather a primitive confusion of words with things. Logic does not dictate which words should be proscribed. If that were the case *rape* would be the penultimate verbal obscenity. Filth does not exist as a characteristic intrinsic to any word. Montagu (1967) explains that *fuck* was an acceptable word in sixteenth century Scotland although it became "obscene" soon after. *Cunt* was a Standard English word for the female pudenda during the Middle Ages, and *shit* was Standard English from the sixteenth to the nineteenth century and then fell into disrepute. The words themselves, then, are not dirty, but we have attached such a label to certain words quite apart from logic and the arbitrary nature of word symbols. Characterizing some words as obscene, profane, dirty, and the like reifies them, makes these words things unto themselves apart from their contextual meaning. There is no clear yardstick, no empirical foundation for making such designations.

Nevertheless, verbal taboos exist and although they are slowly eroding in this country, they remain powerful controllers of verbal behavior in many circles, under various conditions. Understanding the verbal taboo phenomenon is significant for several reasons.

First, reaction to taboo language manifests in a very tangible way a central theme of this book, namely, that language is not a neutral vehicle of communication. Rather, language is a powerful instrument of communication that has an enormous influence on our perception and behavior. Gaining insight into the dynamics of the taboo language phenomenon can help us understand and respect the power of language and encourage us to nurture a rational, prudent attitude regarding language usage.

Second, the taboo language phenomenon is very probably the best example of reification in action. While we may recognize immediately the elementary truth in the statement, "Words are not things anymore than maps are territories," we often forget our general semantics when it comes to taboo language. We forget it at our own peril. Treating words as things can be a very dangerous practice.

Third, taboo language graphically illustrates how context determines meanings of words. Language is a dynamic process not a static entity. The meaning of a word, therefore, is not static but rather subject to alteration depending on the context in which the word is used. Failure to appreciate the complexity of this language process and the importance of responding intelligently to symbols of our own creation, can make us prisoners of our language, victims of our own invention.

Thus, a detailed discussion of taboo language—why we have verbal taboos, the several elements of context that affect our view of the degree of offensiveness of taboo terminology, and the kinds of response we have to such terminology—serves as a kind of case study that illustrates, amplifies, and explains in greater detail and depth, much of what was introduced in the first three chapters.

One final note of preamble should be mentioned here. While I am not insensitive to those who harbor religious scruples concerning "dirty words" and "profanity," and while I realize some people find this subject shocking, embarrassing, and offensive, nevertheless, as you have already gathered by now, no effort will be made to employ circumlocution or to expurgate the taboo words. It would be hypocritical to argue on the one hand that designations of some words as dirty, profane, and obscene are a misuse of language and then on the other hand proceed to lend credence to this reification by avoiding the offending terms, substituting quaint little phrases, applying asterisks, or engaging in other forms of semantic camouflage. A psychiatrist who refuses to listen to a client's problems because he or she finds them "dirty," offensive, "obscene," or embarrassing would be labeled unprofessional at best. Language is the business of those who study and write about improving communication. To pursue it properly requires an intelligent, mature, and frank discussion of language in all forms, not a closed mind and a closed mouth.

TABOO: OUR PSYCHOLOGICAL
TUG-OF-WAR

The word *taboo* is of Polynesian origin but has no exact translation in English. Sigmund Freud (1950) in his work *Totem and Taboo* explains the Polynesian word *roa* is the opposite of *taboo*. It means "common" or "generally accessible." Consequently, *taboo* implies a sense of the unapproachable that is manifested by prohibitions and restrictions. The nature of taboo is one of approach and avoidance, a kind of psychological tug-of-war. On the one hand it means "sacred," and "consecrated," and on the other "uncanny," "dangerous," "forbidden," and "unclean." Eric Larrabee (1955), commenting on "sexual restrictions," puts it this way, "Sex curbs serve a double purpose: to stimulate and to hold back—never too much of either. . . . We live in a state of permanent conflict between our daring and our decency [pp. 672–3]." The forbidden fruit becomes enticing because it is tabooed. It assumes a certain mystique and power over us because of the prohibitions.

This mystique and power makes the tabooed objects dangerous and harmful to those who violate the prohibitions. It is believed that violation of the taboos unleashes magical or supernatural powers that can destroy or punish transgressors.

Verbal taboos illustrate this point quite nicely. Ancient Jews recognized a magical power in the name *Yahweh* and thus formulated a taboo on uttering the "name of God." Failure to abide by this restriction allegedly conferred the power of Yahweh upon the enemy. Gentiles who knew the name of Yahweh could then use the power of the Jews' own God against them.

The religious commandment "Thou shalt not take the name of the Lord thy God in vain" is one of the oldest of recorded verbal taboos. The Bible equates God with "The Word," so blasphemy and profanity are desecrations, a defilement of that which is held sacred and revered. The taboo is a form of verbal idolatry and its violation is an act of iconoclasm. Similar verbal icons have existed in other religions as well. The "true" name of Allah is kept secret as are the names of the Brahman gods and the "real" name of Confucius.

The belief that words and their references are in some way naturally connected allows verbal taboos to thrive. Words become more than mere vehicles of communication. They seem to possess magical powers. By altering the word one alters the thing, so goes the reasoning.

In some African societies, sorcerers are greatly feared and ostracized due to their magical powers. According to Turnbull (1965) sorcerers are believed to use supernatural powers to harm other people by cursing them.

Thus, words and things are perceived to be inseparable. Verbal taboos protect the individual from harm by forbidding the utterance of those dangerous and potentially disastrous words, and they preserve and magnify the magical properties of certain words. Current efforts to censor "obscene" and "pornographic" materials vividly describing sexual behavior demonstrate an analogous fear of the power of words, especially the so-called "four-letter words." Words describing a sex act and the sexual behavior itself become one and the same. In some cases the words become so magical that they alone become feared, apart from any reference to a sex act or offensive behavior.

If verbal taboos are a throwback to a primitive confusion of words with things, then why does a modern, sophisticated society like that of the United States still continue to maintain taboos? The principal reason is that verbal taboos exist to protect society from the dangers of offensive language, which could presumably tear apart the moral and social fabric of a culture. Using "obscene" language challenges the societal values of propriety and decorum and questions societal attitudes concerning sex and biological functions. Profanity challenges religious beliefs. Using tabooed language defies established conventions, demystifies the sacred words, promotes a collapse of established values, and asserts an independence from social control.

Widespread violation of verbal taboos represents a contempt for the taboo or reflects a shifting mood and opinion concerning the taboo itself and behavior it attempts to control. A taboo's worst enemies are disregard and ridicule. Such reactions not only threaten the demise of the taboo but equally threaten to diminish or destroy the moral and social mores that support and breathe life into the taboos.

Those individuals who flout the taboos must be severely punished in order to preserve the status quo. Taboo transgressors tempt others to follow suit. They play upon the ambivalence others experience when confronted with taboos. As Freud (1950) observes, the taboo violators encourage others to copy their actions. Each transgression invites imitation and therefore must be punished.

Failure to ostracize or punish the offender may reveal to others a hidden desire to follow likewise the path of the pied piper of corruption. Perhaps this partly explains the overzealous and disproportionate violence that is frequently loosed upon those who violate taboos. Perhaps such a reaction is an attempt to prove one's allegiance to community standards and values, to erase any hint of desire to imitate the "sinner."

Taboos, then, maintain the status quo and protect society and individuals from the perils of the unknown, the unseen, the desirable, and the unclean. They do this by camouflaging the realities that exist behind the walls of taboo. Death is feared; therefore it is made invisible. Dead bodies are disguised by morticians to look "natural" and "almost alive." Few people during their lifetimes (in industrial societies) have ever touched a dead body. Thus, the mystique surrounding death is fostered. Excrement, the waste product of the human body, is considered "dirty," too foul to discuss openly and frankly. Sex organs are "unclean" yet desirable so they also must remain invisible.

Language taboos are instrumental in maintaining a protective covering, a shield against the perils of exposure. Euphemisms and technical jargon enter the language to camouflage the naked truth. It is not uncommon to hear mature adults making reference to *wee-wee, pee-pee, toidee* or *doing one's duty*. In addition, the sex act is disguised by such misleading phrases as *make love, go to bed,* and *sleep together,* none of which specifies what actually takes place.

Such linguistic concealment exists in other cultures besides our own. The British commonly refer to the toilet as a *convenience* or the *cloakroom*. The Spanish and Italians use words meaning "retreat," the Russians use *abornaya,* meaning "adornment place," and Germans prefer *abort* meaning literally "away place." The Australians, however, have perhaps the most colorful and amusing euphemisms. Powell (1972) cites scores of euphemisms. A sample includes

> *To urinate:* Drain the dragon; syphon the python; wring the rattlesnake; see if the horse has kicked off his blanket; point Percy at the porcelain; trace Terence on the terracotta.
>
> *To have intercourse:* Go like a rat up a rhododendron; boil bangers; play cars and garages; go off like a belt fed motor; have gin on the rocks.

> *Penis:* Beef bayonet; tummy banana; trouser snake; the bishop.
>
> *Toilet:* Throtting pot; chunder box; slash house; wee hoos.

Although euphemisms disguise the territory with misleading verbal maps that merely hint at the truth or deceive outright, technical jargon conceals the reality with labels only vaguely understood if at all by the majority or with Latinate forms requiring a priest for translation. Robert Grave's story of a solder who has been shot in the "ass" is a case in point. When a female visitor to the wards asked where he had been wounded, the solder replied, "I'm sorry, ma'am, I can't say. I never studied Latin." Terms such as *gluteus maximus, tumescence, mycturation, defecation, ejaculation, fornication,* and *copulation* make their referents virtually invisible since many people are unfamiliar with the jargon. The language is antiseptic and sterile. It creates a distance from the subject matter.

Although euphemisms and jargon are not inherently bad as previously noted, such semantic camouflage can create real problems. There are times when a frank and open discussion of such topics as sex and elimination are critical. In such situations (for example, parents explaining the so-called "facts of life" to their children or a doctor explaining a disease of the urinary tract to a patient), misleading euphemisms and technical jargon that obscures and confuses can have serious, undesirable consequences.

Several important ideas have been explored in this brief discussion of taboos. First, taboos are paradoxical, pulling an individual in conflicting directions. They prohibit and entice simultaneously. Second, the prohibitions on certain types of words give such words a power they ordinarily would not possess. Prohibiting their utterance tacitly asserts that these words are potentially destructive in and of themselves. Their mere verbalization becomes the "sin" apart from the referential meaning. The tabooed words become things.

Third, the principal purpose of taboo is protection of society and the preservation of the status quo through social control of behavior. Violations of taboos consequently threaten the social order. It is a dangerous act because the enticing quality of taboos encourages imitation of those who disregard or show contempt for the taboo. Exposure destroys their mystique and power. Euphemisms and technical terminology merely hint at what is concealed behind the curtain of taboo. The tabooed objects remain shrouded in mystery giving them a sinister power and magical quality.

While some taboos such as the one placed on killing other human beings seem highly useful to a society interested in order and the maintenance of its existence, taboos on language are far more troublesome to defend. Such verbal taboos ask us to treat language in a way that is antithetical to its nature as a medium of communication. Words are not things, yet verbal taboos ignore such obvious fact and substitute instead an infantile fear of words. Language should not be feared, although its power should be respected. It is the *misuse* of language, in this case the segregation of a few words out of context as offensive, that should be feared because of the effects it produces—a subject for later discussion.

Before proceeding with a discussion of the factors that influence our perception of certain words as offensive, some distinctions should be drawn between the three principal types of taboo language: verbal obscenity, profanity, and abusive animal terminology (hereafter referred to as *animal abuse*).

Verbal obscenity is a type of taboo language utilizing indecent words and phrases. By *indecent* I mean that which is associated with sex and excretion and is regarded as filthy and foul.

Profanity is a type of taboo language which exhibits an irreverence for that which is an object of religious veneration (Montagu, 1967, p. 101). Obscenity and profanity are often confused, yet obscenity draws upon the indecent whereas profanity draws upon the sacred. Goldberg (1938) makes such a distinction credible by considering the derivation of the terms *obscene* and *profane*. He points out that *obscene* is a Latin derivative that means "beholding filth." *Fane* means a temple, and *profane* means outside or before the temple, thus irreverent or not sacred.

Animal abuse is a type of taboo language which utilizes the names of certain animals for abusive purposes. Although several such terms also fall within the definition of verbal obscenity (for example, *pussy, cock,* and *ass*), many do not (for example, *sow, cow, pig, dog,* and *hippo*), thus justifying a third category of taboo language.

The degree of offensiveness of any of the words that fall into these three categories of taboo language cannot be plotted on a graph. Despite popular conceptions that some words are far more offensive than others, no word separated from its context can be designated as more offensive than other proscribed terms. Several contextual elements influence our perceptions of the degree of offensiveness of any taboo term. Such elements will now be explored.

CONTEXTUAL ELEMENTS OF VERBAL TABOOS
WHO: The Taboo Transgressors

Offensive language does not exist in isolation. It makes a difference who uses such language. There are at least three factors concerning who uses prohibited language that seem to strongly influence our perception of taboo words. They are sex, age, and degree of status.

It has long been a tenet of folk wisdom that women are the gentler sex. Consequently, they refrain from offensive, aggressive language and choose instead the more polite forms of speech. Jesperson (1922) was one of the first to comment on this generally accepted observation of female speech patterns. He asserted:

> There can be no doubt that women exercise a great and universal influence on linguistic development through their instinctive shrinking from coarse and gross expressions and their preference for refined (and in certain spheres) veiled and indirect expression [p. 246].

Wolfram and Fasold (1974) update this view by pointing out that recent studies of linguistic change in the United States indicate that females are frequently responsible for the initial adoption of new prestige forms of language and primarily responsible for perpetuating the prestige norms of language for future generations.

Jesperson's claim that women instinctively shrink from stigmatized forms of language, however, is certainly subject to serious question. Society's definition of women relegates taboo language to the ranks of the "unfeminine"—coarse and offensive expression more properly suited to males. Women who use taboo language are speaking like men and are consequently stigmatized for departing from the societal definition of the female role. It has been taboo for women to use such nonstandard language because it threatens to disrupt the social order. Men have greater freedom to use language flexibly whereas women have greater restraints placed on their language usage. In a male dominated society women are expected to shrink from "coarse and gross expressions" because that is the role they have been delegated. The double standard whereby men can more freely employ taboo language than women reflects an unequal distribution of power. Women do not control men's language (except in respect to observing the rules of propriety of expression when "ladies" are present), but men control the language of women in regards to stigmatized verbal discourse. Failure to observe the "proper" linguistic etiquette marks a woman as rebellious, a threat to the power of men to dominate women. It is small wonder that swearing by women elicits strong reproach.

There are close to a dozen studies (Rothwell, 1977, p. 34) that substantiate the strength of this double standard. As a generalization it seems evident that men use taboo language more often than women as a consequence of social mores. Recent recognition of male chauvinism even in terms of language, however, has apparently begun to loosen the restraints on some of the use of taboo language by women. There are other factors that restrict usage of taboo language by various individuals, but being a woman is one that seems to be losing some of its relevance.

Age is another factor that influences our perception of taboo language. People have basically two reactions to the use of taboo language by young children. Some think it is "cute" and openly laugh when a three-year-old calls them a "shithead." Such a response to a child's using "adults only" language merely encourages further forays into the forbidden realm of offensive language. Others respond with shock and outrage, viewing such words "out of the mouths of babes" as a demonstration of poor parental discipline and guidance.

Another double standard sometimes operates in regard to taboo terminology and age. Those who severely punish young children for using taboo language may quite openly employ taboo terminology themselves. Parents are often surprised and shocked when, upon asking their children where they learned certain "nasty" terms, are informed that their children are only imitating their parents' speech. Again, the issue of power arises. Parents can dominate their children and restrict their language usage because it is the parents who establish the social conventions of behavior. Taboo language, then, becomes an instrument of rebellion against parental control and authority.

Parental patterns of discipline appear to affect children's use of taboo language. In reference to pathological use of obscenity by children, Harrison and Hinshaw (1968) note that extremes at both ends of the discipline scale may result in excessive verbalization of obscenities. Ostensibly a rigid interdiction on taboo language encourages rebellion against such restrictions on freedom, and a seemingly unconcerned and uncaring attitude allows the use of such language to flourish unrestrainedly. In the former case, the child may be striking out against the bonds of conformity in hopes of developing individuality. In the latter case, the child may be trying to shock inattentive parents into noticing his or her very existence. Taboos foster invisibility. Violating societal taboos can produce visibility.

An additional element of this relationship between age and taboo language is that older people tend to respond less favorably to taboo language in general than do young people, owing perhaps to changing social mores. Lewis (1971) found that individuals under thirty years old were much less likely to respond with disgust or anger when obscenities were used at college protest demonstrations than were older age groups—those thirty to forty-nine and those over fifty. Lodle (1972) discovered that subjects over thirty expressed "concern for others" as a major controlling element in a decision to use "dirty words." No other age group exhibited such a concern. How old the speaker is and the age of the receiver influence the perception of taboo language as either offensive or relatively innocuous.

The degree of status an individual possesses is a third factor that affects our view of taboo language. Status is the prestige position or rank one has in relation to others. Traditional "wisdom" assumes that the upper echelons of society, principally because of their exposure to education and "culture," are supposed to develop "refined" attitudes and employ dignified language, whereas the lower-class poor characteristically stoop to coarse and obscene nonstandard language variants. Linguistic research supports this commonly accepted view. Bernstein (1966) and Labov (1972) have demonstrated that a direct relationship exists between socioeconomic status and linguistic choice of speakers. Wolfram and Fasold (1974) cite research which clearly shows that stigmatized forms of speech and language usage are associated with low status groups while socially prestigious variants are adopted by high status groups as linguistic indicators of such status. Verbal obscenity thus becomes associated with "gutter talk," the stigmatized language of the uncouth, the uneducated, and the unwashed.

Those who make claim to high-status positions are expected to speak in dignified language, avoiding stigmatized forms of expression. Many Americans were upset by Harry Truman's penchant for salty language. "Bad language" became an issue during the 1960 Kennedy–Nixon debates, when Richard Nixon piously asserted that Eisenhower had "restored dignity and decency and, frankly, good language to the conduct of the Presidency of the United States."

Two incidents during the Watergate era provide insight into the relationship between status and the reaction to taboo language. It was revealed that two individuals of high status were guilty of verbal taboo violation. Earl Butz, Secretary of Agriculture during the Nixon Administration, reportedly made the following statement in reference to what "coloreds" supposedly want in life: "I'll tell you what coloreds want. It's three things: first, a tight pussy, second, loose shoes; and third, a warm place to shit. That's all [cited in Dean, 1976, p. 57]." Richard Nixon was also guilty of utilizing proscribed language. "Expletive deleted" became a national joke when the Watergate tapes were the subject of public scrutiny. One particular statement, because of its incriminating features, stood out. Nixon's statement, "I don't give a shit what happens. I want you all to stonewall it. . . ." became national news. It is instructive to see how the people reacted to these two statements by high-status individuals.

Generally, there was a mixture of shock and outrage when it was revealed that Earl Butz and Richard Nixon talked like longshoremen. Butz, probably partly because his "joke" was a racial slur as well as a violation of language taboos, was forced to resign his post while under fire from an incensed public. Nixon was forced to resign for other reasons, but the public reaction to the revelation that he liberally sprinkled his private conversations with obscene and profane language was highly negative and hardly dispassionate ("The Public Disillusioned," 1974, pp. 20–27). It was looked upon as a debasement of his high office. Presidents and members of the Cabinet are not supposed to speak gutter language.

Thus, age, sex, and status of the individual using taboo language play an important role in influencing perceptions of proscribed words. Who uses such language does make a difference.

WHAT Is Said: Our Licentious Lexicon

Edmund Leach (1964) formulated an interesting theory which partly explains why some words become taboo. He argues that words become taboo when they fall into an ambiguous intermediate category between two polarities. For instance, bodily secretions are universally tabooed—in particular excrement, urine, semen, menstrual blood, sweat, and mucous. Such substances are ambiguous in the sense that they are "me" and "not-me" at the same time. They are a product of me and yet they are apart from me. In addition, sexual intercourse falls into an ambiguous category because it is an acceptable act only under certain conditions—conditions not universally accepted. Thus, several "obscene" terms have the sex act as their source.

Similarly, religions have created the binary distinction of "this world" and "an other world." God and humans are thus polarities. An intermediate category, however, bridges the gap between God and humans. This intermediate category includes ambiguous supernatural beings who act as links between the two worlds. Incarnate deities, virgin mothers, and mythical monsters that are half human and half beast become objects of verbal taboos. Jesus Christ, for example, was a God-man and his name is a common profanity.

Animal categories of verbal abuse also demonstrate Leach's theory. English-speaking communities have two extreme categories for animals—the tame-friendly animals (sheep, ducks, lambs) and the wild-hostile animals (most animals found in zoos). Animals that fall into these extreme categories do not supply taboo terms that are used as insults. Speakers of the English language do not abuse another person by calling them a "dirty deer," a "raunchy robin," a "zoned-out zebra," or a "pitiful panther." These are not taboo insults. A number of ambiguous categories, however, fall into the apertures of the above binary distinctions. Pets, for example, are beasts that are treated like humans and thus are ambiguous. They can be both wild and hostile in a natural setting, predatory, or they can be domesticated by human intervention. Thus, pets become sources of taboo terms such as *bitch, pussy,* and *ass.* Similarly, some farm animals occupy an ambiguous position because they are regarded affectionately while providing a source of food. Thus swine (pigs) and cock (chickens) are taboo.

Leach's theory helps explain many of our nonrational taboos. It is not, however, the entire explanation. Although providing insight into why certain acts and objects become sources of taboo, it does not adequately explain why only certain terms for these acts or objects are taboo but others are not. *Lord* is not generally taboo but the simple exclamation *God* is. *Sexual intercourse* is acceptable but *fuck* is not, and *kitty* is neither obscene nor abusive while *pussy* can be both.

In addition, not all taboo terms are created equal. It is often asserted, and there is some empirical support available, that certain taboo terms are more offensive than others. Read (1934), Stone (1954), and Montagu (1967) imply that *fuck* is the most outrageous term generally. Sagarin (1962) endorses *cocksucker,* and Rossiter and Bostrom (1969), Lodle (1972), and Baudhuin (1973) empirically verified that *motherfucker* was the most offensive among their student samples. In addition, Rossiter and Bostrom (1969) and Baudhuin (1973) found that sexual obscenities in general were more offensive than excretory obscenities or profanities.

Efforts to discover which taboo terms out of context are most offensive, however, seem ill-conceived. Although generally some terms appear to be more offensive than others, there is a strong idiosyncratic flavor to such determinations. For instance, empirical investigations have revealed that *motherfucker* is the most offensive term, yet it is just as conceivable that *Goddamn* would be more offensive to a strongly religious person or *cunt* to a woman embarrassed by sexual frankness. It is also true that what currently is considered vile and obscene may be perceived innocuously in years to come. The fact that certain words are proscribed, however, contributes heavily to the perception that they are offensive. In essence, these words are offensive because they are forbidden, and they in turn remain forbidden because they are offensive—self-contained circular reasoning in full bloom.

What terms are used obviously has a direct bearing on the degree of offensiveness perceived by listeners. Those who shy away from these taboo terms typically resort to a wide variety of nonsense euphemisms to avoid offense. *Jiminy Cricket, Jeepers Creepers, Criminey, for Criminey sakes,* and similar transmogrifications serve as substitutes for Jesus Christ, Jesus, and Christ. *Golly, gosh,* and *gawd* are veiled alternatives for God; *darn, dern,* and *dadgum* replace *damn* and *dammit; frig* and *friggin'* replace *fuck* and *fucking;* and *son of a gun* sidesteps *son of a bitch.* What is noteworthy about most of these euphemisms is that they have no literal referential meaning. What is a "son of a gun"—a derringer fathered by a shotgun? Who or what is "criminey"?

All of these euphemisms represent acceptable forms of swearing because the taboo terms are merely alluded to but never precisely stated. They are acceptable expletives that serve a swearing function. They are simple exclamations that act as intensifiers for release of frustration or aggression, yet they do not invite the negative reactions so commonly associated with their taboo counterparts. In this respect, society encourages a facade of respectability, the illusion that it is more dignified to merely hint at what one prefers to say rather than state it directly.

In review, not all taboo terms are created equal. Some are more offensive than others. Although generally, sexual obscenities seem to be the most offensive of the taboo terms and profanities the least offensive, the degree of offensiveness is not a static quality of any word. If you assume otherwise, you are reifying.

In 1980, two events occurred that clearly showed how times have indeed changed. A bicycle rider wearing a T-shirt emblazoned with the words "Fuck Iran" casually pedaled down the streets of Eugene, Oregon, with not so much as a ripple of protest, even with some overt support (context makes a difference). The second event was that Barry Commoner, Citizen's Party candidate for President, used the word *bullshit* on one of his radio commercials. Times do change. Future generations may look back on our verbal taboos and their companion euphemisms and laugh loudly at the choices of words we designated as prohibited.

HOW It Is Used

There is a story told about Mark Twain, an experienced swearer, whose penchant for the four-letter phraseology so exasperated his wife on one occasion that she gave him a reflection of what he sounded like by unleashing a torrent of swearwords. Twain allowed her to finish her performance and then dryly remarked: "The words are there, my dear but the music is wanting [in Montagu, 1967, p. 68]."

The paralinguistic aspects of taboo language—tone of voice, demeanor, emotional expression, etc.—can influence how the message is received. You can say, "Fuck you" in a playful, kidding tone of voice, or in a harsh, caustic manner. The response to each variation is quite likely to differ dramatically. Although calling someone a *bastard* may ordinarily invite reprisal, the statement "The poor bastard never got a break" is sympathetic. Abrahams (1964) also notes that among ghetto blacks the most complimentary thing that can be said of a man is that he is a "mean motherfucker" or a "tough motherfucker [p. 261]." Thus, the way in which taboo language is spoken can determine whether such language is just offensive or rather sympathetic, laudatory, or complimentary. If we find ourselves inevitably responding to taboo language as offensive regardless of how it is used, we are then having a signal reaction to taboo words. The affective connotations attached to the taboo terms are superseding their intended meaning. We are setting the offending word adrift from its context, placing emphasis on its connotative meaning in isolation while ignoring its actual usage.

The relevance of context can be seen even more clearly when we consider certain words whose meaning is highly ambiguous, sometimes even when context is considered. You can refer to a private "dick" when in need of an investigator, but it becomes a "private part" when referring to the sex organ. How differently we respond to "don't peter out" and "don't take your peter out." "He played with his balls" leaves everyone in doubt. One can "snatch a kiss" but reverse the order and you have an "obscenity." "Nice pussy" requires further elaboration, "prick" can be touchy, and "cock" is a "barnyard epithet" that does double duty. Unless their usage conjures allusions to sex and excretion, such words can sneak by almost unnoticed but for the occasional snicker of pubescent youth becoming wise to the contradictions of an anxious society. Montagu (1967) cites a limerick that plays upon this double duty that some words perform:

> *There was a young woman named Glass*
> *Who had a most beautiful ass*
> *Not round and pink,*
> *As you might think,*
> *But gray, and had ears, and ate grass* [p. 317].

How frequently taboo language is utilized is another factor that can affect your perception of proscribed language usage. Adolescent peer groups and male groups in the armed forces, to cite just two examples, use the number of taboo words used by an individual in conversation as a criterion for judging masculinity. Males who appear squeamish and offended by profanities, obscenities, and abusive taboo language invite harsh judgments of effeminacy and womanliness. Frequent use and approval of taboo language becomes a sign of masculinity. The fantasy that strong words make strong men is simply naïve reification, yet in ritualistic fashion, weak men often make an attempt to disguise their sense of inadequacy by constant repetition of aggressive swearwords.

While frequency of usage may be viewed by some as a sign of masculinity, a kind of semantic macho, abundant use of proscribed language may result in merely a vague awareness that such language colors the conversation. Studies by Lambert and Jokobovits (1960) and Fillenbaum (1967) demonstrate an anesthetic effect from frequent repetition of some words. Semantic satiation sets in, and once powerful and shocking language becomes hackneyed and impotent. Used solely as intensifiers ad nauseam, a message liberally punctuated with taboo terms can lose its objective sense and become almost comical. Young (1964) cites an appropriate example from an uncertain source, possibly of Australian origin:

> I was walking along on this fucking fine morning, fucking sun fucking shining away, little country fucking lane, and I meets up with this fucking girl. Fucking lovely she was, so we get into fucking conversation and I takes her over a fucking gate into a fucking field and we has sexual intercourse [p. 314].

Fucking obviously is not used here in an obscene or sexual manner. The overabundant use of the term in concert with the more clinical *sexual intercourse,* however, illustrates how repetition can obscure the denotative meaning of proscribed language.

Once again it is affirmed that the context of a word directly affects its meaning. No word is inherently dirty, profane, or abusive. How it is used is an essential ingredient in determining likely reactions to taboo language.

WHY It Is Used

Despite the characterization of some taboo words as *obscene,* and despite their references to sex, taboo language is ordinarily used for reasons other than sexual arousal. With the possible exception of literary use of proscribed words and phrases or perhaps intimate sexual communication, arousal of sexual desire seems a tertiary consideration at best for most practitioners of such prohibited speech. Examination of the several primary reasons why such language enters one's speech will demonstrate that this clearly is the case.

Power and Intensity. The overriding reason for using taboo language is to convey power and intensity. The forbidden nature of such language embues it with seemingly magical powers. Capitalizing on the awkward position verbal taboos impose on an anxious society, the self-styled Yippie leader Abbie Hoffman demonstrated such magical powers of proscribed words during the protests at the 1968 Democratic National Convention in Chicago. Mindful of restrictions on the media concerning explicit reporting of obscene, profane, and abusive language, Hoffman singlehandedly manipulated the three major television networks. How did he achieve such a feat of raw power? Simple: He printed the word *fuck* on his forehead. Cognizant of viewer reactions to such visible "obscenity," the networks had to edit carefully their coverage of Hoffman, for he had the obnoxious magical word obtrusively displayed on his person.

Taboo language conveys a message of great intensity. It adds power to one's speech because it is rebellious, shocking, outrageous, and a repudiation of societal norms of language decorum. Aware that society reacts in signal ways to such language, practitioners are free to exploit such rules of delicacy and "good taste." Hopeful of transmitting a sense of frustration, deep conviction, or passionate commitment to an idea or cause, verbal taboo transgressors use such words to punctuate, add emphasis, and intensify the message communicated. It is audacious, aggressive language when used in this way, and its power is difficult to ignore. It is because it is powerful and intense language that it is used for other reasons as well.

Catharsis.   Virtually any emotionally charged word can provide catharsis—the tranquilizing effect produced by venting our emotions forcefully—and some people will avoid taboo terminology in favor of more "acceptable" expletives. Yet the power of prohibited language to shock and their fugitive existence in the back alleys of societal discourse makes them apt to be unleashed even by many who are outwardly disdainful of such language. Frustration or anger generated by rigid organizations with tight discipline, such as the military service, promotes violation of verbal taboos. Those who have never used profanity or obscenity in their lives may find themselves using it frequently in the army as a means of releasing pent-up frustration and anger kept stifled by demands for unquestioning obedience to authority, sometimes of dubious merit. Covert or overt use of taboo language offers an emotional release, an outlet for aggression. In this way, it serves as a surrogate for physical violence. Unable to strike officers, one can verbally abuse them in private, releasing aggressive feelings encouraged by forced compliance to orders and silence in the face of abuse. Similar patterns exist in business organizations and the like where an unequal distribution of power exists and rigid conformity is mandated.

Unable or unwilling to use taboo language themselves, even in private, some people find catharsis from listening to a shaman. In primitive tribes, the shaman or "sinful" priest or medicine man will commit the outrage, speak the obscenities for others who feel they cannot, thereby relieving their frustrations. The shaman stands outside of almost all of society. From this vantage point sacred cows can be scorned. Lenny Bruce was a shaman. His style of comedy centered on the repulsive, the shocking, the abusive, and the sacred. It seems plausible that his popularity among those who came to be entertained by this "dirty-talking comic" is partly explained by the catharsis that people sought in his performances. Their laughter was their emotional release and their catharsis, and their scorn for the taboos imposed by society that Bruce violated with such impunity, was experienced vicariously (Hartogs, 1967, and Lodle, 1972).

Whether overt, covert, direct, or indirect, the violation of verbal taboos involves intense emotional release. Not only do proscribed words punctuate messages with potency and impact, but they also allow a person to "let off steam" trapped by society's taboos.

Create Attention. This is perhaps the most obvious reason to use forbidden language. Small children sometimes use it to call attention to themselves. Groups with a grievance who feel submerged and ignored by a complacent or insensitive society have increasingly utilized offensive language. For some it is a cry of desperation. Their message has gone unheeded and unheard. Taboo language is intense and jolting, not easily ignored. Shocked as listeners may be, proscribed language cries out for others to pay attention, to see in a new way.

While some may be outraged by the language and ready to exercise punitive action against transgressors, it is a calculated risk to employ such terminology. Some people deem it necessary. To be rejected and scorned and have one's message villified is sometimes more tolerable than to remain unnoticed.

Provoke. Forbidden language can and has been used on occasion to incite a confrontation between disagreeing sides. Such a purpose was most clearly in evidence during the political and social protests of the late 1960s and early 1970s. Verbal obscenity, profanity, and animal abuse terms used by protesters at the Chicago Democratic National Convention in 1968 were clearly intended to provoke a violent encounter with the police (Bowers and Ochs, 1971, p. 70).

The power of taboo language to shock and enrage makes it an

appropriate choice for provoking others to violence. Faced with a steady barrage of verbal villification, police (or almost anyone faced with such abuse) will signally react to these "fighting words" with physical attacks upon the instigators (Rothwell, 1971). Yet such responses can provide a kind of symbolic victory to the agitators. It "proves" the police really are "pigs." If the response by the police seems out of proportion to the provocation, attention may focus on the violent retaliation rather than the abusive rhetoric. This, then, becomes a part of the agitators' gambit. Provoke a violent signal reaction to the verbal invective and then shift the cry *foul* to those who were goaded into disproportionate violence. It is a hazardous venture fraught with dangerous, even tragic, consequences. And as most people have learned from "childhood indiscretions," one does not have to be a radical agitator to feel the sting of a strategy to provoke gone out of control. Parents are not trained like police to resist provocations.

Discredit.   Violation of verbal taboos discredits the taboo, but there is more to it than this. In some cases it is part of a calculated plan of attack upon societal norms and values. Much of the political protest rhetoric in the Vietnam War era incorporated prohibited words as a symbol of rejection of language taboos, standards of civility and decorum, and a "system" that preached national debate and justice for all but allegedly perpetuated racism, poverty, and a multitude of other injustices. Taboo language was seen as an appropriate and powerful attack on societal hypocrisy.

The language of the "establishment" is euphemistic and dehumanizing, it was argued. A system that preaches peace while destroying the tiny country of Vietnam reveals its moral decay and illustrates how impoverished its language has become. Heinous crimes are committed under the guise of *patriotism* or some other convenient abstraction, yet "four-letter words" are considered a more terrible crime. It is argued (with some justification) that the map does not fit the territory. The taboo words are not worse than the violence that is blithely excused. Rejecting the "system" means rejecting its linguistic code with its hypocritical restraints.

There is a strong sentiment for an "honest" rhetoric, devoid of sham, pretense, and euphemistic platitudes that disguise the shameful truth. Since verbal obscenity, profanity, and animal abuse terminology are antithetical to the "establishment" because it has branded such language "taboo," it therefore expresses a rebellion against "the system," an irreverence for the sacred, and a rejection of polite and "rational" discourse that perpetuates injustice. The "system" is discredited by "telling it like it is." The style is irreverent, disrespectful, and caustic. There is a sense of power and delight in speaking the unspeakable, in villifying the sacred objects of respect, of shattering the complacency of the "establishment" with shock rhetoric.

There is a large dose of fantasy, however, in this rationale for using offensive language to discredit. Violating verbal taboos does not "tell it like it is" but only as some selectively perceive it. Proscribed language is not "more honest" than inoffensive language. It is simply bold and outrageous. One does not make more sense by being uncouth, profane, and abusive. Mindless repetition of offensive language may be more a sign of an empty head and a substitute for careful reflection than a sign of honesty, candor, and good sense. At the same time it should be noted that those raising the hue and cry against those doing the discrediting often become more upset by the agitators' language than by the violence and killing the agitators may vehemently deplore. Such a response makes *verbal* violence more unacceptable than acts of physical violence. This hardly stands as a tribute to our claim of rationality.

Redefinition.   Minority groups such as blacks, gays, Indians, Chicanos, and the largest of all minorities, women, have attempted to alter the image and identity given them by the dominant majority, or those in power. It is a vitally important process to redefine negative images especially when such images are inaccurate verbal maps. For blacks it has meant replacing the rigidly stultifying and patently false stereotype picturing them as lazy and shiftless with a more positive image of "black is beautiful" and a more militant rhetoric calling for power. Those who have the power to define are in control.

Redefinition, then, becomes a power struggle. As previously discussed, taboo language has long been viewed in the American culture as a sign of masculinity. It has been taboo for women to use such language because it threatens to disrupt the social order. As Hartogs

(1967) explains, obscenities are a badge of social dominance, and when women speak previously "male" language, they serve symbolic notice that they are assuming male authority status.

In a lesser sense, adolescents symbolically proclaim their adulthood by using adults-only language. Defined by parents as less than adults, as *children,* adolescent youths try to redefine themselves by adopting language exclusive to adults. It is, of course, only a symbolic gesture analogous to women's struggle to redefine themselves. Adolescents do not become adults simply by adopting some of the superficial verbal accoutrements of adulthood. Women likewise do not shed their subservient role merely by employing aggressive taboo rhetoric. Language would be truly magical if such were the case. More than style is required to gain power and self-determination. Using taboo language, however, can be an effective strategy for gaining recognition of a new image identity and stature, one that is contemptuous of the established order, because it is immediately noticeable and carries impact.

Identification.   The use of proscribed language sometimes serves the purpose of establishing identification with a group or individual. It is an attempt at social solidarity. Adolescents (usually male) sometimes adopt such language to be "one of the group." Hartogs (1967) asserts that upper class executives may also use dirty language in front of workers with lower class status to demonstrate that they are "just like them." Ross (1960), in a simple empirical observation, also suggests a relationship between use of swearwords and identification with the group. Conklin (1974) claims that using a word like *shit* or *fuck* is one of the signs of a feminist in this society. It is a symbolic gesture of acceptance of an ideology and a value structure of certain groups. It is a symbol of oneness with the group. It may prove worthiness to join the group or simply to maintain membership because taboo language may serve as a pledge of allegiance and militancy. It has functioned in such a fashion for young white "radicals" trying to demonstrate their solidarity with blacks (Rothwell, 1971).

One of the best examples of taboo language used to establish identification with a group is the verbal skill game played by young male ghetto blacks variously termed *the dozens, sounding, playing the dozens, the dirty dozens,* and other more local labels. The function of the game is to establish a "rep," an ethos within the group. It is a contest of one-upmanship where the best "rappers" are looked up to by the group. Kochman (1969) points out that "ability with words is apparently as highly valued as physical strength [p. 33]" among ghetto blacks. When one is goaded into physical violence as a response to verbal attack, the status of this individual is diminished.

Verbal obscenity plays a central role in such verbal combat. The contest often begins with an obscenity such as "Fuck you," which may elicit the standard retort, "Fuck your mother," or the less common, "Man, you haven't even kissed me yet [Kochman, 1969, p. 33]." Since the object of this verbal skill game is to out duel your opponent and win the admiration of the group, verbal obscenity serves the useful purpose of providing a strong arsenal of insults that attack opponents' vulnerabilities and encourage them to "blow their cool."

Use of taboo language is obviously not the sole method of establishing identification with the group. If using such language were all that was necessary to gain admission to a group, infiltration by outsiders and "enemies" would be child's play. Use of proscribed language is also not enough to sustain membership in a group. In addition it is quite obviously an inappropriate means of identification with many more "traditional" groups in our society.

Taboo language is thus utilized for a variety of purposes, the least of which is to arouse sexual interest. As circumstances change, the reasons one uses such language often change. Unquestionably, why proscribed language is used does affect both the sending, receiving, and ultimately the content of messages.

WHERE It Is Used

Using obscene, profane, and abusive language, even in a clinical way, in schools, courts of law, churches, on public stages, and in other locations whose norms dictate a more sedate type of language is shocking in its violation of long-held standards of "public decency." While many people deplore the use of taboo language in public, they nevertheless use it quite freely in private. Nykodym and Boyd (1975) found that the subjects they studied used verbal obscenity more frequently when alone and less when in the presence of strangers.

There are, however, exceptions to the norm that use of taboo language in public is more serious than in private. In some public places and situations taboo language is expected, even encouraged. Taverns and public restrooms provide forums for proscribed language because they are relatively unobtrusive whereas downtown shopping centers are normally inappropriate forums for shouting obscenities.

Exceptions regarding verbal behavior are also different. In the military the expectation is that language normally interdicted will be used bountifully.

The issue of public versus private use of sanctioned language is a more complex one than these simple observations indicate. The legislative and especially the judicial branches of government, and on occasion the executive branch, have all become embroiled in the controversy, "Where do we draw the line?"

Legal and professional restraints placed on offensive language involve complex judicial decisions and precedents. Where such language is used is but one factor contributing to such restraints, but a highly important one nonetheless. An examination of these restraints shows an interplay between all the various factors that influence a person's perception of sanctioned language.

While judicial interest in obscenity dates back to the nineteenth century, it was not until the *Roth* (354 U.S. 476 [1957]) decision that the United States Supreme Court attempted to define obscenity and delineate guidelines for where to draw the legal line. As stated more directly in *Memoirs* (383 U.S. 413 [1966]), the *Roth* decision established three standards for obscenity. First, the dominant theme of the work taken in its entirety must appeal to a "prurient interest in sex." Second, such references to sex must be "patently offensive" when applying "contemporary community standards." Third, the work must be "utterly without redeeming social value."

The *Roth* test did little to clarify obscenity standards for the courts, law enforcement officials, and legislatures. The use of such terms as "prurient interest," "patently offensive," and "contemporary community standards" proved to be elusive verbal maps upon which to guide judicial determinations of obscenity. Justice Harlan in *Ginsberg* v.

New York (390 U.S. 707 [1969]), stated that "anyone who undertakes to examine the Supreme Court's decision since *Roth* . . . would find himself in utter bewilderment." The *Roth* test of obscenity was applied to language in literature in three major court cases. One dealt with D. H. Lawrence's classic in erotica, *Lady Chatterly's Lover (Grove Press, Inc.* v. *Christenberry,* 276 F. 2nd 433 [2nd cir. 1960]). A second case involved Henry Miller's novel *Tropic of Cancer (Grove Press, Inc.* v. *Gerstein,* 378 U.S. 577 [1964]). A third case considered John Cleland's *The Memoirs of a Woman of Pleasure (Memoirs* v. *Massachusetts,* 383 U.S. 413 [1966]), better known as *Fanny Hill,* a book first printed in England in 1749 containing vivid descriptions of sexual activity but no conventional "dirty words." In all three cases a majority of the justices ruled the works acceptable for public consumption and outside the obscenity standard.

Following these court decisions it seemed clear that any language, euphemistically suggestive or "patently offensive," was not by itself sufficient grounds to censor a printed work. "Dirty words" by themselves do not make a work obscene. What actually does constitute obscenity in concrete instances was a matter still befuddling the justices.

In a rare about-face, the Supreme Court, hoping to establish a more applicable and concrete obscenity test, muddied the obscenity issue with a series of decisions, most notably *Miller* v. *California* (413 W.S. 15 [1973]). Recognizing that the *Roth* test was "unworkable," the majority once again established three standards for determining obscenity. First, "community standards" of "prurient interest" and "patent offensiveness" need not be national uniform standards, but rather state or even local standards (Haan, 1978). Second, which acts are potentially obscene should be spelled out by state or federal legislatures. Third, the "utterly without redeeming social value" test was replaced with "serious literary, artistic, political, or scientific value."

Miller suffers from the same affliction associated with its predecessor *Roth.* Although purporting to be specific and clearly defined, it is not. Determinations of the relevant "community standards" are inevitably subjective and grounded on the selective perception of judges and jurors. Efforts by the court to provide a "few plain examples" of obscenity, became mired in high-level abstraction. Terms such as "ultimate sexual acts" and "lewd exhibition of the genitals" may sound concrete but allow wide differences of opinion and interpretation. They are merely vague descriptions. "Patently offensive" also remains unexplained. Justice Brennan argued in *Jenkins* v. *Georgia* (418 U.S. 167 [1974]) that as long as *Miller* remains the test of obscenity "one cannot say with certainty that material is obscene until at least five members of this Court applying inevitably obscure standards, have pronounced it so."

While *Miller* has changed the formula for obscenity, nothing in its construction or official attempts to clarify its standards indicates that offensive language *alone* is sufficient reason for banning a printed work. Offensive language by itself is not legally proscribed when used in a book, magazine, pamphlet, and similarly printed matter.

The same holds true for newspapers. In *Papish* v. *the University of Missouri* (410 U.S. 667 [1973]) the Supreme Court ruled that the term *motherfucker* even when printed in a headline was not "constitutionally obscene." The material must be considered as a whole and the entire standards of obscenity articulated in *Miller* must be applied. In other words, context is the guiding principle in any determination of legally proscribed language.

Radio and television were accorded special treatment, however, by the Supreme Court in 1978. Ruling on a case involving the broadcasting of a satirical spoof of "bad words" by comedian George Carlin on radio station WBAI in New York City, the Court decreed that due to the obtrusive nature of radio (and presumably television as well), such "indecent language" cannot be aired over radio during regular daytime hours when children might be listening. Justice Stevens of the Supreme Court argued for the majority, however, that "Indecency is largely a function of context—it cannot be adequately judged in the abstract. Indeed, we may assume . . . that this monologue (George Carlin's) would be protected in other contexts ["FCC Allowed," 1978, p. 1A]."

Although Supreme Court decisions and Section 1464 of the United States Criminal Code, which reads, "whoever utters any obscene, indecent, or profane language by means of radio communication shall be fined no more than $10,000 or imprisoned no more than two years or both," serve as important inhibitors of offensive language usage on radio and television, other factors also play an important role.

Given the commercial nature of such media, self-censorship is exercised. Worried about alienating their listening and viewing audience, and ultimately inducing the wrath of sponsors, radio and television have largely avoided taboo language. Even late night talk shows are punctuated with "bleeps" or brief periods of silent conversation, alerting audiences that a language taboo was violated.

Sitting in the background insuring that television stations will perform the necessary exorcism of offensive language is the Federal Communications Commission. The power to revoke licenses when stations' programming is deemed contrary to the public interest makes the FCC a potent agency to be reckoned with.

Although newspapers are relatively unrestricted concerning taboo language, they also are highly sensitive to commercial interests. Despite its newsworthiness, a spot check by the Associated Press bureaus throughout the United States revealed that only two newspapers printed verbatim the Earl Butz "joke" referred to previously ("Papers Cautious," 1977). Many papers, however, did print the Nixon "I don't give a shit" quotation (Rothwell, 1977).

The movie industry has a long history of self-censorship beginning with a "Production Code" in the 1920s and 1930s which forbade "four-letter words" and "profanities" in motion pictures. It was not until 1961 and the movie *The Connection* that the word "shit" was introduced into the vocabulary of movies. It created a storm of controversy. A few years later *Who's Afraid of Virginia Woolf?* assaulted audiences with a host of forbidden terms as no previous film had. Other movies soon followed suit when it became clear that such language did not jeopardize the commercial success of a movie. The industry, recognizing the futility of its effort to censor the language in movies, since it had no legal authority to do so, resorted to its now well-established rating system to guide viewers (or warn them) rather than censor content.

Restrictions on the use of taboo language in a public forum not specifically involving mass media have been gradually eroded by the Supreme Court. Rutzick (1974) notes that the Court has drawn a tight line of constitutional protection around the use of such language excepting but one area of concern. Offensive language that incites a violent response, so-called "fighting words," in a face-to-face confrontation is unprotected speech. This "fighting words" rationale for censoring public expression of certain words tacitly recognizes that such words can incite signal reactions in the form of violence. Protection of public morality and regard for the sensibilities of offended listeners, two previous concerns of the Court, have been rejected as justifications for censorship of offensive language in public.

This so-called reformulated *Chaplinski* model (Rutzick, 1974) grappled with the issue of offensive language that was not used in a sexual or erotic manner. The case of comedian Lenny Bruce, however, introduced another element into the issue of constitutionally protected speech.

In a three-year period prior to his death in 1966, Bruce was arrested on obscenity charges several times. His comic routines were frontal assaults on societal mores. Bruce was accused of using lewd and indecent language that "debased sex." He urged the Court to recognize his routines as socially important, thereby under the *Roth* test absolving him of the crime of obscenity. After protracted litigation, Bruce was found innocent of obscenity charges, eighteen months after his death from a morphine overdose. His routines were judged to have some socially redeeming qualities.

Legal and professional restraints placed on offensive language emphasizes the flexibility of language and the importance of considering such language in its proper context. What is said and where such language is used make a critical difference. Words that escape sanction when printed in books, magazines, or newspapers can be legally prohibited on prime time radio and self-censored by an industry such as television. In each case it is presumed that the nature of the media of transmission alters the effects of such language.

In addition, who uses "bad words" (Nixon and Watergate), how offensive words are used—in a profane or obscene manner as opposed to a spontaneous outburst, for instance—and why they are used, such as to incite violence from listeners or simply to entertain and produce laughter, are factors that determine whether offensive words will be legally and professionally sanctioned.

On the whole, legal interdiction of offensive words has been loosened considerably over the years. With the exception of broadcast media and public incitement to violence, criminal prosecution for using conventionally tabooed terminology is no longer the rule. Because most uses of such language do not appeal to prurient interest and are not fundamentally erotic, *Miller* seems difficult to apply and will not likely reverse the gradual trend toward relatively unrestricted language choice.

Professional restraints, however, while virtually nonexistent in the areas of movies and books, still remain stringent in such areas as newspapers, television, and radio. The fear of legal repercussions has contributed to some of this stringency while sensitivity to audience reaction that might affect commercial interests accounts for the rest.

EFFECTS

A point that has been consistently stressed is that the effects of using offensive language are a result of a conglomeration of elements all interacting to greater or lesser degree in any one context. The who, what, where, why, and how of offensive language bear directly upon the ultimate effects such language will have on an audience.

Why proscribed language is employed, however, does offer a useful gauge of the intended effects. The purpose becomes a type of yardstick upon which to measure the effectiveness of sanctioned language. For instance, if it is intended to provoke violence, then a measure of its effectiveness would be observable violence. If the intent is to gain attention, then you would try to determine the degree of attention aroused.

All purposes for using taboo language are potential effects, and to the extent that the purpose is achieved one can claim effectiveness (ignoring, of course, values implicit in each purpose). Thus, the intent may become the result or effect. It may intensify messages, create attention, provoke violence, discredit the icons, sacred cows and shibboleths of the controlling majority, provide cathartic release, re-define persons or groups, and establish solidarity and identification with a group.

The provocation of violence, however, seems to be the principal effect of such language. Greenberg's (1976) study of language intensity correlates taboo terms with perceived aggression. Categorizing 35 sentences into seven levels of verbal aggression, Greenberg reveals that the ten sentences found to be most aggressive by subjects all contained obscenity, profanity, or animal abuse terms. Conversely, none of the ten least aggressive sentences as rated by subjects contained any taboo language.

Physical violence is the most frequently noted effect of taboo language. A child may be spanked for using such language. Calling someone a *bastard* or a *motherfucker*, when intended as an insult, may result in an extended stay in the hospital.

Two significant protest demonstrations in the late 1960s and early 1970s show the relationship between sanctioned language and incitement of violence. The first occurred during the 1968 Democratic National Convention in Chicago. The report by the Walker Commission details numerous instances of verbal obscenity and violence it apparently precipitated. Daniel Walker (1968), the director of the Chicago Study Team that wrote the report, notes in the preface: "Extremely obscene language was a contributing factor to the violence described in this report, and its frequency and intensity were such that to omit it would inevitably understate the effect it had [p. ix]." Bowers and Ochs (1971), using the Walker Commission as a primary source, claim that verbal obscenity was probably the tactic that incited the "police riot."

It is of course plausible that Chicago police merely used the outrageous language as a pretense for pulverizing a few "freaks" and "hippies." Even here, though, offensive language was at least an indirect cause of violence.

The protest at Kent State University in the spring of 1970 is another instance where sanctioned language has apparently played a role in provoking violence. James A. Michener (1971) in a careful and detailed recounting of the shooting of 13 students by Ohio National Guardsmen, argues:

> Worse, in a way, than the missiles were the epithets, especially when launched by coeds. A steady barrage of curses, obscenities, and fatal challenges came down upon the Guard, whose gas masks

did not prevent their hearing what they were being called. Girls were particularly abusive, using the foulest language and taunting Guardsmen with being "shit-heels, motherfuckers, and half-assed pigs [p. 33]."

Michener concludes that the obscenities contributed to the slaying of four students and wounding of nine others. He also claims that verbal obscenity, especially from women students, was instrumental in alienating the local citizenry. Violation of language taboos incites an intense, frequently aggressive response.

If the report of the Walker Commission and the Michener account are correct even to a degree, you can see the power of verbal obscenity. Its capacity to incite verbal or physical violence is a two-edged sword. Michener's account clearly supports the observation that students in general never anticipated the kind of response they received from the National Guard. It is a hazardous rhetorical strategy. Even when used simply for cathartic release, shock, anger, and even physical reproach are not unlikely actions from even casual auditors.

In addition, although taboo language is sometimes used as a strategy of redefinition (for example, when women assert control over their language behavior), it can backfire. Guardians of the status quo may seize upon the "dirty language" as proof of the degeneracy and filth of those using such language. They are then capable of claiming that the language defines those using it as less than human and thus worthy of contempt and worse.

Another related effect is that verbal obscenity, given the conservative view of mass media like television and radio concerning such language, limits access to the mass media. In some cases verbal obscenity may limit access to media unintentionally, and in others by design. In either case, the message is watered down and filtered, scrubbed of its intensity and capsulized into some generalized description like "and obscenities were used." The message is altered. The rage is gone. All that remains is the dry, emotionless report devoid of direct quotation. Separated from its live context, the verbal obscenities may seem less justified, morally reprehensible to some. Where the obscenity appears and how it is reported can radically alter the effect it has upon auditors.

Another corresponding effect that grows out of the polarization created by using verbal obscenity to discredit or provoke is an obvious block to engaging in dialogue. This may be intended, but it nonetheless merits mentioning because of its communication implications. Verbal obscenity draws attention but frequently to itself. The language becomes the only message filtered through. Communication is difficult when the issue becomes language choice rather than more central concerns (although in some instances language choice may be the important issue to both sides). Issues such as racism, morality, justice, and so forth, can be easily obfuscated when attention is drawn to the rhetorical style and when the rhetorical style becomes the content and the issue.

WHEN TO USE TABOO LANGUAGE: LINGUISTIC SENSITIVITY

It is not imperative that you use taboo language to prove your linguistic emancipation and your semantic sophistication. It is a matter of personal choice. Some of you may choose to avoid taboo terminology entirely. Such a choice does not constitute language misuse. I am not embarking on a campaign to promote universal swearing.

It is inevitable, however, that many, perhaps most of us will use proscribed language. Since the consequences of violating verbal taboos can be quite serious, and since this book is concerned with language misuse and malpractice, let me offer some thoughts regarding what I consider to be a rational, sound approach to taboo language usage—one which flows from my previous treatment of verbal taboos.

First, those who believe it is always wrong to use taboo language should realize that they have made a value judgment, a moral decision which is not grounded in a rational assessment of the nature of language. The indiscriminate evaluation of certain forbidden words is an instance of reification. Such reification can make us prisoners of our own language because we shackle ourselves to a rigid, inflexible response to such language. We signally react with disgust, anger, hatred, or even violence whenever we hear proscribed words. No rational assessment of the message is required. We are thinking with our glands, not our brain.

Second, those who believe that offensive language should never be proscribed and everyone should be free to use such language whenever the mood strikes are equally prisoners of language. Asserting that it is your right to say whatever you please using whatever language you choose has no basis in law and is an infantile view of communication and language. It may gratify us to shock people with offensive language, but it is pretentious and self-indulgent when that is the only reason it is used.

Prohibitions on language usage, however, should rarely be matters of law. What we are principally dealing with here is linguistic sensitivity—analyzing your audience and considering the entire communication picture before consciously choosing how to phrase your message. Linguistic sensitivity requires an intelligent appraisal of the purpose of the message, the audience that receives the message, and the occasion. There is no simple formula such as "It's always wrong" or "It's never wrong."

Consider two examples. Should you allow your child to use taboo language? The answer, of course, is easy if you take one of the extreme positions. Then again all decisions are easy if we take a dogmatic point of view, one guided by two-valued thinking (for example, "good" versus "bad").

Personally, I find the question far more complicated. Since I see nothing inherently wrong with taboo language from a linguistic and rational point of view, I am inclined to say "yes" to the question. But I wouldn't be pleased if a child of mine learned words such as *shit* or *fuck* before learning *mom* and *dad*. Call it pride if you will, but I believe a child needs to become linguistically sophisticated enough to appreciate the power of language and be able to analyze an audience before I would want them making decisions regarding the use of taboo terminology. At that point, perhaps by adolescence, the choice is theirs and so are the consequences.

The second example hits very close to home with me. Should a teacher use verbal obscenity or profanity in the classroom? Ask most school boards or parents and it would hardly seem an issue. And yet again I see it as a complex question. I have had many occasions in the college classroom to discuss language as an instrument of communication. Taboo language is a relevant and significant issue which I believe should be discussed in such a classroom setting. So the answer to the question is "yes" and "no." Yes when the purpose is educational, such as illustrating the power of language and principles of effective language use. No if it is merely to shock or seem "hip" and "with it." The primary school classroom also seems too early for such a discussion for reasons already explained in the first example.

Ultimately, each of us must make his or her own linguistic choices. There should be no glib formulas for language choice. Communication contexts are too complex for such simplistic decision-making to be relevant, reasonable, and appropriate.

SUMMARY

Whether you decide to use taboo language is probably less important than how you react to its use by others. A rational, sensible approach to such language considers the entire context, the who, what, where, why, and how of proscribed terminology. It is this complex context which determines the meaning of the words. As communicators, both senders and receivers, we should be sensitive to such contexts. Signal reactions to symbols of our own creation make us the slave not the master of our language.

THE LANGUAGE
OF VIOLENCE
AND THE KILLING POWER
OF WORDS

The pages of human history are soaked in the blood of battlefield carnage. Despite virtually universal protestations by nations large and small that war is abhorrent, humankind inexorably marches toward its own funeral. It has been estimated that in the last 5,000 years, only two hundred and ninety-two were without war. There have been almost 15,000 wars resulting in the deaths of 3.6 billion human beings, almost equal to the present world population (Bobrakov, 1973). Yet this orgy of bloodletting has not produced satiation, probably because we have lost our capacity to be horrified.

Recitation of aggregate deaths from previous centuries of collective violence pale into insignificance in an age when the prospect of a return to the Stone Age is not a mere fantasy of science fiction writers but rather a real possibility. Nevertheless, talk of doomsday rarely elicits more than a yawn, a shrug, or at most a fleeting expression of concern.

Part of the problem is that war and killing have become evermore impersonal. Where once we brutalized one another with clubs, knives, and swords, like slow-witted Neanderthals, now members of the nuclear weapons club can, in a fit of pique, bequeath our planet to the cockroach with a simple push of some buttons. Even in our "limited" wars victims often remain faceless nonentities. Bombs dropped from 50,000 feet appear as puffs of smoke and no more. Lifton (1972) notes that the trend in "conventional" warfare is toward an equally impersonal automated battlefield, where soldiers are replaced by machines and electronic circuitry that initiate the killing by remote control. Human "enemies" will be mere blips on a TV screen. There will be no "war crimes" nor "atrocities" but rather "computer errors" or, as one military spokesman termed it in testimony before a Senate committee, "a nontargetable activation."

Numbers of "enemy" dead and wounded, produced by our technological warfare, read like a census report. Such "casualty counts" have no human features. They do not bleed or suffer, feel grief or anguish, nor do they personalize the rage, hatred, loathing, agony, and fear associated with human slaughter.

War has become so abstract that we now "think the unthinkable" and use computers to calculate the likely consequences of a nuclear cataclysm. Not only has technology screened us from the ugliness of war, but our language has also been used to depersonalize killing, legitimize mind numbing levels of violence, and blind us to the realities of armed conflict.

Nevertheless, we have not yet reached the point where we can entirely escape the ravages of war. Vietnam, for instance, triggered a decade of domestic violence and few remained dispassionate about our role in the war. Vietnam is a chapter in history most Americans would prefer to forget, however, along with our history of collective violence against such groups as the Indians and blacks.Nevertheless, a significant lesson can be derived from careful scrutiny of such events, namely, that language can serve the cause of peace or war, nonviolence or violence. Used carefully and skillfully, it can be our most powerful tool for reversing the accelerating spiral of impersonal mass violence. Misused, language can be our own worst enemy, an implement of our collective suicide.

While presidential commissions, social scientists, philosophers, theologians, and other interested parties have carefully examined many causes of violence, the role language plays in producing and perpetuating collective violence has been largely ignored. This strikes me as a rather enormous oversight. Our chief means of describing incidents of mass violence, our primary medium of information exchange, our principal vehicle of persuasion, our fundamental instrument of negotiation, and our prime means of lying, deceiving, and distorting the truth has received scant attention as both a cause and partial solution to mass violence. The manner in which misuse of language makes collective violence more tolerable and acceptable and even fosters sometimes withering levels of brutality and killing is the subject of this chapter. At a time when collective violence is becoming increasingly impersonal, and language has become the handmaiden of apologists for mass murder, an earnest discussion of the language of violence seems urgent.

WHAT IS VIOLENCE?

This may appear at first blush to be a rather elementary, even trivial, question to pose. Surely we all know what violence is. In the abstract it refers to the dictionary definition—an exercise of physical force to abuse, incapacitate, or injure a person or damage and/or destroy property. Seems clear enough, right? Unquestionably shooting people and beating them up would have to be labeled *violence*. Yet a study by Blumenthal and her colleagues (1972) shows a rather remarkable lack of consensus among American males concerning which acts should be so labeled. Almost 1400 men between the ages of sixteen and sixty-four were asked to designate certain acts as either *violence, not violence,* or both. Fifty-seven percent of the respondents labeled police *shooting* looters *not violence* and 30 percent labeled police *beating* students as *not violence.* Conversely 58 percent of the same group designated draft card burning *violence* and 38 percent so designated student protest in and of itself.

In a subsequent study Blumenthal and her associates (1975) asked American males whether holding a protest meeting without a permit was violence. Sixty percent chose the *violence* end of a seven-point continuum from *violence* to *not violence;* 32 percent were on the extreme edge of the *violence* side of the continuum.

In an effort to discover the source of this rather surprising mis-labeling of relatively innocuous acts as *violence* and potentially injurious and lethal acts as *not violence,* Blumenthal and others used Osgood, Suci, and Tannenbaum's semantic differential technique referred to in Chapter Two. In addition to the three dimensions of this technique (evaluation, activity, and potency), Blumenthal added two additional dimensions, necessary-unnecessary and avoidable-unavoidable.

Agreement on the semantic meaning of "violence" was not universal but was significant. Generally, subjects agreed that violence is "fierce, strong, unnecessary, avoidable, and bad." Apparently, if a specific act is seen as possessing these qualities it is designated as *violence,* but in the absence of one or more of these qualities it is not deemed *violence.* For example, police shooting of looters may be perceived as unavoidable, necessary, and even good given the nature of looting, even though it may be perceived simultaneously as fierce and strong. It is thus labeled *not violence.*

What we are dealing with here is not the objective denotative meaning of violence (that is, use of physical force to abuse, incapacitate, or injure a person or damage or destroy property), but rather its subjective connotative meaning. It is a volatile not a stable verbal map. An individual labels an act *violence* when he or she selectively perceives that act to be neither legitimate, good, nor necessary. What constitutes violence thus becomes the mere reflection of each individual's view of the world at a particular moment.

Such subjective meaning for the word *violence* is like the story about the psychiatrist giving a Rorschach inkblot test to a client. When asked to identify the image produced for each inkblot, the client responds to the first, "a couple making love," to the second, "a nude woman silhouetted behind a shower door," and to a third, "a couple walking naked hand-in-hand." The psychiatrist pauses, then remarks,

"Mr. Smith, you seem to have an obsession with sex," whereupon Mr. Smith indignantly retorts, "What do you mean? You're the one showing me the dirty pictures." Violence, like dirty pictures, is in the eye of the beholder when connotative meaning serves as our conceptual map.

What constitutes violence in people's minds is not a trivial issue. There are at least two serious consequences of this reliance on connotative meanings of violence. First, violence for purposes of retaliation and social control is encouraged. The Blumenthal (1972 and 1975) studies found a direct relationship between the labeling of certain acts as *violence* and the levels of retaliatory physical force advocated. Additionally, the more respondents tended to label police acts as *not violence*, the higher the levels of injurious physical force deemed reasonable for social control.

Violence has negative connotations (that is, bad, unnecessary), so in order to rationalize harmful, even lethal, behavior considered necessary, good, and unavoidable, a kind of semantic prestidigitation is employed whereby such acts are simply labeled *not violence*. Language thus serves a magical function, in effect defining undesirable acts out of existence. As a result, violence (as denotatively defined) is fostered. Blumenthal (1972) observes that

> . . . if one defines police actions as violent, one is less likely to advocate such measures in the control of disturbances. Defining injurious or even deadly actions in other terms makes them easier to recommend and justify, a phenomenon of language and social action that has been especially observable in the politics of war and persecution [p. 90].

A second consequence of depending on connotative meanings of violence as a conceptual blueprint is that nonviolent protest will be discouraged and violence to achieve social and political goals will be encouraged. If society does not label acts as *violence* or *not violence* according to objective conventional definitions, which are then applied in a consistent manner, protesters are unlikely to draw such distinctions either. If a peaceful march or picketing is met with the same response as rock throwing, firebombing, or gang raping, then those with a grievance will choose strategies not so much on the basis of nonviolence but rather according to what means will produce the quickest results.

When nonviolent protest is met with physical abuse, beatings, club-bings, or even shootings as occurred in the early labor movement, the Civil Rights movement, and the era of Vietnam protest, advocates of nonviolence often become radicalized into accepting violence as a legitimate means of achieving their goals.

Thus, the connotative meaning of *violence* produces a rubber yardstick that promotes the use of physical force. Despite agreement at the high levels of abstraction that violence connotes that which is bad, unnecessary, and avoidable, the yardstick bends to individual self-interest. Graham and Gurr (1969) in their report to the National Commission on the Causes and Prevention of Violence note that Americans regard as violence anything that is contrary to personal or subgroup concerns, and have applauded or ignored acts of violence such as lynchings and murders when personal interests were served. This double standard is abetted by mislabeling relatively innocuous acts as *violence* and acts of brutality and inhumanity involving physical force as *not violence*. It is Orwellian doublethink in action. Violence is *not violence*. It is like a map of New York City applied to San Francisco, Chicago, Philadelphia or any other territory that strikes one's fancy. Its utility lies in confusing and muddling rather than clarifying and guid-ing. Mislabeling acts as *violence* or *not violence* can only perpetuate and promote primitive solutions to problems.

IDENTIFYING OUR ENEMIES: NOW YOU SEE THEM, NOW YOU DON'T

The United States has witnessed two periods of national hysteria in this century. The first was the "Red Scare" that followed on the heels of World War I, and the second was "McCarthyism" of the Korean War period. Although both instances graphically demonstrate the dangers inherent in waging war over ill-defined abstractions, the former in-stance clearly precipitated mass violence whereas the latter example generally produced outrageous violations of individual rights but comparatively little overt violence. The "Red Scare" is thus of more central interest to us here.

Robert K. Murray's (1955) definitive study of the "Red Scare" provides the relevant details concerning the relationship between signal reactions to vague language labels and violence. *Bolshevist* (the forerunner to *Communist)* was the signal word of the Red Scare era. It was an indiscriminate label that purported to identify the enemies of America, but no attempt was ever made to understand what the word meant. In the popular mind a Bolshevist could be anyone from a twitchy-eyed bombthrower to an advocate of nudist colonies or merely someone holding a contrary point of view. Union members, Socialists, and foreigners were common targets of abuse.

Bolshevism was an invisible enemy that spawned hatred, bigotry, repression, and mob violence. The American Civil Liberties Union estimated that there were at least fifty mob riots during 1919 related to the hysterical public paranoia concerning Bolshevism (p. 181). The answer to Bolshevism provided by the "super-patriots," who were in the vanguard of this exorcism of the "Red menace," was "100 percent Americanism." One vague abstraction was answered with yet another fuzzy abstraction. Slogans substituted for clear, precise thinking and careful investigation. America slept uneasily at night convinced that the evil Bolshevists were hard at work plotting America's demise.

The spectacle of a nation that espouses civil liberties and tolerance engaging in a frenzy of witch hunting was not exactly a venerable moment in American history. In retrospect, the whole incident seems like a comic opera except for the violence that erupted as a result of this national panic. It clearly points, however, to the peril created by imprecise use of language labels.

There are other historical examples of the relationship between collective violence and inexact identification of an enemy. During World War II Japan was clearly our enemy. Pearl Harbor destroyed any illusions about that. Yet all Japanese were not the enemies of America. This mistaken belief led to the forceable incarceration of 112,000 Japanese living on the Pacific coast. Seventy-one thousand were citizens of the United States by birth, yet were stripped of their possessions and imprisoned in camps located in desert areas of several Western states. Guarded by soldiers and surrounded by barbed wire and machine guns, the Nisei endured a Spartan existence. A "Jap" was a "Jap" no matter what the citizenship. Yet Nisei were later allowed to fight and die as American soldiers (the 442nd Regiment or Nisei outfit received more than 18,000 individual decorations for valor during the war [Hosokawa, 1969]) while their families lived in relocation camps.

A similar situation occurred in Vietnam. In order to "prove" we were winning the war, body counts of dead "enemy" soldiers were compiled. The problem was identifying ally from enemy when making such counts because the North and South Vietnamese were indistinguishable from each other, at least by physical characteristics. This also made it difficult at times to know whom to shoot, so killing in some instances became indiscriminate.

One solution to this problem of enemy identification was articulated by a GI who had been at My Lai (quoted in Lifton, 1971): "If it's dead, it's V.C.—because it's dead. If it's dead, it *had* to be V.C. and of course, a corpse couldn't defend itself anyhow [p. 42]." An American captain, when asked how he determined that the man he had just shot running out of a hut was a Viet Cong, replied, "Son, I know he's a V.C. by the nine bullet holes in his chest [Quoted in Schell, 1970, p. 19]."

The official army report on the My Lai massacre listed 128 "enemy" dead. Corpses offer no refutation. Some of the slaughtered were babies, making the label *enemy* inexact at the very least.

The absurdity of such tautological thinking whereby any dead Vietnamese is labeled an enemy because he or she is dead was pointedly summed up by Richard Goodwin (quoted in Donovan, 1970) during the war:

> If we take the number of enemy we are supposed to be killing, add to that the defectors, along with a number of wounded . . ., we find we are wiping out the entire North Vietnamese force every year. This truly makes their continued resistance one of the marvels of the world [p. 174].

At home, civil strife produced similar problems of enemy identification. Intangible labels such as the *establishment,* the *system,* the *military-industrial complex,* and the *power structure* became signal words, slogans for those opposed to the War and other social ills. So-called *establishment figures,* when branded as the cause of America's problems, tended to retaliate with equally simplistic allegations that domestic turmoil was the work of *hippies* and *radicals.* Such labels soon became reified and took on an independent existence. It is difficult to know what precisely people were identifying. Who belongs to the establishment? Anyone who possesses power? And to which one of the competing *establishments* do you refer? What is *the system?* Is it democracy that is the enemy here or simply those making decisions and legislating? What is a *hippie?* Anyone with long hair who wears beads and funny clothes?

Protesters and their rivals were often guilty of dead-level abstracting throughout the war. The enemy remained an abstraction, so amorphous and ill-defined that all were free to plug in their own prejudice and pet group (the military, corporate executives, politicians, "pigs," "rednecks," and the like) as the cause of the war, racism, poverty, or crime.

The irony of ritually mouthing such indiscriminate abstractions as *the system* and *the establishment* as causes of social evils and collective violence is that these same or similar trigger words were used to mobilize an entire nation to an orgy of violence by history's most notorious mass murderer, Adolph Hitler. As Bosmajian (1974) notes, Hitler identified the enemies of Germany in such ambiguous and hollow phrases as the *Red Dragon, Jewish bastardization, non-Aryan blood poisoning,* the *parliamentarians,* and the *democratic-Marxist Jew.* All these hateful sounding abstractions were then lumped together into yet another abstraction *das System.*

The Nazi propagandist Franz Six explained the rationale for creating the specter *das System.* As he observes, *das System* became an easily understood formula, a popular slogan, a call to battle against the economic conditions in Germany at that time. The hatred of the unemployed worker and the over-taxed farmer could be channeled in one direction. *Das System* was an abstraction that could have meant the Republic, the Marxist, or the Liberal government. It did not matter. The masses could be unified against a common enemy, driven on by National Socialist agitation.

A signal reaction to *das System* was the goal and it mattered not, rather it was prudent, that the German people responded to an invisible enemy that generated hatred and malice. The Jew, as a supposed chief architect of *das System* became a main target of violent oppression produced by such contrived malevolence. The result is history.

To battle abstractions is to fight ghosts. Violence is frequently the offspring of this quest to destroy bogey men and demons. We do have enemies but until we can more carefully specify and precisely identify them, we will continue to behave like a punch-drunk fighter swinging at shadows, and many innocent people will be victimized by such indiscriminate labeling practices.

IMAGES OF THE ENEMY: COWBOYS AND INDIANS REVISITED

Enemy and *ally* are rather fragile categories subject to the pragmatics of politics and power brokerage more than accurate perceptions of people and nations. The image of the cruel, treacherous, inhumane, vicious little bucktoothed "Jap" of World War II has succumbed to perceptions of Japanese as industrious, cultivated, and charming people worthy of our respect and friendship. The Russians were "courageous allies" in World War II; then they engaged in confrontation with the United States and assumed a less admirable image. And of course the Germans have see-sawed between being a fierce, ruthless enemy and a steadfast ally.

World circumstances to be sure have changed markedly over the years, influencing our perceptions of certain groups. These perceptions, however, tend to be gross, indiscriminate stereotypes that characterize all members of a nation in certain ways based primarily and perhaps exclusively on actions of their leaders. Gallup polls (1966) in 1942 and again in 1966 revealed that Americans' perceptions of people of various nations changed rather dramatically. In 1942 Germans and Japanese were characterized as warlike, treacherous, and cruel. None of these adjectives were used to describe Russians. In 1966, it was the Russians who were characterized as warlike and treacherous and such adjectives were absent from descriptions of Germans and Japanese.

Here is an example of stereotypes changing, yet they changed in gross extremes, making it improbable that the people of any of these nations had radically transformed from ruthless barbarians to lovers of peace and freedom and vice versa. One stereotype replaced another and the stereotypes were based on perceptions of nations as "enemies" or "allies." This two-valued orientation resurrects the worn-out movie cliche of the bad guys versus the good guys. There is no room for a middle view. If you are an enemy you must be thoroughly evil and sinister and if an ally a few black marks may tarnish the image of a good guy, but such inconsistencies can be conveniently overlooked because you are on "our side."

This two-valued view of the world was demonstrated in a study reported by Frank (1967). College students were presented with fifty statements concerning belligerent and conciliatory actions taken by both the United States and the Soviet Union. Half the students were led to believe the acts were those of the Soviet Union. Significant differences in evaluations of the same act were noted when comparing the "Russian" group with the "American" group. For instance, on a scale from 0 to 6, 0 being very unfavorable and 6 highly favorable, scores on the statement "The U.S. (Russia) has established rocket bases close to the borders of Russia (the U.S.)" were 4.7 for the U.S. version and 0.5 for the Russian version. "The U.S. (Russia) has stated that it was compelled to resume nuclear testing by the action of Russia (the U.S.)" averaged 4.2 for the U.S. version but 1.0 when attributed to Russia. Less dramatic differences in evaluative reactions were recorded when conciliatory acts were considered but differences were still significant.

When a nation or people have been labeled as *enemy*, our perceptions of them tend to become gross stereotypes. The world then is divided into friends and foes. Enemies are thoroughly bad, and acts seen as peaceloving when initiated by the good guys are redefined as warlike and treacherous when initiated by the bad guys. The inevitable consequences of such a cowboy mentality is a shootout at high noon except now the world can ill afford to play spectator passively waiting for the showdown to take place. In the nuclear age there are no real spectators.

Our images of "the enemy" are very much like riding a roller coaster. We manifest peaks of two-valued thinking characterized best by the "Cold War" cliches that are resurrected from time to time, and we exhibit troughs where we ride the rails of seeming good will, perhaps best characterized by the almost euphoric acceptance of detente during the Kissinger years. Recognition of China, her entrance into the United Nations, trade with China and Russia, a SALT agreement with the Soviets, joint ventures in space, and the like have all served to erode indiscriminate stereotypes and reveal a more multivalued orientation, a more complex perception of our "enemies."

The Russian invasion of Afghanistan and problems in Poland, coupled with the Reagan Administration's flirtation with Cold War rhetoric, intensifies the pressure to return to a two-valued image of the world. Such an orientation is fraught with danger. It encourages dogmatism, the unqualified belief in the absolute correctness of one's perceptions. Simplistic solutions are concocted for complex problems. In the international arena, this can quickly degenerate into an evangelistic fervor to destroy the enemy, to opt for firepower as the panacea for our international ills. It remains to be seen whether this return to two-valued conceptions of the world is merely temporary breast beating for catharsis and political advantage or whether it signals our return to a cowboys-and-Indians mentality.

As Conover and others (1980) point out, such two-valued thinking (*mirror imagery,* as they term it), once triggered, may stubbornly persist among the populace even after its political utility has vanished. "In effect, the persistence of mirror imagery within the public after a conflict has been resolved may place severe constraint on the manner in which a country's leaders may pursue peace" [p. 335].

How our leaders interpret events for us (Conover and others, 1980) and how gullible we are in accepting extreme interpretations of events are two critical factors in the formation of two-valued thinking on the international scene. What information we are fed and how critically we consume this information are important elements in the two-valued equation.

The Conover (1980) study notes that in some instances individuals and events are black and white. By any conventional definition we apply, Hitler was most assuredly a ruthless aggressor. There seems to be little quarrel with this evaluative assessment. This, however, probably represents the exception, not the rule, in international affairs. It is important to develop a sense of openness to changing events, a desire to reassess our evaluations of nations and peoples, and a willingness to entertain a more complicated perception of the world than a simple "It's them against us" formula allows.

LEGITIMATION OF VIOLENCE: IT WAS MY DUTY AND BESIDES, THEY DESERVED IT

I have already noted that conceptions of violence typically depend on whether we view certain acts as legitimate or illegitimate. Physical force to protect political institutions is normally considered legitimate whereas similar physical force aimed at destroying these same institutions is designated as illegitimate. Although the method of physical force used in both instances may be identical, the act of those threatening existing political institutions is far more likely to be labeled *violence* than similar acts initiated against enemies of established order and power. The Blumenthal studies also clearly establish the link between perceptions of legitimacy and levels of physical force deemed acceptable.

Ultimately, the process of legitimation whereby we deem certain behaviors to be good, moral, righteous, and in conformance with accepted principles, rules, or standards (Ball-Rokeach, 1973, p. 101), is a power struggle. Those who wield power tend to define their brand of physical force as legitimate. Even mass murder when ordered by those in authority is viewed as acceptable by many. Kelman and Lawrence (1972) reported that in a nationwide survey by the Roper Organization, 58 percent of Americans felt William Calley should not have been tried for his involvement in the My Lai massacre during the Vietnam War. Among those respondents who opposed Calley's trial, 83 percent gave "doing his duty" as the reason for such opposition. In addition, 67 percent felt most people would follow orders and shoot villagers, and

58 percent said they would shoot women and children if ordered to do so by those in command.

If those considered legitimate authority order a massacre, it is to be obeyed because the order is deemed legitimate although not necessarily wise or even moral. Those who disapprove are declaring the act illegitimate despite the fact that legitimate authority issued the order.

It should be noted that legitimacy does not necessarily equal legality. Although there are some vague references to international law attached to justifications of acts of war or challenges to their legitimacy, no nation feels compelled to sacrifice what it views as its "national interest" simply because violation of international law is alleged. While legality certainly acts as a legitimizer of physical force, even illegal acts are characterized as legitimate in some circumstances. A study of the police conducted by Westley (1970) revealed that 66 percent of the police surveyed gave an illegal basis (for example, disrespect for police, to obtain information, or when you know he is guilty) as justification for the use of force, while only 8 percent of the police provided a legal basis (for example, to make an arrest) for using force. More recent evidence from the U.S. Commission on Civil Rights and the Justice Department reveals a similar pattern ("Police," 1978). When it serves our purpose almost any act, no matter how vile and outrageous, can be rationalized as legitimate and therefore acceptable.

Language plays a critical role in this process of legitimation. Several language strategies used to legitimize violence will be considered here. They are dehumanizing our enemies, labeling killing *humane,* employing semantic camouflage, claiming self-defense, and appealing to ideals.

Dehumanization—Our Lethal Labels

Zimbardo and Ruch (1977) define dehumanization as the "psychological erasure of human qualities (p. 647)." Human beings are devalued, bestialized, and viewed as nonhuman or subhuman. When they are excluded from the human species, it becomes rather simple to treat them as mere objects, playthings, or targets for our contempt and hostility. Crushing a cockroach is not considered violent or illegitimate because bugs are devalued. This is a symbolic process that says slugs, ants, and spiders are "lower forms of life" and thus insignificant when compared with humans. Thus, rats and rabbits are injected with lethal doses of drugs and chemicals to determine toxic levels before those drugs or chemicals are used on humans for therapeutic and curative purposes. Likening certain categories of human beings to lower forms of life excuses, even encourages their violent control or extermination. History is replete with examples of such legitimized mass violence.

Most notable perhaps is Hitler's attempted genocide of the Jews. In what was characterized as the "Final Solution," Jews were systematically cremated, gassed, given acid showers, surgically experimented upon, starved, beaten, tortured, and treated with all manner of sadistic brutality until six million of them died. Their crime was "poisoning" the Aryan race. These "parasites," "bacilli," "disease carriers," "poison spreaders," "vermin," and "maggots in rotting flesh" (Hitler, 1939) had to be excised from the Fatherland as one would lance a boil, thereby removing the infection and restoring "racial purity" to the German people.

Richard Grunberger (1971) describes some of the dehumanizing language used in the concentration camps:

> The standard phrase used by SS record clerks for new arrivals at Dachau was "Which Jew-whore shit you out?"—a question designed to elicit the name of the inmate's mother. At Belsen the female warders talked of handling so and so many new "pieces of prisoner per day" and the correspondence between IG-Farben's drug research sections and the Auschwitz Camp authorities referred to "loads" or "consignments" of human guinea pigs [p. 330].

Grunberger goes on to explain that "the incessant official demonization of the Jew gradually modified the consciousness even of naturally humane people," creating an indifference among the German populace to Jewish torment because the Jews were "not real people [p. 466]."

The extent of this callous indifference by the German people toward the Jew is reported by Moses Moskowitz (quoted in Opton & Duckles, 1970) in 1946. Commenting on a survey of German opinion he observes:

> The most striking overall impression is the absence in the German of any emotional reaction toward Jews, be it positive or negative. It was shocking at times to listen to people decrying the evils of Nazism, reciting the horrors of concentration camps . . . without one word of sympathy for the victims [p. 15].

Clearly, the systematic dehumanization of the Jew, the labeling of the Jew as a subhuman invited no sense of kinship with these fellow human beings. Destroying the Jew was like killing a fly.

Similar mass murder and violence have stained American history. America's first inhabitants, the Indians, characterized as "savages" and "barbarians," were driven from their land and slaughtered by the thousands. It is an historical fact that the practice of scalping was used not just by Indians, but also by their white oppressors as a means of proof in order to collect bounty for killing Indians. The United States War Department advocated the extermination of the Indian (Krout, 1965). Bosmajian (1974) provides a litany of examples of the rationalization of Indian slaughter because they were "uncivilized savages." Some Indian tribes became extinct while others managed to eke out an existence on desolate reservations. Indians, who were dubbed the "vanishing Americans," fell in numbers from approximately 850,000 at the time of Columbus to about 220,000 by 1910—largely the product of treatment by the white settlers and the U.S. government.

Blacks were also accorded similar treatment. Virtually from its inception the American colonists acquired slaves from Africa. What began as a small enterprise in human commerce soon burgeoned into a huge business. By the eighteenth century America had a slave population of more than 700,000. By 1850 it leaped to 3.2 million and by the Civil War it had grown to nearly 4 million.

In order to justify the glaring contradiction between Revolutionary America's espousal of freedom and equality and its participation in human bondage, the black slave was defined as subhuman—a "beast," an "ape," an "uncivilized heathen," a "savage brute," an "inferior race."

Dismissed as less than human, blacks became property to be owned, merchandise to be bought and sold at slave auctions. Even the U.S. Constitution (Article I, Section 2) recognized the slave as merely "three-fifths of all other persons" in designating the formula for apportioning Representatives to Congress.

Treatment of the slaves was nothing less than inhuman as befits "property." Wrenched from their home in Africa by slave traders looking for a profit in human flesh, the slaves were crammed into ships, forced to endure indescribable conditions during the two-month "Middle Passage" across the Atlantic. They were cargo, valuable as property but not as human beings. If the safety of the ship was threatened during the "Middle Passage," the human cargo was jettisoned and those fed to the sharks were labeled "goods" or "chattels" for insurance purposes (Austin, Fenderson, and Nelson, 1970). Loss of half the slaves from disease on board ship was not unusual. It has been estimated that as many as 50 million Africans died as the result of three-and-a-half centuries of the slave trade with North America and the West Indies (Meier and Rudwick, 1966, p. 33).

When the slaves arrived in America their conditions improved but slightly. Some were treated paternalistically by slaveholders while others were subjected to sadistic cruelty, but "few adult slaves had ever completely escaped the whip [Meier and Rudwick, 1966, p. 59]." Commercial breeding of slaves commensurate with their animalistic status was a common practice in the South. Black women who held promise of fertility, referred to as "good breeders," brought a high price when auctioned.

The eventual emancipation of slaves freed them from the bondage of institutional servitude but not from the brutality of whites. Lynching as a means of keeping the "nigger" in his place reached its peak in the 1890s, averaging about 150 a year and higher, diminishing only slightly well into the twentieth century. Major riots by whites against blacks occurred during and immediately following the First World War. By this time the pattern was well established. Blacks were "inferior" and deserved to be treated as beasts and savages. While the plight of blacks has improved markedly in recent years, racism and its attendant violence have not been erased from the face of America.

The relationship between the semantic dehumanization of individuals and groups and collective violence is likewise apparent during periods of war. As Frank (1967) explains:

> The ferocity of war is both made possible and enhanced by the denial of humanity to the enemy: he becomes a statistic, an abstraction, and a beast, and the perception of him as subhuman reinforces the conviction that, like an animal he is impervious to reason and will respond only to punishment. This discourages searching for means of peacefully resolving the conflict [p. 185].

President Truman's justification of atom bomb attacks on Japan illustrates this point. A few days after Truman introduced the world to the atomic age, he wrote a private letter to Samuel McCrea Cavert (Bernstein, 1975, p. 61). In it he referred to the Japanese as "beasts" who deserved to be treated accordingly. Dehumanizing the enemy legitimized unloading history's most terrifying weapon.

In war our enemies have been labeled *gooks, chinks, Japs, dinks, slopes, slant-eyes,* and other dehumanizing characterizations. An American pilot typified the feelings of many U.S. soldiers when, speaking on a televised interview in 1965, he argued that his Vietnamese victims were "like vermin, like animals. You shoot them down." Lyndon Johnson reputedly made a similarly insensitive reference to the North Vietnamese during the war: "Without air power, we'd be at the mercy of every yellow dwarf with a pocket knife [quoted in Lewallen, 1972, p. 37]."

The Kelman and Lawrence (1972) study shows the relationship between dehumanization of the enemy and acceptance of violence and mass murder in Vietnam. Thirty-seven percent felt that Calley's actions at My Lai were justified if the victims were communists; 47 percent responded affirmatively to the statement, "Calley's actions were justified because it's better to kill some South Vietnamese civilians than risk lives of American soldiers." Additionally, 53 percent believed "it would have been better to kill some German civilians than risk lives of American soldiers" during World War II.

The value of human life is gauged by which group you belong to. In war, all humans are not created equal. This point of view is reminiscent of a statement by U.S. Senator Richard Russell of Georgia in 1968 concerning nuclear war. He remarked that "if we have to start over again with another Adam and Eve, then I want them to be Americans."

History speaks eloquently of the senselessness of the slaughter of millions of innocent people whose crime consisted of membership in a group despised by those wielding power. The semantic derogation of the Jews was a significant factor leading to the "Final Solution." Unquestionably, killing "bacilli" was less anguishing than murdering human beings. The pirating of Indian land and the massacre of thousands was more palatable by redefining them as "savages" unworthy of human rights and decent treatment. Black "chattel" stirred little sense of remorse or moral outrage when they were brutalized and butchered, for they were "property" not people. *Gooks,* which literally refers to "sludge," "slime," and "liquid filth," offers no redeeming image in our minds but instead invites loathing and revulsion and ultimately death to those so labeled.

Clearly, language labels that dehumanize can be lethal. Killing is made easier when human qualities have been erased from our victims.

"Humane" Killing—Choosing Our Poison

The esoteric debate concerning which methods of killing are "humane" and which "inhumane" has commanded human attention for centuries, yet this debate has degenerated into a casuistic exercise in chauvinistic labeling. The underlying assumption of the argument is that if certain methods of killing are "humane," they are legitimate and therefore acceptable; if "inhumane" they then become "atrocities" and are illegitimate and unacceptable, even contemptible.

States that have capital punishment terminate the lives of their victims in different ways. Some states use hanging, others use firing squads, and still others kill by gassing or electrocution. There are also proposals to kill by injection in some states, making capital punishment a bit more palatable to some because it is "humanely" accomplished. Arguments concerning which of these methods is the most "humane" are common.

The humane killing debate reaches its zenith, however, in regards to warfare. Nazi genocide of Jews was labeled a "war crime." Methods they used to accomplish this end were labeled "inhumane," bestial. The disembowelings, beheadings, and various other hideous methods of killing people performed by the North Vietnamese were labeled *atrocities.*

Typically, those who argue the "humane-inhumane" thesis are not comparably repulsed by acts of their own country. The world was shocked and outraged by the inhumanity of Hitler's bombing of Rotterdam in World War II, but the Allies were not similarly appalled by the firebombing of Dresden, a nonmilitary target where 135,000 civilians were massacred. Incinerating Jews in ovens was an *atrocity* but incinerating Vietnamese with napalm rarely produced equivalent horror. Americans who brand Nazi officers as sadists and criminals typically do not apply such labels to American pilots and crew members who dropped atom bombs on Hiroshima and Nagasaki.

The Wright Institute (Opton, 1970) conducted intensive interviews with several dozen subjects concerning their reactions to the My Lai Massacre. When asked to compare My Lai and Nazi genocide of the Jews, one respondent stated:

> Oh, it's not the same as their dirty cruelness. I guess it's similar in a way. . . . They killed women and children. It doesn't make sense . . . Like, the Nazis, they used showers with acid in the water or something like that, and that was really horrible. Our men are just shooting people [p. 67].

When Kelman and Lawrence (1972) asked subjects to compare William Calley's action at My Lai and bombing raids that also killed Vietnamese civilians, 51 percent of those who approved of Calley's trial replied that the two were different, whereas 32 percent of the total sample felt this way. Most of these subjects argued that killing civilians in bombing raids is "accidental" while Calley's action was "intentional murder."

The distinction that killing civilians in a bombing raid is "accidental" but shooting them as in My Lai is intentional and therefore inhumane is a tortured argument at best. If bombing Hiroshima, Nagasaki, and Dresden "accidentally" slaughtered civilians, then the

Germans' bombing of civilians in London would also have to be termed an "accident." It makes about as much sense as an accidental rape. If you drop a bomb you must expect civilian casualties. The killing of civilians is the inevitable consequence of virtually any bombing raid even upon so-called military targets. Knowing full well that this is the case, it is linguistic gymnastics to claim such deaths are unintentional.

The whole debate regarding which methods of killing people are humane and which are inhumane is an odd issue to be concerned with in the first place. It is nothing short of macabre to be anguishing over which forms of extermination are more acceptable. It assumes killing is acceptable as long as it is done in the proper fashion. It boggles the mind to even contemplate a "humane" bayonet thrust or a "loving" shot in the head.

The principal problem with trying to determine humane from inhumane killing is the criteria for distinguishing the two from each other. Is selective killing more humane than indiscriminate killing? Was Calley wrong because he failed to identify his victims as actual enemies? How then can we exonerate those who bomb cities? When has bombing ever selectively killed only combatants but spared non-combatants?

Is slow, painful killing inhumane but swift relatively painless killing humane? If so, practically all weapons of war would have to be abolished as inhumane since virtually all of them are capable of producing very slow, agonizing deaths.

Then, of course, there are weapons such as the neutron bomb which decimate humans but leave buildings standing. Somehow that strikes us as inhumane and wicked. It is unquestionably a strange proposition to argue that we need a weapon that indiscriminately destroys humans but spares edifices. But the neutron bomb is inhumane because it incinerates humans in the invisible fire of radiation not because buildings would remain as grim testimony of human stupidity.

Finally, it has been alleged that weapons of mass murder are inhumane but weapons that are less efficient killers are more humane. Chemical and biological warfare are considered to be in the former category whereas rifles are in the latter. It is noteworthy that although many have argued that weapons of mass destruction are inhumane, the human tolerance for horror has risen with each successive generation of weapons technology. At various times in history the sword, poisons, asphyxiating gasses, contact mines, torpedoes, and other delightful instruments of death have been branded inhumane by world leaders, peace tribunals, and the like (Wells, 1967). Lumsden (1979) notes that the St. Petersburg Declaration of 1868 and the Hague Declaration of 1899 banned exploding, incendiary, and expanding bullets but only in wars between European armies. It was argued that such weapons were necessary in colonial wars in order to defeat "savages."

We should have internalized the message that this whole exercise is a futile and empty gesture about the time Hitler proclaimed that attacking an enemy by air was "inhumane." As weapons became more sophisticated, more terrifying, and more destructive, weapons previously branded inhumane suddenly seem humane by comparison. The verbal yardstick is quite elastic.

Nevertheless, the debate continues. The United Nations held a special conference on inhumane weapons from September 10th to the 28th, 1979. The greatest weapons of mass murder, nuclear bombs, were excluded from the discussion for obvious political reasons.

Numbers are not the issue for most people, however. Killing over 100 Vietnamese at My Lai was labeled a *massacre* and branded criminal, but the systematic demolishment by heavy American bombing of a thriving community of 50,000 people on the Plain of Jars in Laos during the same war never produced a war crimes trial. Physical proximity to the victim seems to be a more important determinant of "humane–inhumane" labeling than the number of victims.

The problem with killing lies not with the weapons but with the killing itself. To argue that some methods of destruction are "humane" merely legitimizes and encourages human carnage. The phrase "humane killing" seems contradictory. By what tortured line of reasoning do we argue that respect for life, compassionate concern for other human beings (common denotative meaning of the word "humane") is promoted by labeling certain methods of killing people "humane?" If people don't want to die, how is it compassionate (humane) to kill them? Is this not doublethink? It seems more vital to discuss ways of preventing killing rather than debating the proper or improper techniques for inducing death.

On the issue of war and mass violence *humane killing* is a language map without a territory; a reification.* There is no objective, empirically based criteria by which we can apply such a label. As Wells (1967) explains: "While we may wish that all not be fair in war, humanitarian considerations seem incapable of giving us the criteria by which to judge such fairness or unfairness [p. 125]." Ultimately, we make judgments of "humaneness-inhumaneness" according to nationalistic concerns. It is usually the enemy that commits "atrocities" while we steadfastly refuse to accept our own handiwork as "inhumane." When we truly embrace the view that killing human beings in war, domestic strife, and the like is inherently "inhumane," the techniques for accomplishing human slaughter will also bear such a label. At this point, we may then consider pursuing alternate strategies for resolving intergroup conflict.

Semantic Camouflage: Sanitizing War

Thomas Merton (1969) makes the observation that:

> Warmakers in the twentieth century have gone far toward creating a political language so obscure, so apt for treachery, so ambiguous, that it is good only for war. . . . It does not invite reasonable dialogue, it uses language to silence dialogue, to block communication, so that instead of words the two sides may trade divisions, positions, villages, air bases, cities—and of course the lives of the people in them [p. 112].

The separation of the act of killing almost completely from the idea of killing by means of technical, impersonal, and euphemistic language ranks as one of the chilling contributions of modern warfare.

We no longer kill people but rather we "liquidate," "waste," "lawn

---

*Humanitarian interest regarding issues such as "mercy killing" involve human dignity and definitions of life and death, concerns that are irrelevant to mass violence. A case might be made for "humane" forms of inducing death in specialized cases, but no such case can be supported for instruments and techniques of mass violence.

mower," "hose," "dust," "barbecue," or "terminate with extreme prejudice." We engage in "protective reaction strikes" not aggressive air assaults, "incursions" not invasions, "search and destroy missions" not destroy and then search, and "limited air interdiction" not heavy bombing. We hit "targets of opportunity" with "antipersonnel weapons" rather than bombing noncombatants caught in the middle. "Accidental" bombings that kill women and children are excused as "target misidentification." Even the term *war* is avoided. The Korean War was labeled a *police action* and the Vietnam War was referred to as the Vietnam *conflict* during the initial years of U.S. escalation.

The weapons of mass murder are also depersonalized and given linguistic disguises. In Vietnam we "treated" the forest with "herbicides" or "defoliants," making it sound as innocent as killing weeds in a vegetable garden. Yet, a report by the National Academy of Sciences based on research authorized by Congress and undertaken by forty-seven scientists and special consultants, concluded that the systematic use of these "weed killers" for "routine improvement of visibility in jungle areas" and for "resource control" destroyed 36 percent of the mangrove marshes, breeding grounds of fish for the Vietnamese diet. The report also noted that part of the inland tropical forests, along with crops, was destroyed. These forests "will not spontaneously recover for well nigh a century, if at all (Karnow, 1974, p. 19)." There is even speculation that some Montagnard children died as a direct result of the "defoliation," and American soldiers have claimed that a variety of ailments they have suffered since returning home from the War are directly related to the spraying of "agent orange." (Both of these claims, however, are difficult to prove so they should be considered with caution.)

CS, the chemical powder used in modern forms of tear gas, was also widely used in Vietnam for "riot control." Yet as Clarke (1972) argues, "Unless B-52 bombers are accepted as a legitimate means of riot control, it soon [becomes] clear that CS [is] being used for something quite different [p. 145]." Its real purpose, as later revealed by the Defense Department, was to flush out "enemy" troops into the open where they could be mutilated by fragmentation bomb bursts.

Pretty soon this cosmetic surgery of our language led to *smart bombs* and *clean bombs,* disguising the results of using such weapons. The tolerance for sloppy language usage, however, was sorely tested when a

U.S. major offered his now famous rationale for shelling the town of Bentre in February, 1968. "It became necessary to destroy the town in order to save it." The major would be a poor person to have around if you needed emergency first aid.

Although presidents are sometimes given to hyperbole, a truly extraordinary insensitivity to accurate language usage was demonstrated by Richard Nixon ("Text," 1972) when on May 8, 1972, he stated: "Throughout the war in Vietnam the United States has exercised a degree of restraint unprecedented in the annals of war [p. 6A]." Presumably, Nixon meant that because the United States did not use the full range of destructive power at her disposal (that is, nuclear weapons) and did not invade North Vietnam we therefore manifested "restraint" that was "unprecedented" and thus admirable. The degree to which we have become numbed to the horror of modern warfare, however, is revealed by this willingness to call fearsome levels of violence *restraint.* Juxtapose this characterization by Nixon of our role in the Vietnam War with a few chilling facts and the phrase *unprecedented restraint* appears wholly inappropriate.

According to a task force report to Senator Edward Kennedy's Judiciary Subcommittee on Refugees (see Karnow, 1974, and "Peace with Honor," 1974), 3.6 million Vietnamese soldiers and civilians on both sides were killed or wounded and approximately 10 million Vietnamese were made homeless sometime during the eight years after U.S. escalation of the war in 1965. The war left almost 900,000 Vietnamese orphans, 83,000 amputees, 40,000 blind or deaf, and 8000 paraplegics. A majority of these casualties were the direct result of massive bombing by the U.S. Thirty billion pounds of explosives, almost triple the total quantity of bombs dropped in all the theaters of World War II, wrought havoc on this tiny strip of Asian geography. According to Westing (1978), U.S. forces delivered a total firepower of 17,800 kg per enemy soldier killed in Vietnam. This compares to 5,600 kg in Korea and 1,100 kg in World War II. In addition, the National Academy of Science report stipulates that the U.S. unloaded 18.8 million gallons of "herbicides" on more than 25 million acres of South Vietnamese landscape, over 10 percent of its entire land area. The devastation of the natural environment of South Vietnam by the U.S. was itself an unprecedented act of war.

The question whether the United States was justified in precipitating such devastation in Southeast Asia was debated at length throughout the war. My concern here is not to redebate this issue but instead to illustrate how language was used to disguise the actions we did undertake. By any objective standard, by the conventional meaning and use of the phrase, the level of violence unleashed by the United States in Southeast Asia cannot be accurately termed *unprecedented restraint.* Rather, the awesome level of sustained violence by the United States during its involvement in Vietnam was itself unprecedented in the annals of warfare. It is yet another instance of language used to disguise an unpleasant truth.

Language misused can cloud our thinking and disguise the reality of violence and warfare. It can create a psychological detachment from the horror that is war. In this way we become numb to human suffering that inevitably accompanies violent conflict.

When collective violence is separated from its consequences, scrubbed of its emotion, we can be transformed into coldly efficient killers.

Heinrich Himmler, one of the chief architects of the Holocaust, could boast, "To have gone through this and yet remained decent, that is what has made us great." The Holocaust was permitted largely because the Jews were dehumanized and the German people chose to accept the rationalizations and semantic smokescreen offered by Hitler and his henchmen that camouflaged the reality of genocide.

But that was Germany four decades ago. Despite our record of violence in Vietnam, surely we would never seriously entertain thoughts of actual genocide. Surely we have learned the lesson of history; or have we? If language were used carefully, calculated to produce just the right signal reactions, would Americans now subscribe to genocide? Mansson (1972) conducted a study that was replicated by Carlson and Wood (1974). The results were nothing short of startling. Students were presented with a carefully worded appeal by a professor to cooperate in the extermination of the "mentally and emotionally unfit." Appeals to subjects' intelligence, allegations of an impending crisis of overpopulation, reference to a "scientific solution," and recognition of humanitarian concerns that painless methods be utilized (that is, "humane" killing) were made. Two-thirds of the subjects approved of the "scientific solution" when the threat was described as imminent, while two-fifths endorsed it even if the threat was a century down the road.

Had the subjects been asked to disapprove Hitler's extermination of the Jews it is likely all 570 subjects would have done so, perhaps vehemently. Yet, when presented with an analogous act, subjects reacted to such labels as *unfit,* and *scientific solution* and not to the reality. Emotional reactions and profuse justifications following the experiment when its purpose was revealed support this interpretation. Subjects did not perceive it as a Hitlerian act of genocide, but rather a reasonable solution to a troublesome problem. If a person can be so easily seduced into advocating killing, then we are indeed in serious trouble. Parents beware! Carlson and Wood (1974) discovered that 29 percent of their subjects supported the "Final Solution" (that is, extermination) even when applied to their own families.

Perhaps when faced with the actual situation, we would not behave in accordance with our expressed attitudes. But the parallels to Hitler's "Final Solution," "Jewish problem," and elimination of the "unfit" surely warrant our attention. We can be fooled into believing our cause is righteous and sensible. We can fall prey to the double-thinkers, reifiers, and euphemizers who with antiseptic phrases and sterile language camouflage the tragedy and human agony wrought by mass violence. We can become anesthetized into accepting killing as the solution to conflict and social problems because we allow ourselves to be deceived, and we choose to hide from the unpleasant realities cloaked in bloodless language.

Claiming "Self-Defense"

Probably the most frequently used justification of violence is self-defense. The Blumenthal (1972) study indicated strong support for such a justification. Eighty-nine percent either strongly agreed or agreed somewhat that killing another person in self-defense is legitimate. Even if the object of attack is not a person, but personal property (for example, a house), 58 percent condoned killing the offender.

Self-defense is a highly-valued right in this country and internationally. It has become a relatively empty phrase, however, because typically all parties in a conflict accuse the other side of aggression and picture themselves as victims of belligerence. Osgood (1960) found that when people from eight different countries were asked to describe themselves, all considered themselves peace-loving, despite the fact that several of these countries were bitter enemies. During the Southeast Asian War, the U.S., North Vietnam, South Vietnam, Cambodia, and Laos all claimed self-defense. In the Middle East, Israel, Egypt, and the Palestine Liberation Organization have asserted self-defense. Even the Russian invasion of Afghanistan was justified as an effort to defend the Afghan regime from "rebel" forces. In the silly-putty world of international conflict, offense is characterized as *dynamic defense,* retaliation is tediously excused as *self-defense,* and no country owns up to the role of *aggressor.*

White's (1977) analysis of the Arab-Israeli conflict illustrates some of these semantic problems which occur on the international scene. Each side perceives the four major wars (1948, 1956, 1967, and 1973) as "aggression" by the "enemy." The Arabs perceive the wars of 1956 and 1967 as examples of blatant Israeli aggression because Israeli troops fired first and invaded Arab territory. The other two wars, 1948 and 1973, were instances of Israeli provocation despite the fact that Arab troops initiated the hostilities. The Israelis, on the other hand use the same rationale except it is the Arabs who were guilty of naked aggression in 1948 and 1973, and it is the Arabs who provoked hostilities in 1956 and 1967. Thus, both sides are aggressors and innocent victims of provocation at the same time.

The problem is fundamentally a semantic one. The term *aggression* has acquired two conflicting definitions (White, 1977). Actual initiation of large-scale hostilities is one definition, but the second definition, substantial provocation prior to large-scale hostilities, serves as the antithesis of the first verbal map. What inevitably happens, then, is that one side attacks the other, a charge of *aggression* is made, and this is refuted by a claim of *self-defense* by reason of provocation. A build-up of force can be a *provocation.* A terrorist attack can be a *provocation.* Threats, bluster, almost anything that might appear *potentially* aggressive can act as a rationalization, a justification for attacking another country in "self-defense."

Vested self-interest is a primary motivation of acts of war, and "self-defense" has become merely a convenient excuse used to legitimize actions viewed as vital to a nation's self-interest. It is a dangerous semantic game nations play when they initiate hostilities and then claim provocation.

As nations continue to arm themselves to their teeth, the prospect that one nation will perceive such militarism by another nation as threatening increases. If we continue to define *aggression* as provocation, then even preparations for war become aggressive. The likelihood of a preemptive attack in "self-defense" becomes increasingly probable. What is to prevent nations from perceiving a build-up of armaments, even if only to "deter" attacks, as "aggressive" not "defensive"?

In the nuclear age we have now reached the point where Strangelovian logic asserts itself. Consider this question: If the United States becomes convinced that Russia is preparing for a nuclear attack on America, would the United States be justified in striking Russia first? Would this then be self-defense? Or what if Russia did launch a full-scale nuclear attack on the United States? Would the United States be justified in reciprocating in kind? Would this be self-defense or retribution?

As long as nations subscribe to two conflicting definitions of *aggression*—actual initiation of hostilities, and a potential or perceived threat of aggression—then the whole concept of "self-defense" takes on an Alice-in-Wonderland quality. Everyone and no one is guilty of aggression because there are two conflicting verbal maps for "aggression." It is little wonder the rationalization for hostile military attacks are virtually endless.

Appeals to Ideals

It was pointed out in the first chapter that humans will fight and die for symbols of their own creation. Certain abstractions we call ideals such as peace, freedom, democracy, patriotism, honor, justice, and the like are capable of producing signal reactions in the form of violence and killing. It was once quite fashionable for "gentlemen" to spill one another's blood in duels to the death over matters of "honor." Honor was a prime motivating factor at the battle of Verdun during World War I. A terrifying investment of human life was made in an endless struggle to defend "national honor" when strategic significance of this slice of geography had long since vanished (Horne, 1966). American disengagement from Vietnam was made more difficult because we steadfastly pursued a vague abstraction—namely "Peace with Honor." We became involved in World War I ostensibly "to make the world safe for democracy." "National interest" has been trumpeted as the rationale for international blood-letting, and "patriotism" has helped sustain a warrior mentality among belligerents during innumerable conflicts.

In October 1968, *Fortune* magazine (Seligman, 1969) conducted a survey of young people between the ages of eighteen and twenty-four, a group most susceptible to the effects of the Vietnam War. They were divided into two sections, non-college educated and college students, and were asked what ideals were worth fighting for. "Patriotism" affected 28 percent of the college students versus 46 percent of the noncollege group. "Fighting for our honor" was considered worthwhile by 64 percent of the noncollege group and 31 percent for the college students. "Protecting the national interest" was supported by 73 percent of the noncollege sample and 52 percent of the college group. These findings can be interpreted in a number of ways, but the point worth noting here is that even among groups most vulnerable to the ravages of an unpopular war in progress, abstract ideals have relatively strong support as justifications for involvement in war. Surveys among groups not so directly affected by the war probably would have revealed much stronger sentiment for defending these ideals.

In the abstract, these ideals can produce highly charged signal reactions. They can serve as legitimators of collective violence. Yet fighting for symbols creates some vexing questions. As we lockstep to the beat of the drummer's pulsepounding call to arms, do we really have a clear conception of what these symbols actually mean?

What, for instance, is "patriotism?" Samuel Johnson once remarked that it is "the last refuge of a scoundrel." Leo Tolstoy (1967) defined patriotism as "the exclusive desire for the well-being of one's own people (p. 106)." Viewed in this way, patriotism is simply selfish nationalism. Is patriotism "love of country?" If so, can an individual refuse to take up arms against an "enemy" and still claim to be "patriotic" or must a "patriot" always be willing to kill for his or her country? And what is "honor" and "national interest" and who should define these vague abstractions? Can you specify what these ideals refer to and would others have such an understanding or are we simply responding to code words for violence, tuning into our private connotations?

As it currently stands, the symbols we commonly fight and die for are ambiguously defined. They are mere connotations in our minds with unclear and often unspecified referents. We have reified these "ideals," often demanded uncritical conformity and knee-jerk compliance to symbols. Those who attempt to establish a dialogue in hopes of clarifying these concepts and perhaps redefining them are often branded as "traitors," "cowards," or "un-American."

The time seems long overdue for the people of this and other nations to spell out these vague principles. Those justifying policies and actions as "patriotic" or "honorable" or in the "national interest" should be challenged to specify how they are honorable, patriotic, or in the national interest. A critical eye should then be trained on any such rationale offered. Only by intelligently challenging the cosmic justifications of violence so frequently offered by world leaders can we determine what it is we are really fighting for or against and whether it merits the support of the American people. Simply dusting off time-honored justifications for collective violence and reciting them with ritualistic fervor should not substitute for intelligent discussion of the consequences of armed conflict and the appropriateness of violence as a solution to disagreements.

Recapitulating briefly, legitimation of violence has a direct relationship to levels of violence advocated and employed. Language plays a central role in the legitimation of violence. By using language to dehumanize our enemies, "humanize" methods of killing, camouflage the horror of war and disguise the human suffering that is the legacy of violence, by claiming self-defense when we initiate hostilities and by appealing to vague abstractions we call ideals, we promote, encourage and make possible fearsome levels of violence. When language maps are inaccurate representations of territories, when language labels can substitute for reason, and when vague abstractions divorced from clear referents become primary justifications for killing, language then becomes the seductive mistress of the bellicose and belligerent. Violence is glorified and killing is seen as a "final solution" to social and political problems.

ANACHRONISTIC WORDS OF WAR: TO THE "VICTORS" BELONG THE SPOILED

The language of the nuclear age is heavily ladened with words and phrases more suited to a time when conventional warfare produced winners and losers and total war did not threaten human extinction. Although conventional wars are still fought, these engagements are always conducted in the shadows of threatened nuclear weapons exchange when the so-called "superpowers" are involved. We have not adapted our language to the reality of nuclear weapons, rather we speak a language characteristic of the pre-atomic era. Consider just a few examples.

In the name of "security" the world now rests precariously on a colossal powder keg. Russia and the United States are engaged in an arms race, each one attempting to establish "nuclear superiority" or "equivalence" (depending on the political climate and level of paranoia floating about). It is a remarkable paradox that at a time when the ability to annihilate an opponent has long since been reached, nations can still speak of gaining "superiority" over each other by stockpiling more nuclear weapons.

The world's arsenal of nuclear weapons has reached such gigantic proportions that it is difficult for the human mind to grasp the extent of the destructive power available in the world today. According to the Center for Defense Information (Sivard, 1975), the global stockpile of nuclear arms amounts to approximately 60,000 megatons of TNT, roughly 15 tons of explosive power for every human being on earth.

During World War II and the Korean War combined, approximately 3.1 megatons of explosive power were unleashed by all combatants (Legault and Lindsey, 1976, p. 38). Thus, if we could compress

World War II and the Korean War into a single day, the world's nuclear arsenal is equivalent to the aggregate firepower of both of these wars unleashed in one lump sum each day, day after day for 53 *years*.

Despite the awesome levels of military power available, the inventory of destructive armaments continues to accumulate. U.S. Senator Mark Hatfield (1979) of Oregon estimated that even with the SALT II agreement between the United States and Russia, which died from lack of United States ratification and shows few signs of resurrection at this writing, by 1985 the two superpowers will have stockpiled the equivalent of *2 million* Hiroshima bombs. In 1980, the United States alone had 10,000 strategic nuclear weapons. By 1990, that figure will rise to at least 19,000 unless "defense" policies are significantly altered (Wicker, 1980).

Nations of the world spend roughly $500 billion per year on the military, and this is increasing each year at a phenomenal rate. In the United States alone, the Reagan Administration projects a $343 billion military budget in 1986 and $1.5 trillion spent on the military in the five-year period 1982 to 1986 (Sheils and others, 1981). Even accounting for expected inflation, this represents a 67 percent increase in military spending during that time period.

The military "inferiority–superiority" debate has become a meaningless abstraction. Nations have no sense of how much weaponry is enough. Our notion of "security" is appropriate for an earlier era when the number of planes, ships, bombs, guns, etc. would likely produce a "victor" and a "vanquished." In regards to nuclear weapons that has all changed.

Nevertheless, it is the nature of the Catch-22 language of international affairs which allows nations to label the capacity to annihilate an enemy several times over as "inferior" simply because they have less aggregate destructive power than their foes. No longer is it sufficient merely to exterminate an enemy. Now you must be able to duplicate the act many times over. This "overkill" capacity that the superpowers possess presumes that it is necessary to the preservation of "national security" to be able to more than annihilate your nemesis. This is tantamount to killing a fly with a hand grenade, dynamiting your house, and then calling in an air strike on the whole neighborhood just to make sure the fly is really dead, nay, deader than dead.

As the debate on military "superiority" becomes more abstract, arguments seriously advanced for increases in "defense" spending make less and less sense, yet they may appear to be quite reasonable. For instance, it was discovered that Russia spends a higher percentage of her Gross National Product on "defense" than does the United States. Many people, upon hearing this, worried that the United States was "falling behind" the Russians in military strength.

Former Senator Eugene McCarthy, in a speech at Western Washington University in November 1980, proposed a unique solution to this "problem." He suggested that we wipe out the pickle industry (a multimillion dollar industry). It would reduce our Gross National Product (G.N.P.), thus making the percentage of our G.N.P. that we spend on the military higher. "Security" would then be a matter of reducing G.N.P., not increasing military spending.

McCarthy's facetious solution applies equally well to a companion argument aimed at "proving" the U.S. plays second fiddle to the Russians' military might. Instead of the G.N.P., some have discovered that the Russians spend a higher percentage of their budget on the military than does the United States. Take such "logic" to its absurd conclusion and we find that eliminating government expenditures for health, education, and welfare would *increase* our military power. When you're lost in abstraction-land, almost anything appears sensible until someone yanks you to the ground and forces you to see the implication of your arguments (those vague abstractions).

The debate on military "inferiority–superiority" is further blurred when we speak of "defense" at a time when the distinction between "offensive" and "defensive" weapons has become obscured. It used to be true that most weapons could be used for offensive or defensive purposes. Planes could repulse an attack from an aggressor, tanks could repel an invading army, and so on. With the exception of the AntiBallistic Missile System (A.B.M.), a weapon of dubious capabilities, nuclear weapons are exclusively offensive. Launching our nuclear arsenal in retaliation will not thwart a nuclear attack from Russia once initiated. If Russia decides to begin Armageddon, we are quite helpless to defend ourselves. The most we can do is swap missiles. This is hardly "defense." Nothing is protected and no American lives are saved by the posthumous annihilation of an enemy.

The new concept of "defense," therefore, is really the threat of retaliation. This threat of massive retaliation or "mutual assured destruction" (MAD) is supposed to provide a "deterrent" to World War III. Thus, our "offense" has become our "defense." We are threatening to destroy people in order to save them. While we may be convinced that our building of nuclear weapons is merely for "protection" (that is, defensive), how can we convince anyone else that this is so? As the superpowers become ever more bloated militarily, it becomes increasingly difficult to convince anyone that all this nuclear hardware is exclusively for "deterrence."

In fact, Jimmy Carter's Presidential Directive 59, leaked to the press during the 1980 Presidential campaign, maps out a new nuclear strategy that clearly envisions the prospect of a limited nuclear war over a long period of time with winners and losers (Buckley, 1981). So much for the rationale that nuclear weapons are exclusively for deterrence.

Called *counterforce*, this new strategy targets Soviet missile installations, military bases, even Soviet headquarters and the Kremlin. This is a significant departure from the previous strategy (MAD) that targeted Soviet cities and industrial complexes.

As Slater (1980) argues, counterforce may make nuclear war more likely by making it seem, however fantastic, more rational and controllable. Already there is evidence of this psychology emerging. George Bush told *The Los Angeles Times* during his campaign for the Presidency in 1980 that there could conceivably be "a winner in a nuclear exchange." This was not unlike a statement attributed to U.S. strategists Colin Gray and Keith Payne at the Hudson Institute, who argued that "the U.S. must possess the ability to wage nuclear war rationally" ("Physicians' plea," 1981, p. 22). It would be interesting to hear what guarantees these advocates of "rational nuclear war" can offer so that either side in such a conflict would see the wisdom of restricting the war to a limited nuclear exchange while large portions of each party's homeland are being selectively demolished. What prevents counterforce from going MAD?

It will also be difficult, to say the least, to convince the Soviets that our counterforce strategy is for deterrence only. It looks alarmingly offensive. Why target missile silos and Soviet command headquarters, and why develop increasingly accurate missiles capable of striking within a few hundred feet of a target or closer still, when our goal is "defense" and "deterrence"? Does this not appear amazingly like a first-strike capability aimed at knocking out Soviet weapons before they can retaliate?

The whole idea of a rational limited nuclear war is illusory, to put it kindly. In what possible sense would such a war be "limited," given the awesome destructive power and radioactive fallout of even one nuclear missile? What's more hundreds or even thousands rained upon an enemy's missile installations? In what sense is it "rational" to even contemplate nuclear war of any kind, strategic or general?

In any case, the efficacy of our strategy of deterrence, whether it be MAD or counterforce, is difficult to measure. There are those who firmly believe that MAD and counterforce have prevented and will continue to prevent a cataclysm. The proof offered is that nuclear war has never occurred in more than three decades since such weapons were developed, and it is unlikely to do so in the future.

Such "evidence," however, calls to mind the old story about a man who walked around incessantly snapping his fingers. When asked why he did this, he replied that it kept the tigers away. Informed there never had been any tigers in that part of the country, he happily exclaimed, "See, it works." The only way we will know if nuclear stockpiling fails to prevent World War III will be when it is too late to correct the mistake (and too late to repeat it). We will never know for sure whether, in the absence of such a calamity, we escaped such a fate because of or in spite of our strategy of "deterrence." This fragile "balance of terror," however, is a far cry from the conventional meaning we attach to "security." It is a highly dangerous game we are playing, and unless we start updating our language of warfare to more accurately reflect the realities of the nuclear age, the game will look more and more like Russian roulette.

SUMMARY

Language must be an accurate reflection of that which it represents. It should be clear from this analysis that language has not been used prudently regarding the problem of violence. *Violence* labels are designated where no empirical basis exists for making such attachments. Acts of physical abuse and serious injury, even death, are legitimized as "not violence." We excuse awesome levels of violence by dehumanizing victims, designating methods of killing as "humane," claiming "self-defense," appealing for signal reactions to "ideals," and camouflaging the terror of violence with technical, impersonal language that sanitizes a very messy business.

Our enemies are poorly defined abstractions. They are seen in gross stereotypes which are outgrowths of the "enemy" label we hang on them. The world becomes a battleground between good and evil and no one has to guess which side every nation claims to defend. Our labels are rubber yardsticks bending with the expediencies of world and domestic politics. Sometimes these labels reflect a world no longer in existence.

Making our language maps accurate representations of the territory, concentrating on language strategies that picture violence as illegitimate rather than seeking ways to legitimize it, using language to picture problems and nations in a multi-valued not a two-valued framework, and specifying the denotative meaning of vague abstractions and cosmic justifications of violence according to clear, objective, and empirically based criteria wherever possible, will prove valuable in one's quest for a peaceful world. Unfortunately, this is not a panacea but a mere beginning. Causes of violence are many. Careless and inappropriate use of language is merely one of those causes. But language is our chief means of dialogue, negotiation and bridge building between rivals. It seems like a fruitful place to begin eroding the forces of violence and killing.

CHAPTER 6

THE LANGUAGE OF RACISM AND SEXISM

There are many examples of language that stigmatizes. The semantics of racism and sexism, however, offers a fertile ground for examining the libelous labeling and linguistic dehumanization of whole groups of people.

These two areas, race and sex, have much in common when considering stigmatizing semantics. First, the dehumanization is at least partially based on imagined, not real, differences between favored groups and stigmatized groups. Second, a status hierarchy, a kind of caste system exists whereby dominant groups in society dehumanize less powerful groups. Third, individuals stigmatized for their race or sex are considered subhuman and thereby worthy of psychological and physical abuse.

It is a picture all of us are familiar with in varying degrees, but a closer examination will reveal that language misuse and malpractice plays an important role in the perpetuation of racism and sexism.

RACISM: THE CONSEQUENCES OF LIBELOUS LABELING
"Race": Our Modern Mythology

"Races" do not exist! Does this surprise you? I would guess that such a statement would strike most people as the sheerest sort of nonsense. Of course "races" exist, you might protest. Do my eyes deceive me or is that not a black man and an Oriental woman walking down the street? There's your proof that "races" exist.

I can understand that it will take no small effort to convince most of you that "race" is a modern myth, given birth in the latter part of the eighteenth century (Montagu, 1974) and nurtured by ignorance and expedient self-interest. Nevertheless, the concept of "race" as commonly understood and used in everyday discourse is an empty abstraction, a reification of a symbol that does not correspond to anything factual or real. It is a figment of our imagination, a fanciful notion.

I said "as commonly understood and used," "race" is a myth. There is one sense in which the concept of "race" is not a myth. To a geneticist, "race" is a statistical concept referring to a population which differs in the frequency of certain genes from other populations. This very restricted definition of "race," however, although valid, is probably not a very useful basis for classifying humankind, as we shall see.

The common conception of "race" bears little resemblance to such a restricted genetic definition. As conventionally used, the term *race* refers to a homogeneous group of individuals who are characterized by an aggregate of genetically determined traits which individually and collectively distinguish such human beings from individuals in all other groups (Montagu, 1974). The mythology of "race" becomes apparent when we examine this common conception of "race" piece by piece.

Consider first the notion that "races" are homogeneous groups. Here we have the allness problem Korzybski referred to. Because we observe a few readily apparent physical characteristics which some humans have in common, we lump them together in a group, then assume they are alike in most other respects as well. One black man is essentially like all other black men. Because genetics or inheritance plays a part in this racial lumping together of individuals, there is a sense of permanence, of immutability which attends racial classifications. It is as if such racial classifications were a discovery in nature, not an arbitrary invention of humankind.

The fact is that although humans have much in common with each other by virtue of their membership in the human species, humans are noteworthy for their great diversity and variability. Once you go beyond the basic similarities which go with the territory *homo sapiens:* two arms, two legs, basic organs, and so forth and begin attempting to divide humankind into subspecies known as "races," problems immediately occur.

Racial designations assume substantial similarities that exist among individuals so classified beyond the fundamental equipment which comprises humans in general. Such is not the case. Although a few arbitrary, noticeable similarities exist in any "racial" group (for example, skin color and hair texture), a significant diversity exists within the so-called "race."

This only stands to reason when you consider that the statistical possibility that any two individuals will have an identical genetic makeup, excluding identical twins, is virtually incomprehensible, namely, one followed by 3000 zeroes (Farb, 1980, p. 234). Each human being is therefore unique.

Given the uniqueness of each human being, diversity within any arbitrarily designated group is bound to be great. If an individual from one geographic population (for example, Africa, Asia, or Europe) is chosen at random and compared to another individual from a different geographic population also selected at random, the genetic difference between these two individuals will be about 35 to 40 percent. Significantly, when two individuals from the *same* "racial" population are chosen at random and compared, the genetic difference is nearly as great—almost 30 percent (Farb, 1980, p. 259).

A technique for precisely measuring the differences between individuals called *electrophoresis* shows in another way the substantial diversity of human beings. Electrophoresis measures the proteins in the human body. These proteins are genetically controlled so they reliably indicate human variation. Such a measurement will reveal approximately 200,000 differences in the proteins of any two randomly selected Europeans, Africans, Chinese, or other members of "racial" groups. Compare the supposed extremes *between* "racial" groups, however, such as a European ("white race") and an African ("black race") and the difference in proteins is only slightly more than the 200,000 found when comparing individuals from the same population (Farb, 1980, p. 259).

What this all means is that a "pure race" is a fiction. Human beings are so thoroughly mixed genetically that the whole racist concept of "racial purity" was and is a simple-minded notion.

Secondly, the notion that a "race" is a homogeneous group of individuals is also a myth. The genetic differences between members of a so-called "race" are very nearly equal to the differences between members of supposedly distinct "races."

Nevertheless, there are some obvious differences between "races." Are they significant in kind if not in quantity, thereby justifying the concept of "race"? Hardly!

Interest in racial classification emerged from nineteenth century class prejudice (Montagu, 1974). It wasn't "race" which determined class, rather it was class which led to "race." Racism, the belief in the superiority of some "races" over other "races," is therefore the product of a caste system, of social stratification.

American blacks, for instance, were not considered members of any "race" when they were originally enslaved. They were, however, members of the infidel slave class. This was a *social* not a biological designation. When slavery was attacked as "inhumane" a justification for the perpetuation of such an institution had to be found. Biological "inferiority" as manifested by physical differences became that justification. Blacks "deserved" slavery because they were physically or biologically inferior to members of the "white race." Since the physical or biological differences remain constant, the social position of blacks should remain that of a lowly slave, so it was argued. Class status thus produced "races," and differences between "races" justified social stratification.

Ironically, the differences between "races" would melt into oblivion, leaving only differences between individuals if it weren't for this caste system. The caste system that produced racism in America also led to rigid restrictions on "cross-racial" breeding. Social barriers "protected" the "superior white race" from putrefaction by the "inferior black race." Interracial breeding (miscegenation) was forbidden by law in the South in order to keep the "superior race" pure. Thus, the physical and biological differences between the "races" were maintained, not because "race" determines fixed differences, but because social barriers prevented "race" mixing.

As Montagu (1974) points out, if blacks were freely permitted to marry whites, the apparent physical differences between the two groups would eventually disappear. Like the fist that dissolves in the air when we open our hand, so also does "race" vanish when we open our minds to the facts.

The choice of characteristics used to distinguish "superior races" from "inferior races" further demonstrates how exceedingly ludicrous this whole racial business is. The most common characteristic chosen is skin color. Classifying "races" according to skin color is like categorizing books in a library by the color of their covers. What value would there be in such an artificial grouping? What would it tell us about the content and substance of the book itself?

Skin color or any other physical characteristic is a superficial human trait which reveals nothing significant about the content of the group. We might as well have a freckle-faced "race," a short or tall "race," maybe a bow-legged "race," or how about a bald-headed "race" or perhaps a protruding belly button "race." These are all inherited physical traits which no one seriously suggests should be the basis of racial designation yet who can be heard laughing at the suggestion that a "black race" or "white race" or "yellow race" exists?

A case could be made for this approach to human classification, however, if it could be shown that by knowing certain populations are similar in skin color, a cluster of less obvious but important human traits could then be assumed to exist in that population. The common definition of *race* includes such a belief in this "aggregate of genetically determined traits."

Unfortunately for the disciples of race classification human variation follows no such orderly pattern. Despite the persistent belief that human variation is concordant, that is, human characteristics exist in aggregate and vary together, the facts show otherwise. As Ehrlich and Feldman (1977) clearly document, variation in one characteristic does not permit the easy conclusion that predictable variation in other characteristics will necessarily follow. Evidence cited by Ehrlich and Feldman shows that skin color, for instance, is not an accurate predictor of such other characteristics as height, shape of the head or nose, nor of the distribution of A, B, and O blood-group genes. The point is that black persons in parts of Africa can and do vary widely even on relatively unimportant yet easily observable physical characteristics from black persons in other parts of Africa, America, or some other geographic location. Such *discordant* variation is true of all other human populations as well. Thus, defining race on the basis of one characteristic is obviously a silly business.

So how many characteristics are enough? The question is actually quite meaningless. It assumes that clear divisions between human populations can be identified on the basis of physical and biological traits. How dark must your skin be in order to be included in the "black race?" At what point is your nose no longer narrow? When do you exhibit heavy body hair?

Human beings are so mixed regarding their heredity that between groups differences exist only in a comparison of extreme types and even these groups manifest few truly distinct differences. Physical traits such as darkness of skin, thickness of lips, and so forth are not discrete entities. Such traits are gradations on a continuum from more to less—not thick *or* thin, black *or* white, and so forth.

The geneticist's definition of "race," as previously noted, recognizes that human differences are not discrete entities, easily lumped together in explicit categories. The geneticist's conception of *race*, however, is not terribly useful except perhaps to the geneticists. The frequency of certain genes exhibited by a human population does correspond to a reality of sorts, but it is a statistical reality, an abstraction that points to no one person. For instance, Navaho Indians of New Mexico as a group exhibit blood type O in 77.7 percent of their population, at least in the sample of Navahos blood-type. Obviously, no single individual within this group, or any group for that matter, would be a typical Navaho if frequency of type O were the basis for the categorizing. No single individual possesses 77.7 percent type O blood. It's 100 percent type O or 100 percent of some other discrete blood type. Frequency of genes can be displayed by a whole population but not by a single individual. It is analogous to the "average American couple gives birth to 2.2 children." That is a statistical "reality" but hardly a biological possibility. Thus, no American couple is truly average by that criterion, nor any other statistical average.

The futility of trying to categorize human populations according to "races" can be illustrated by looking at previous attempts. Farb (1980) notes that one scientist, after a life long effort, classified human populations into nine "geographical races": American Indian, Micronesian, Polynesian, Melanesian–Papuan, Asiatic, Australian Aborigine, Asiatic Indian, European, and African. Problem was he was forced to recognize thirty-two other "local races" which didn't fit into the nine main "races." Many other "local races" could also be classified that fall between these thirty-two "local races," and so it escalated.

Farb cites other classification schemes, one which lists more than two hundred "races," one which stuffs all of humankind into only three races (European or Caucasoid, African or Negroid, and Asiatic or Mongoloid), and an estimate by some human biologists that a *million* "races" might be identified depending on the criteria used.

Human populations are simply not discrete, homogeneous groups composed of aggregates of inherited traits. It is a fiction, a myth to suppose such a "reality" exists. The U.S. Census Bureau discovered this when they attempted to identify Mexican Americans.

In 1930, the U.S. Census Bureau classified "Mexican Americans" (referred to as "Mexicans" only) as an "other race" along with Indians, Negroes, and Orientals. Thus, Mexicans were not considered part of the "white race." By 1950, the Census Bureau identified "Mexican Americans" according to Spanish surnames. Persons with Spanish surnames were now classified as "*white* persons of Spanish surname." In twenty years, Mexican Americans had, by the simple declaration of our Census Bureau, been transformed from a nonwhite "other race" to members of the "white race."

By 1970, the Census Bureau threw in the towel and allowed

persons to specify their "race" as they saw fit. The same held true in 1980. This merely recognized the futility of trying to classify human populations that are inherently indiscrete into discrete "races." The issue of race identification becomes even more confusing and contradictory when we examine common references to the "Jewish race," "German race," "Japanese race," and so forth. Nationality, language and culture, and religion are vague criteria laypersons often use to identify "races." The presumption is that such "races" are homogeneous groups exhibiting common physical traits and behaviors.

The language and cultural basis of "race" identification exemplified by references to the "Anglo-Saxon race," the "German race," or the "Aryan race" is silly in the extreme. Hitler's so-called "Aryan race" was not a "race" at all. Rather, the term *Aryan* refers to a group of Indo-European languages which includes German, English, Latin, Slavic, Greek, Armenian, and even Sanskrit (Benedict, 1959). Despite Nazi propaganda that equated "Aryan" with certain "preferred" anatomical characteristics, no such relationships exist. Language is a learned behavior, not an inherited trait. There is no unity of physical characteristics, biological traits, and mental ability among speakers of Indo-European languages. Where similarity of characteristics appear among speakers of a language, it is because of geographic isolation and not the language.

The absurdity of classifying "races" according to language can be easily shown. Those who carelessly label people as members of a "linguistic race" typically accept physical differences as criteria for "race" classification as well. Thus, a black person of the "Negro race" who happens to speak German as a first language appears to belong to two "races"—"Negro" and "German." If that same "German Negro" were to have children, and those children, because of physical separation, learned French instead of German, would they then be members of the "French Negro race"? The whole idea is of course preposterous. The same arguments hold true for classifications of race on the basis of nationality.

"Race" classification on the basis of religion (for example, "Moslem race," "Islamic race") is an equally meaningless designation. The "Jewish race" is a case in point. Strictly speaking, a Jew is a person who embraces the Jewish religion. The nonsense nature of "religious races" was illustrated several years ago when the entertainer Sammy Davis Jr. "became a Jew" by accepting membership in the Jewish religion. Sammy Davis Jr. appeared to belong to two races—"Negro" and "Jew"—one inherited and the other volunteered for. If all one has to do is sign up to be a member of a "race," where are the limits to what we call "race"? Should we take seriously references to the "Catholic race," the "Protestant race," or the "Mormon race"?

Most people, however, laughed when jokes were made about Sammy Davis Jr.'s "becoming" a Jew, because they considered Jews an easily distinguishable "race" of people exhibiting common physical and behavioral traits, not simply adherents to a religion (although the distinction between the two definitions of Jews are rarely offered). Supposed common physical traits of Jews include a long hooked nose; dark complexion; black, frequently wavy hair; and short to middling stature. Behavioral traits, allegedly include aggressiveness, intelligence, peculiar gestures, and a certain quality or air of "Jewishness." The belief is that Jews universally share such inherited "racial traits." This is utter fiction. Montagu (1974) marshalls persuasive evidence to prove unequivocally that persons classified as "Jews" because of membership in the Jewish culture do not exhibit anything resembling uniformity of physical characteristics. Biologically speaking, this type of Jew is a heterogeneous population manifesting great diversity of physical characteristics. Montagu also notes that the aggregate physical characteristics that supposedly distinguish a Jew from members of other "races" are traits manifested in much higher frequencies among non-Jewish populations of the Near and Middle East and the Mediterranean.

The behavioral traits attributed to Jews of the world are not inherited. They are the products of culture. Not all Jews exhibit such cultural traits since some, because of outside cultural influences, are less affected by ancient Jewish beliefs and traditions. Those who do have been strongly influenced by their environment not their heredity. Jews are sometimes readily identifiable in a given population in the same way that members of other cultures such as Americans, Italians, and Germans are oftentimes easily identified. Their learned patterns of behavior do not blend perfectly with other cultures. Yet this hardly qualifies Americans, Italians, Germans, or Jews as members of a "race." Persons or groups of persons are visible as Jews not because of their physical traits, but because of certain cultural traits they have acquired in a Jewish community.

The common conceptions of "race" are colossal fantasies. Such "races" do not exist, and yet the fiction is perpetuated by an ignorance of the facts. It is a significant fiction, one which serves as the basis of virulent racism.

Racist Mythology at Work

Bertrand Russell once said, "Most of the greatest evils that man has inflicted upon man have come through people feeling quite certain about something which, in fact, was false." Although the existence of "races" as commonly defined is a fiction, the belief in "race" persists. Racism, the offspring of this elaborate myth, has produced one of these great evils Russell alluded to. Fortified by the illusion that the "white race" is superior to other "races," especially intellectually superior, all manner of inhumane treatment has been visited upon allegedly "inferior races."

The social reality spawned by "race" mythology cannot be denied even though the biological "reality" is a myth. It is small solace, I'm sure, to the Jews, Indians, and blacks, to know that the attempted genocide, enslavement, torture, and brutality they were forced to endure were products of a fallacious belief in the existence of "races" reminiscent of treatment accorded "heretics" and "witches" who were believed to be Satan incarnate.

Mythical beliefs are highly resistant to change, but even the most intransigent ones have been known to die out. We no longer burn witches. In fact, witch hunts have fallen into disrepute even when applied to more contemporary political hobgoblins. Religious heretics are likewise no longer barbecued for their sins although they may be rhetorically roasted in public and/or private, or excommunicated and "sentenced" to the more long-lasting but less immediate fires of eternal damnation.

It is a frustrating task, however, to combat a myth that has long been believed and acted upon. Facts are ignored or distorted. Issues become confused. In some cases, the mythology is camouflaged with abstractions, scientific "evidence," and the like.

The issue of "race" and intelligence is such a case. From the inception of I.Q. tests purporting to measure a poorly defined abstraction called *intelligence,* results of such tests have been ceremoniously reported as proof of the innate mental inferiority of blacks, Indians, Mexican-Americans and other "racial minorities."

Two of the best-known proponents of this point of view are William Shockley, an electrical engineer and Nobel Prize–winning co-inventor of the transistor, and Arthur Jensen, a well-known educational psychologist, both of Stanford University. The Jensen–Shockley hypothesis argues that blacks, the group of primary interest, are innately inferior to whites in intelligence and this is the product of genetic inheritance. Were this to be found true, the implications for black people in this country and throughout the world would be enormous.

Aside from the heavy stigma attached to the label *stupid* and *inferior,* effects on the self-esteem of blacks, especially black children, and likely consequences on job-hiring practices in white-collar professions, our own history and that of other nations, most noticeably Nazi Germany, portends the frightening prospect of renewed calls for a eugenics program—controlled breeding to "improve" humanity. Compulsory sterilization of blacks (and other "inferiors" for that matter), laws against interracial marriages, and similar regulations are not inconceivable once the majority white population believes that scientific evidence proves blacks are hopelessly and inherently inferior and that such "mental incompetents" are a burden and threat to the wellbeing and progress of the human species. Recall the results of the Mansson (1972) and Carlson and Wood (1974) studies previously cited where the extermination of the "mentally and emotionally unfit" was accepted by a startling number of subjects.

This new wave of "scientific racism," as Farb (1980) terms it, is fortified by studies showing that blacks score an average 15 points lower than whites on I.Q. (intelligence quotient) tests. Jensen, who incidentally does not advocate the above treatment of blacks and argues against race discrimination in his book *Bias in Mental Testing* (1980), nevertheless claims that research demonstrates that only 5 of the 15 point difference between "races" can be explained by environmental factors. The remaining 10 points, Jensen argues, is due to heredity. Thus, blacks are asserted to be innately inferior intellectually to whites, and such "scientific" findings will easily be accepted unequivocally as fact by the uninformed and the bigoted.

The arguments against the Jensen–Shockley hypothesis are plentiful and complicated. The evidence refuting this hypothesis is abundant. It is not possible to present more than a brief sample of such arguments and evidence. Nevertheless, even a brief sample will highlight its weaknesses.

First, *Jensenism,* as the Jensen–Shockley hypothesis is often dubbed, accepts without question the "reality" of "races." In fact, virtually all the research Jensen cites as "proof" of the truth of his hypothesis classifies "races" on the basis of skin color (Vernon, 1979, p. 246). Jensenism is therefore grounded in fallacy. It begs the question. That which must be proven first, namely, that distinct "races" exist, is taken for granted.

Second, the concept of *intelligence* is a vague abstraction. Various psychologists have identified anywhere from 2 to 120 special abilities such as verbal comprehension, perceptual speed, and reasoning as indicators of intelligence. So what is this thing we call *intelligence?* What combination of special abilities must a person have to be considered intelligent? And is it right-brain or left-brain "intelligence" we're identifying?

Some psychologists have skirted this whole issue and defined intelligence as whatever intelligence tests measure. This, of course, is a circular definition and thus never answers the central question. It also assumes that I.Q. tests are flawless.

Third, I.Q. tests measure special skills taught in North American and European schools. As Farb (1980) points out, since we don't know for sure what intelligence is and since I.Q. tests measure academic skills, such tests should probably be called A.Q. (academic quotient) tests. I.Q. test scores do correlate with academic achievement but they are culture specific and thus biased against people of different socioeconomic backgrounds from that of the dominant white group (Farb, 1980, and Montagu, 1974).

So before we even consider the research on differences in I.Q.

scores between blacks and whites it becomes apparent that Jensenism rests on a precarious theoretical foundation. It certainly won't take an earthquake to make the Jensenist hypothesis crumble. Let's examine some of the relevant research.

To begin with, Ehrlich and Feldman (1977) point out that there is no way to measure "genetic I.Q." What it comes down to is, fundamentally, how you determine that it is your genes and not your environment that has resulted in the level of "intelligence" measured by I.Q. tests. Even genes are affected over time by environmental influences.

Although genes are responsible for giving all humans the fundamental material necessary for human intelligence (that is, a brain that is human in size and make-up as opposed to one the size and composition of a dinosaur), *differences* in intelligence are markedly affected by environment. If genes are more important than environment in accounting for such differences, as Jensen asserts, and blacks are intellectually inferior because of their genes, then you would expect, as Shockley has asserted, that as "black genes" increase, intelligence decreases. As near as anyone can measure, that is not the case.

Vernon (1979) cites several studies which show that presence or absence of "white blood group genes" in "black" children did not correlate with I.Q. scores. Ehrlich and Feldman (1977) cite a Canadian study which shows that subjects judged as "half-black" on the basis of their ancestry averaged *lower* I.Q. scores than those judged "three-quarters black." In another study (cited in Ehrlich and Feldman, 1977, p. 129), 68 percent of "gifted black children" had *more* black than white ancestry. If "white genes" produce greater intelligence, then the gifted black children should have had more white ancestry than black.

Finally, studies on the influence of environment on I.Q. scores refutes the Jensenist position that heritability is paramount, that nature not nurturance accounts for lower I.Q. scores among blacks and other minority groups.

Some studies reveal that when black and white children share the same high-quality environment for at least one year, I.Q. scores for the two groups are virtually identical (Ehrlich and Feldman, 1977). In some instances—nonverbal tests of intelligence—blacks score higher.

Enriching the environment for children can also have a marked effect on I.Q. scores. Ehrlich and Feldman (1977) conclude from an examination of the research that improving the environment for a child can raise I.Q. scores anywhere from 16 to 40 points (p. 154). Since blacks have experienced lower quality environments than whites on the whole, it is not surprising that they generally score somewhat lower than whites on I.Q. tests.

To reiterate, Jensenism is a bogus issue. It begins with a myth, advances to a vague abstraction *(intelligence)*, measures academic ability but mislabels it *intelligence*, asserts "genetic I.Q." can be measured when it can't be done, then concludes that blacks are inherently inferior intellectually despite the evidence that convincingly demonstrates the strong influence of environment on I.Q. scores. Myths are truly resistant phenomena if such pseudoscientific nonsense disguised as credible scientific inquiry can still be seriously entertained. Nevertheless, the fallacy of "race" and its offspring "racism" continues to encourage the dehumanization of ethnic minorities.

"Race" versus "Ethnic Group"

Voltaire once remarked that "as long as people believe in absurdities, they will continue to commit atrocities." The belief in "race" is an absurdity that has produced some of history's most outrageous atrocities.

The term "race" itself stands as an obstacle to clear thinking on the subject of human differences. "Race" is a trigger word that incites a signal reaction. It is a verbal map that leads our thinking astray, points us in dangerous directions, and muddles our minds. During the Middle Ages, erroneous belief in "evil humors" as the cause of disease directed thought toward bleeding as a "cure." The erroneous belief in "race" points us in the direction of looking for biologically determined differences especially in "racial" intelligence, and instituting eugenics programs to "purify" and protect the "superior races."

Montagu (1974) argues that we should purge *"race"* from our vocabulary and replace it with the term *"ethnic group."* According to Montagu, an ethnic group refers to population groups that maintain their physical and cultural differences from other population groups by means of geographic and social barriers (p. 441). Thus, an ethnic group may be a nation, a people (the Jews), a group bound together by a religion (the Amish), groups bound together by a caste system who share common physical features (American blacks), or a language group (the Dakota Indians). Such groups may exhibit greater frequency of certain genetic characteristics and physical traits than other populations, not because they are a "race," but because they have been isolated and consequently share a common gene pool.

It is of course naïve to believe that racism could be eradicated by eliminating the word "race" from our vocabulary and substituting "ethnic group." Such verbal magic equates words with things. Yet Montagu persuasively argues that there are several advantages to be gained by replacing "race" with "ethnic group."

First, it is not a mere verbal sleight of hand. It is a correction of a serious error in thinking. "Ethnic group" is not simply "race" in a different set of clothes. The term "ethnic group" calls for a different perception of population groups than does the term "race." "Ethnic group" shifts the emphasis to the influence of culture and environment upon human development, both mental and physical. Where the term "race" erroneously imputes a kind of biological determinism upon human groups, the phrase "ethnic group" represents no such biological fallacy. "Ethnic group" does not ignore the role of heredity in the development of human differences; it simply places heredity in its proper cultural and environmental context, something "race" does not do.

A second advantage of "ethnic group" over "race" is that it eliminates the obfuscating and dangerous connotations surrounding the term "race." When the term "race" is used, the question "What do you mean by 'race'?" is rarely, if ever, asked. "Race" is so familiar to us that we assume our private meaning for the term corresponds to the facts, to something real. The phrase "ethnic group," however, is not so familiar to us and encourages questions concerning its meaning. "Ethnic group" thus has educational value.

Anthropologists at one time referred to nonliterate groups as *savages.* The term has been excised from the anthropological vocabulary because the connotations of inferiority and negative judgment attached to the term *savage* were seen to be reflections of ethnocentrism, not empirical facts. Even the term *primitive* is being abandoned and replaced with the less value-loaded term *nonliterate* for essentially the same reason, namely, the inaccuracy of the verbal maps. Thus, precedents do exist for replacing an inaccurate and misleading term such as "race" with the more accurate and neutral phrase "ethnic group." Since "races" do not exist except as a statistical abstraction but "ethnic groups" do, the change seems an eminently intelligent one.

SEXIST LANGUAGE: THE SEMANTIC STIGMATIZATION OF WOMEN

Martin Luther once commented that "God created Adam lord of all creatures, but Eve spoiled it all." The stigma attached to women started early. As a co-conspirator with Satan, Eve tempted poor Adam into sharing that fateful apple with her, thereby damning the entire human species to a life of rush-hour traffic, stagflation, and valium vacations.

Although the story of Adam and Eve stuffing their faces with forbidden fruit doesn't have to be taken literally but rather can be treated as Biblical mythology, males as a rule have taken the bit about their being "lord of all creatures" quite literally. This male supremacist mythology is remarkably similar to racist mythology. Male supremacist and racist arguments have much in common. As Montagu (1977) notes, virtually everything that has been asserted about any so-called "inferior race" has been asserted by men about women. Women have been branded as less intelligent than men, childlike, emotional, irrational, uncreative, and the list goes on and on. In times past, women in the United States were not even accorded the legal status of *person*. Reminiscent of the U.S. Constitution's definition of blacks as only three-fifths of a person, the U.S. Supreme Court ruled in 1894 that it was reasonable for a lower court to rule that the Virginia bar could deny entry to women because a woman was not legally a person (in *re Lockwood* 154 U.S. 116 [1894]).

Women's nonperson status in fact as well as in law has been demonstrated perhaps most graphically in the field of psychiatry. In the mid-nineteenth century, doctors "cured" so-called illnesses of sexuality such as nymphomania, ovariomania, or uterine madness by cauterizing the "diseased" woman's clitoris or simply removing her ovaries (ovariotomy) or clitoris (clitoridectomy). Masturbation was the primary indication for such surgery, but as Gena Corea (1977) evidences in her book *The Hidden Malpractice,* a multitude of symptoms such as indigestion, insomnia, back pain, depression, headache, anemia, a "desire to run away from home or become a nurse," heart palpitation, and "eating like a plowman" could invite mutilation of the female sex organs. Although concern about "masturbation insanity" (Szasz, 1970) also led to mutilation of male genitalia, it is clear that women were the principal victims. Women's sexuality was an expendable commodity.

The minds of women have also been considered expendable. At least two-thirds of psychiatric patients receiving electroshock treatments for "mental illness" have been women. As Schrag (1978) points out, the effects of such treatments are severe. Excruciating pain during and after treatments, memory loss, sheer terror, and a zombie-like state are some of the results of shock therapy.

If shock treatments don't work well enough there is always psychosurgery. Lobotomies, where sections of healthy brain tissue are surgically excised to alter emotional and behavioral states, have been most often performed on women (Breggins and Greenberg, 1972). Such operations destroy a victim's creativity. As Dr. Peter Breggins (1972) observes, however, a remarkably large percentage of female lobotomies have been justified on the grounds that creativity is "an expendable quality in women." Lobotomized women who return to housework are considered evidence of the "success" of the "treatment."

Most women have escaped the ravages of the psychosurgeon's knife, and our attitudes concerning female sexuality have certainly changed. Nevertheless, despite marked improvement in women's position in this society, women still suffer a daily dose of psychological maiming by being depreciated, trivialized, and excluded from positions of status and power. Sexist language both reflects this male supremacist thinking that puts woman "in her place" and reinforces it. While sexist language can discriminate against men by defining them in ways that limit their human potential (for example, men are "aggressive," "macho," and "analytical" but must not show emotion), clearly the principal victims of such language are women. Men have the power to define women in man's image. The exercise of this power to define women in ways that are dehumanizing constitutes the subject of this next section.

Defining Women: In Man's Image

Depreciation. Studies of sex role characteristics (see Broverman and others, 1970; Chafetz, 1974, and Birnbaum and others, 1980) have presented a negative picture of women and a generally positive picture of men. Despite the fact that these studies included both male and female subjects, women were described with predominantly negative connotative words such as *dependent, subjective, illogical, petty, fickle, frivolous, vain, shallow, passive,* and *gossipy,* while men received such predominantly positive descriptions as *independent, objective, active, adventurous, skilled in business, confident, trustworthy, logical, experienced,* and *practical.* As a whole, stereotypically feminine traits are usually perceived as less socially desirable than stereotypically masculine traits. For instance, even positive traits assigned to women such as *idealistic, gentle, tender, soft,* and *innocent* are frequently derided as impractical and signs of weakness.

Such dichotomous stereotyping of males and females reflects the predominance of two-valued thinking in our society. Men and women are viewed as opposites. Recent research into the concept of androgyny, the idea that individuals can be *both* masculine and feminine without contradiction, reveals, however, some fundamental popular misconceptions concerning sex-role stereotyping.

First, masculinity and femininity are not opposite ends of the same continuum; rather, they are separate dimensions (Spence and others, 1975). Confusion on this point stems primarily from a misunderstanding of the differences between sex and gender. As Walum (1977) explains, sex refers to the biological aspects of persons such as their anatomy and physiology, whereas gender refers to the psychological, social, and cultural components. Sex is revealed at birth whereas gender is learned within the context of culturally condoned and prescribed behaviors and characteristics considered appropriate for men to be "masculine" and women to be "feminine." When we confuse gender with sex it does not appear natural for an individual to manifest an integration of both masculine and feminine traits.

Psychiatrists, psychologists, and social psychologists have long assumed that society and the individual are better off if sex-specific differences are learned and maintained. Sandra Bem (1972), however, after reviewing the sparse research on this issue, concludes that heavy emphasis on gender appropriate behavior may in fact be harmful. Maccoby and Jacklin (1974) found that girls exhibiting strong masculine traits and boys exhibiting strong feminine traits tend to do better on intellectual activities than do boys and girls manifesting gender appropriate traits. Spence and others (1975) discovered that androgynous students (high scores on both masculinity and femininity) had the highest self-esteem of any group studied, while persons low on both masculinity and femininity had the lowest self-esteem, and persons high on one dimension but low on the other were in between. Schwartz (1979), using clinical examples, argues that gender-specific role identification severely restricts emotional and sexual intimacy, whereas androgynous loving is the maturest form of an intimate relationship. Bem (cited in Walum, 1977) also found that nonandrogynous subjects were far more anxious and less competent when performing a variety of tasks, especially those demanding qualities typically associated with the opposite sex. While this research is not conclusive it does strongly suggest that viewing men and women as opposites greatly restricts the human potential of both sexes (see Bem, 1979).

Nevertheless, the prevailing attitude (albeit generally eroding) in our society, especially among males, is that men must act their part and women theirs. Men who display stereotypically feminine traits may be labeled *effeminate,* whereas women who display stereotypically masculine traits may be labeled *unfeminine* or *mannish.*

While all such labels are pejorative, negative connotations associated with such labels have a different source for men than they do for women. Since a woman's role is not valued, the label *effeminate* ridicules males for being "weak" and seemingly unable to act out the strong masculine image society carves out for them. Labels such as *unfeminine* and *mannish,* on the other hand, ridicule women for wanting to assume a stronger image and act out more assertive behavior. Sex role stereotyping thus demands that men appear strong and dominant while women remain weak and submissive.

Two-valued thinking sees androgyny, then, as an attempt to diminish men by asking them to adopt "weak" feminine traits. Such thinking does not consider that there is strength in both gender specific clusters of traits for male and female. When women are coerced or manipulated into accepting an inferior role solely because of their sex, then they are dehumanized, and "femininity" is not a pedestal for exalting women but a pit for trapping them.

The depth of this "femininity" pit can be deduced in several ways. A study by Broverman et al. (1970), for instance, reveals the classic Catch-22 women are faced with when trying to free themselves from the shackles of negative stereotyping that imprisons them in rigid, socially undesirable female roles. A group of seventy-nine psychologists, psychiatrists, and social workers (forty-six male, thirty-three female) were asked to describe a "mature, healthy, socially competent adult man," a "mature, healthy, socially competent adult woman," and a "healthy, mature, socially competent adult person" by choosing from a list of bipolar stereotypic behavior traits or characteristics. There was general agreement that a mentally healthy *adult* closely parallels a mentally healthy *male*. The picture of a mentally healthy woman, however, bore little resemblance to that of a mature, healthy adult. Mentally healthy women supposedly differ from mentally healthy men by being *more* submissive, easily influenced, dependent, excitable in minor crises, emotional, conceited about their appearance, and *less* adventuresome, aggressive, competitive, and objective. "Healthy" women also dislike math and science. As Broverman and others observe, "This constellation seems a most unusual way of describing any mature, healthy individual [p. 5]."

Thus, the woman's role is negatively valued, yet if women attempt to exhibit behaviors appropriate for mature, healthy adults they are branded not only as "unfeminine" but also as mentally unhealthy. They must remain as less than mature competent adults in order to be perceived as healthy.

Obviously what we have here is a semantic straitjacket for women. The more they try to wriggle free from the constraints of their negatively valued roles, the tighter they are bound by the assignment of a mental illness label. It is little wonder women experience depression more frequently than do men.

Even our terms of disparagement and abuse reflect a monumental contempt for women with no equivalent contempt for men. Muriel Schultz (in Thorne and Henley, 1975) identified almost 1000 words and phrases describing women in a sexually derogatory manner, yet there is but a fraction of this number describing men in such a fashion. Farmer and Henley (1965) discovered over 500 terms in English which are synonyms for *prostitute* but could find only 65 synonyms for the male counterpart *whoremonger*.

Schultz (in Thorne and Henley, 1975) also cites scores of "perfectly innocent terms" that may begin with a neutral or positive connotation but gradually acquire negative connotations and eventually end as sexual slurs when applied to women. *Broad, nymph, whore, wench,* and *hussy* are some examples. Also, some titles of honor and respect have become debased for women but remain exalted for men. *Madam, mistress, lady,* and *dame* have all acquired degraded meanings but no such fate has befallen parallel male titles such as *master, lord,* and *sir.*

Animal metaphors applied to people reflect the same bias against women. Nilsen (in Nilsen and others, 1977) observes that to call a man a *dog* may mean he's shrewd ("sly dog") or fortunate ("lucky dog") but when a woman is a *dog* she's simply unattractive. A man may be "cocky" but a woman revealing self-confidence is likely to be called a "cocky bitch." *Bull* connotes sexual prowess in males but *cow* has no redeeming social meaning when applied to women. *Pig* is a rare exception to this pattern. It is highly negative when assigned to either sex. *Sow,* however, is an abusive metaphor reserved for women. In addition, women have a corner on the market for such animal metaphors as *vixen, cat, pussy, bat, chick, hen,* and so forth.

Descriptions of men and women exhibiting parallel behavior also reveal this same pattern of semantic stigmatization. For instance:

He's inquisitive.	She's nosy.
He shares information.	She gossips.
He discusses.	She chatters.
He explains.	She complains.

He's cool.	She's frigid.
He's reflective.	She's moody.
He's a lover.	She's a tramp.
He's sexually potent.	She's a nymphomaniac.
He's resolute.	She's stubborn.
He loses his temper.	She's hysterical.
He's thorough.	She's picky.
He suffers mid-life crisis.	She's menopausal.
He's analytical.	She uses feminine logic.
He's an eligible bachelor.	She's a spinster.
He's become a bachelor again.	She's become a divorceé.
He's forgetful.	She's scatterbrained.

The way in which women are described in the mass media, compared with descriptions of men, is yet another reflection of the semantic dehumanization of women. A woman's appearance and physical attributes receive paramount attention whereas a man's position and stature in society is a primary object of attention. Women are typically described as "blondes, brunettes, redheads" (can you picture men being described as "baldies, greyhairs, or blackheads"?), "curvy, petite, and shapely," and so forth. Foreit and others (1980) discovered that newspaper coverage of women was more likely to include a description of women's personal appearance and attire than newspaper coverage of men. Women are valued for their sexuality and beauty, not their intellect or capabilities.

Certainly we do not always speak kindly about men and pejoratively about women in our society. Nevertheless, our language reflects a disproportionate number of highly abusive terms for women and reinforces the attitude that women are valuable only for their bodies and the sexual favors and nurturance they can provide men.

The female role is not highly valued while the male role is esteemed. Our sexist language puts woman "in her place" by diminishing her, abusing her, and describing her as a second-class human being. As Montagu (1974) points out in his book *The Natural Superiority of Women*, the evidence strongly suggests that women's capabilities are at least on a par with those of men and in several ways may be superior to men's. The real issue is not one of intrinsic potential. Rather, the real issue is power.

Linguistic Invisibility.   The fact that women do not wield power in our society is reflected in their linguistic invisibility. Consider first a woman's surname (read that *"sir"* [male] name). When a woman marries, which is the usual course of events even today, she normally assumes her husband's surname. A woman thus integrates her identity with that of her husband. Her identity is now that of wife to her husband. Historically this has meant that a married woman became the property of her husband

William Blackstone's *Commentaries on the Law of England,* a document that enormously influenced the American legal system, defined women as inferior to men, and married women, according to Blackstone, had no "being or legal existence" whatever. The American Civil Liberties Union, arguing in *Hoyt* v. *Florida* (368 U.S. 57 [1961]), summarized Blackstone and the legal status of women in the United States. According to the ACLU, women have been

> chattels, in effect slaves, their legal existence suspended during marriage, with limited freedom of movement, little right to property or earnings, no control over their children, and no political or civil rights, of any kind. Blackstone's quip (slightly paraphrased) that "Husband and wife are one and that one is the husband," was no idle jest. At the very moment when a man met his bride at the altar and said to her, "With all my worldly goods I thee endow," he was actually taking every cent she possessed. . . . He could beat her with a stick "no bigger than the wedding ring." All this on account of her "defectum sexus."

A married woman had no legal identity.

On various occasions the courts in this country have decreed that in certain circumstances a woman cannot legally use her maiden name even if she so chooses (De Crow, 1974, and Bosmajian, 1979). Married women have been forced in some states to register to vote or to vote under their husband's surname. Refusal to do so has meant disenfranchisement. The U.S. Supreme Court as recently as 1972 upheld an unwritten regulation in Alabama which stipulated that a married woman could not be issued a driver's license in her maiden name. Statutes that prescribe formal procedures for changing one's name frequently exempt married women. When a man changes his surname, his wife's surname is automatically changed whether she wants it so or not.

Historically, then, women in this country have been treated as legal nonentities. The identities of married women have been submerged into those of their husbands. It took over two centuries to significantly erode legal sexism in the United States. Vestiges of it still remain, however.

Women are linguistically invisible in ways other than legal. When references are made to *man* or *mankind,* women are forced to wonder whether such generic references really include women. Prescriptive grammarians assert that when the sex is unspecified, *man, mankind,* and personal pronouns such as *he* and *him* incorporate both sexes. Research suggests, however, that in actual practice, such generic references produce images of males, not females. Nilsen (1973), using a picture-selection technique with one hundred children from nursery school through seventh grade, found that *man* in the sentences "Man must work in order to eat" and "Around the world man is happy" was interpreted by most subjects, male and female, to mean males, not females. Schneider and Hocker (1972) discovered a similar result. Several hundred college students were asked to illustrate different chapters of a sociology textbook being readied for publication. Half the students were assigned chapter headings such as "Social Man," "Industrial Man," and "Political Man" to illustrate with pictures from magazines and newspapers. The other half were given chapter headings such as "Society," "Industrial Life," and "Political Behavior." Images of males only, excluding women from participation in these areas of life, were evoked in a majority of the minds of students, male and female, who were given "generic man" titles as measured by the pictures they chose for illustration. Corresponding titles without the generic man reference evoked images of both male and female.

It is little wonder that generic man references translate into primarily male images. Men can always assume they are included in the term *man* and *mankind,* yet women can never be certain of their inclusion.

The term *man* operates on two levels of abstraction, the gender-specific and the generic. This is where the problem lies because two contradictory propositions surface when using the term *man.* The gender-specific use of *man* provides the proposition that "woman is not man," while the generic use of *man* stands on the proposition that "woman is man." This wouldn't cause much confusion if it were clear when the gender-specific and when the generic were being used. A sentence such as "All men are created equal" is said to be a generic use of the term *man,* yet historic evidence clearly reveals that women, who had no property rights and no vote, were not originally included in this quotation from the Declaration of Independence. It was a gender-specific reference masquerading as a generic reference.

We cannot know for certain in which sense the following sentences are being used:

1. Man is a superior creature.
2. Man invented the wheel.
3. All men are mortal.

The picture is confused further by adding generic he, him, or his references. For example, "Man is the master of his own destiny" could be a generic reference to both sexes according to grammatical rules, yet it defies such an interpretation. What we ask women to believe is that "Man is the master of his own destiny" also conveys the meaning "Man is the master of *her* own destiny" as well. Such allegedly generic references demand a mental two-step. First we gain an image of maleness, then we must add femaleness into the picture. Clearly, we stumble after the first step excluding women from our mental image.

Taken individually, specific instances of semantic depreciation and linguistic exclusion of women evidenced here may seem relatively inconsequential, at least to male readers. The important point to realize, however, is that language usage reflects and reinforces prevailing attitudes and norms. In the case of women, sexist language practices exhibit a monumental contempt for over half of the world's population. Women in this country have been doormats, and their vehement attacks on sexist language signal an unwillingness to allow men to step on them any longer. Eliminating sexist language practices as an aid in putting women in their rightful place, in equal partnership with men, is clearly warranted.

Desexing the Language

The linguist Otto Jesperson (1923) proudly proclaimed that English is "the language of a grown-up man, with very little childish or feminine about it [p. 1]." Whether Jesperson's assessment of our language is accurate or not matters little. What does matter, however, is the long prevailing attitude expressed by his linguistic assessment. That which is "masculine" should be valued while that which is "feminine" should be demeaned.

In Chapter One, I discussed the Sapir-Whorf hypothesis and concluded that, although we are not prisoners of our language unless we victimize ourselves by careless language practices, we are nevertheless strongly influenced by the affective elements of our language. Our language also guides our thinking, acting as a verbal map. In addition, it can help us see what might otherwise remain hidden in the absence of a readily available lexicon. Desexing our language is justified from all these perspectives.

First, the semantic depreciation of women unquestionably affects their self-image. Studies clearly reveal that women consistently have low expectations of their abilities and lower self-esteem than men (Zimbardo and Ruch, 1977). Sexist language, of course, is only one force diminishing the self-esteem and self-concept of women, but it seems inconceivable that a steady diet of linguistic depreciation would have little or no effect on women's self-assessments. The message has been trumpeted loudly and clearly for centuries. Women are trivial, worthless, and insignificant by the male standards of our society, except for their sexuality and nurturance capabilities. As Blaubergs (1978) observes, our sexist language not only reflects prevailing sexist attitudes and stereotypes but also reinforces and fortifies such attitudes.

Second, desexing our language will call attention to the fact that women have been discriminated against. Nonsexist language makes women more visible, thereby making them more difficult to ignore. The language becomes inclusive, not exclusive. New verbal maps are constructed challenging us to see in a new way.

This new visibility was illustrated by the change from Miss or Mrs. to Ms. as a standard form of addressing women. It helped spotlight discrimination against women. It was a small, seemingly insignificant change, yet it fomented a national debate and captured the attention of the mass media.

Rather than waiting patiently for language to reflect social change that is slow in coming, women are increasingly desexing the language to effect change. While changing sexist language patterns will not by itself eliminate sexism in our society, continued use of sexist language can only help perpetuate the dehumanization of women. If we don't clean up our language, then we are unlikely to clean up our act. Sexist language reinforces male supremacist attitudes and nourishes stereotypic thinking.

Many people have argued that changing sexist language patterns is too troublesome and produces awkward, clumsy alternatives. Those who take such a position typically find nothing very clumsy about referring to women as *man* or *he, him,* and *his.*

Desexing our language is actually quite simple once we are committed to doing it. I have had very little difficulty writing this book in nonsexist language. It merely requires a commitment and a bit of practice. It soon becomes second nature.

So what kinds of changes should we make in our language in order to desex it? Blaubergs (1978) examines two approaches. The first is circumvention, or the elimination of gender-specific terms and/or the substitution of neutral terms. The following samples based on Blauberg's analysis illustrate how circumvention works:

Sexist	*Nonsexist*
1. *Terms of disparagement:* chick, broad, slut, piece, and the like	Eliminate such references.
2. *Generic references:*	
	a. *Use indefinites*
man, mankind	human, humankind
chairman	chairperson
businessman	business executive
policeman	police officer

b. *Circumlocutions*

postman	letter carrier
farmer and his wife	a farm couple
man-made	synthetic
common man	average person

c. *Pluralization*

he, him, his	they, them, theirs
	(can also use he or she,
	him or her, his or hers)

3. *Nonparallel usages:* *Make parallel*

men and girls	men and women
man and wife	husband and wife

4. *Sex stereotypes:*

housewife	avoid it
the weaker sex	eliminate it
best man for the job	best person for the job
manhole	sewer lid

5. *Trivializing:*

lady lawyer	lawyer
career girl	career woman
astronette, jockette	astronaut, jockey
poetess	poet

A second approach to sexist language actually doesn't desex the language. Rather, it marks gender, thereby increasing the visibility of women. For example:

1. *Generic references*

salesman	saleswoman or salesman when gender is known
congressman	congressman, congresswoman
he, his, him	use femine she, hers, her
	for example, "The office worker. . .she"

2. *Gender indefinite*

poet	poetess
actor	actress
astronaut	astronette

3. *Parallel usage*
   ladies and gentleman   Reverse the order
   sons and daughters   for example, wives and husbands
   husbands and wives

Circumvention has the advantage that it truly desexes the language while gender marking obviously highlights sex specification. I personally am more comfortable with circumvention as a strategy for making language less sexist. The decision regarding which strategy to use, however, is a political one. Gender marking may prove to be a more effective strategy to combat sex stereotyping and create linguistic visibility for women. Circumvention simply neutralizes the language as regards gender.

In actual practice you may decide to use both strategies, depending on the context and circumstances. Ultimately, linguistic changes that are easiest to make will generally prove to be the most productive.

Concocting new terminology such as *huperson* or newly coined common gender pronouns such as *thon, tey, ve, xe, jhe, hesh,* etc., all proposed by various people, usually fail to catch on *(Ms.* is an exception) and may merely invite ridicule.

Stephan Kanfer (1972), for instance, in an article in *Time* entitled "Sispeak: A Msguided Attempt to Change Herstory," offers a typical example of such ridicule in the extreme, ridicule which occupied poets and pundits of the mass media for quite some time. In part, Kanfer parodies:

> Cartoonists and satirists have suggested that the ladies were Libbing under a Msapprehension. Their inventions were Msanthropic and Msguided attempts to change herstory. . . . Shedonism, girlcotting and countessdowns were to be anticipated in the liberated 70s. As for the enemy, he could expect to be confronted by female belligerents inviting him to put up his duchesses. He would find, in short, that his gander was cooked [p. 79].

While such satirical swipes at efforts to desex the language can be great fun, the fervor with which males protest such language changes is noteworthy. If the issue is really as trivial as many have claimed, then why all the ruckus? Nonsexist language merely produces greater accuracy of communication.

Miller and Swift (1976) cite an ironic example of male outrage precipitated by the common sexist practice of using *she* when referring to a primary or secondary teacher. As more men entered the teaching ranks their annoyance at being referred to as *she* mounted. By the mid-1960s, some of these angry young male teachers were claiming that the use of *she* in reference to teachers was partly responsible for their poor public image and low salaries.

When the roles are reversed, men experience the frustration and anger that inevitably result from such linguistic exclusion. Yet somehow it is supposed to be trivial to exclude women whereas it is a matter of vital importance when sexist language affects men.

SUMMARY

The language of dehumanization affects all of us, some directly, others indirectly. How we treat each other is a gauge of what kind of society we hope to build. The semantic stigmatization of ethnic minorities and women results from a status hierarchy bolstered by mythical and fallacious beliefs in the inferiority of such groups. Racist and sexist language sustains this mythology and encourages a continuation of the ignorance and wrongheadedness that is so essential to prejudice and discrimination.

PSYCHOLABELING:
The Semantics
of "Mental Illness"

One of the remarkable qualities of humankind is our ability to organize our perceptions into classification systems. Such systems order our experience, show relationships, note differences between ideas, objects, phenomena, etc., and provide us with a cognitive blueprint which steers our thinking in certain possibly insightful directions.

As our previous discussion of *race*, however, clearly warns, no classification scheme is infallible, and some are decidedly more dangerous than others. It is not a matter of which classification system is right or wrong, good or bad, for that is a value judgment we make on the basis of what we as a society or group decide is desirable and worthwhile. It does matter, however, which classification system, which model, which verbal map we choose to represent our view of reality. A classification system that bears little or no resemblance to the reality it purports to represent will be confusing or even dangerous.

The choice of a model, a verbal map, is a value judgment, but one that should be made in terms of which classification system or systems best meet the goals we deem desirable. For instance, if our goal is to reduce human pain and suffering, then a classification system which exacerbates human anguish will fail to achieve the goal.

My purpose here is not to debate which goals or values our society should espouse. My task is less complicated than that because I happen to agree with the basic principles (goals or values) that this country espouses. For example, the United States clearly advocates curing the sick and reducing human suffering. The fact that we haven't been overly successful on this score has less to do with morality and ethics and more to do with semantics than many would guess.

The problems and pitfalls of a classification system which aims to assuage human distress yet often aggravates such conditions is the subject of this chapter. The process of labeling people "mentally ill," or what I shall call psycholabeling, while nobly intended, has proved to be a source of no small human distress rather than a map showing us the road to less anguish and misery.

"MENTAL ILLNESS":
LABELING THE NEW LEPROSY
Fear and Loathing
of the "Mentally Ill"

When a person is diagnosed as "mentally ill," it amounts to a social kiss of death. While attitudes toward the "mentally ill" have softened somewhat, no significant transformation has occurred to substantially lessen the social stigma attached to people tagged as mentally diseased.

The stigma attached to "mental illness" labels is manifested by public denigration of those so branded, and by the self-deprecation that "mental patients" exhibit as a result of their public rejection and the belief that they are "ill."

Evidence of the magnitude of public denigration accorded the "mentally ill" is voluminous. Numerous studies cited by Sarbin and Mancuso (1970) and Farina and others (1971) substantiate the claim that the "mentally ill" are social lepers. This body of experimentation variously reveals that those designated "mentally ill" are less acceptable as friends and neighbors than dope addicts or ex-convicts, are described as more worthless than blind people and lepers, are pitied, feared, degraded, and isolated, and are often viewed as weak-willed, unassertive malingerers. One study (Tringo, 1970) measured the social acceptability of twenty-one disability groups. The least "preferred" of the disabled were the "mentally ill."

The President's Commission on Mental Health (1978) concludes that "mental patients" or former "mental patients" suffer discrimination in housing, hiring, employment, divorce, and custody proceedings, jury duty, professional licensure, public service, security clearance, and even voting (p. 1876). A comprehensive review and analysis of the over 100 studies conducted to examine public attitudes toward the "mentally ill" was undertaken by Rabkin (1977) for the President's Commission on Mental Health. Although some of these studies reveal a softening of negative attitudes toward the "mentally ill," Rabkin concludes that a large segment of the American public "continues to be frightened and repelled by the notion of mental illness, although it is becoming less socially acceptable to say so." Rabkin further concludes that in the abstract, "mental illness" may be viewed in an acceptable light but when faced with specific situations that directly affect them, lay persons are fearful of "mental patients."

For instance, a community survey in California (Hazelton and others, 1975) found only 17 percent of those questioned agreed that "mental patients are not dangerous." Visions of knife-wielding, depraved, psychotic murderers frequently depicted in movies and on television with maximum dramatic effect and pulse-pounding suspense serve to color in black public attitudes against the "mentally ill."

Do the "mentally ill" deserve to be stigmatized or are we responding to stereotypes of "mental patients" that are for the most part empirically groundless? Consider the most significant stereotype of the "mentally ill" just alluded to, namely, that they are dangerous.

Virtually all short- and long-range studies of "mental patients" strongly refute such a stereotype. For instance, Rappeport and Lassen (1965) reveal that a study of 5583 discharged "mental patients" showed an arrest rate of 6.9 per 1,000 arrests compared with 99.7 for the general population. They report a similar study of 10,247 "mental patients" whose arrest rate of 122 was dwarfed by the arrest rate of 491 for the general population.

Even psychiatrists fall victim to exaggerated fears regarding the dangerousness of "mental patients." Cocozza and Steadman (in Rice, 1977) studied 257 men indicted for felonies but found mentally incompetent to stand trial. A total of 118 psychiatrists labeled 154 of these men (60 percent) "dangerous." In a three-year period, however, only 14 percent of the "dangerous" group were arrested for violent crimes following their release while 16 percent of the innocuous group were so arrested. Psychiatrists not only grossly overestimated the threat posed by mental patients but were also unable to accurately predict which group of "mental patients" would be dangerous and which would not. As Shah (1975) concludes, the overwhelming majority of the "mentally ill" who are incarcerated in mental institutions for the protection of society do not engage in dangerous behavior following release despite stereotypes to the contrary.

Regarding most other stigmatizing stereotypes of the "mentally ill," these also prove to be more fantasy than fact. As Farina and others (1971) point out, the "mentally ill" are not only negatively evaluated, they are also blamed for nonexistent shortcomings. In addition, a person labeled "former mental patient" is accorded harsher treatment than this same person receives when presumed to be reasonably "well adjusted" (Farina and others, 1966).

The evidence reveals that people are responding more to the negative connotations associated with the psycholabels than to actual behavior witnessed (Sarbin and Marcuso, 1970). Nunally (1961), for instance, using a semantic differential, found that connotations associated with "mental health problems" such as "neurosis" and "insanity" included "worthless, dirty, dangerous, cold, unpredictable, and insincere" (a description of someone to put on your hit list but certainly not your Christmas list). With such negative connotations it should not be surprising that so many people fear and loathe the "mentally ill."

Obviously, such profound public denigration of the "mentally ill" warps the self-estimation of those branded as social lepers. They believe what society tells them. Crumpton and others (1967) found that "mental patients" viewed themselves as akin to criminals and sinners.

Ellis (1967) argues that such self-deprecation can lead to a kind of self-fulfilling prophecy. Branded as sick, rejected and ostracized for their "mental disease," victims of such dehumanization will likely feel a sense of hopelessness and begin or continue to act in a sick manner. It is clear that those labeled "mentally ill" are social pariahs, not because as a group they deserve to be treated like slugs in a dinner salad, but because of the strongly negative connotations associated with the sickness semantics of the psychiatric field.

Considering how damning psycholabels can be, accurately applying such labels (assuming they will continue to be used) becomes enormously important. If we cannot distinguish "sanity" from "insanity" or "mental health" from "mental illness," then the whole psycholabeling system provides us with a dangerous cognitive blueprint. Rather than building our knowledge and insight of more effective ways to deal with "mental disorders," it will lead us into blind alleys, trapping us into thinking we are helping people with unfortunate problems when in fact we are victimizing the very people we seek to help.

Are There Only Cuckoos in This Nest?

Eight individuals (a psychology graduate student, three psychologists, a pediatrician, a psychiatrist, a painter, and a homemaker), none of them with any psychiatric problems, gained admission to twelve different psychiatric hospitals in 1972. These twelve mental institutions were located in five different states on the East and West coasts. They represented a cross section of psychiatric institutions in this country from dilapidated, understaffed facilities to brand-new, well-staffed hospitals. One was private, the others were publicly supported.

This was not some clandestined raid on mental institutions to spring the "crazies" and create havoc in the streets. It was the initial step of an experiment conducted by Stanford University psychologist David Rosenhan (1973). Rosenhan wanted to test whether those supposedly in-the-know professionals in the field of psychology and psychiatry, could distinguish between individuals who are sane and those who are not.

These eight pseudopatients gained admittance by complaining to the admissions staff at each hospital that they had heard voices that said "empty," "hollow," and "thud." As Rosenhan explains:

> The choice of these symptoms was occasioned by their apparent similarity to existential symptoms. Such symptoms are alleged to arise from painful concerns about the perceived meaninglessness of one's life. It is as if the hallucinating person were saying, "My life is empty and hollow." The choice of these symptoms was also determined by the *absence* of a single report of existential psychoses in the literature [p. 251].

Beyond alleging these symptoms and falsifying their identities for protection from later stigma, these eight pseudopatients made no alterations in their life histories. Since their histories and current behavior revealed no signs of pathology except for the alleged voices, the experiment was strongly biased in favor of detecting sanity.

Once admitted to the cuckoo's nest, the pseudopatients acted as they normally would given their surroundings. No symptoms were feigned, and when asked they told the staff that they felt fine and no longer heard voices. Rosenhan forewarned the pseudopatients that they would have to gain their freedom by their own devices—essentially by demonstrating their sanity.

Despite the objective evidence of normality, none of the eight pseudopatients was ever discovered as an imposter. Instead, they were hospitalized from seven to fifty-two days (average of nineteen days). Eleven of the hospitals diagnosed the pseudopatients as "schizophrenic." The remaining pseudopatient was alleged to have "manic-depressive psychosis."

Upon discharge, the pseudopatients' records simply said "schizophrenia *in remission*." It is clear from the hospital records and the fact that the pseudopatients' "illness" was never questioned by *any* staff member, that the professional staffs believed the pseudopatients were not cured but simply experiencing a temporary remission of their symptoms.

There is a first-rate irony in this study. While it apparently never occurred to the trained professionals that the pseudopatients were in fact quite sane, many patients in these hospitals—supposedly real, live, in-the-flesh "lunatics"—frequently detected the sanity of the pseudo-patients. During the first three admissions of pseudopatients, when accurate totals were compiled, 35 of a total of 118 patients on the ward voiced suspicions, some vigorously. Common remarks included, "You're not crazy. You're a journalist or a professor [referring to the continual notetaking of pseudopatients]. You're checking up on the hospital." The fact that the inmates often appeared to recognize sanity when they witnessed it but trained professionals did not, causes you to wonder who should play the doctor and who the patient.

Some have argued that Rosenhan's study was a set-up, proving very little because you would reasonably expect only the "mentally ill" to seek help from a psychiatric institution. One such critic is the general semanticist Neil Postman (1976). In his book *Crazy Talk, Stupid Talk,* Postman debunks the whole study by Rosenhan as rediscovering the wheel. Of course, says Postman, the hospital setting predisposes the doctor to assume that only crazy people would try to gain admission to a mental hospital. That is analogous, argues Postman, to saying that if a waiter sees a person enter a restaurant, sit down, and ask for a menu, the waiter will naturally assume the customer wants to eat.

Postman's analogy, however, is a false one. There is a critical point of difference between the two situations. Surely there are ways the customer in the restaurant can easily convince the waiter that his presupposition is erroneous. Who would be considered irrational in this situation, the customer who insists he or she merely wants a cup of coffee and isn't hungry or the waiter who insists the customer's appetite is "in remission" so he or she better order a full meal so it will be ready when the "symptoms" inevitably return?

On the other hand, once admitted to a mental hospital, what could patients possibly do or say that might prove their sanity to the satisfaction of the staff? While Rosenhan's pseudopatients *sought* admission to the hospitals, thousands of people are involuntarily committed to such institutions. How will errors in diagnosis ever be determined if our yardstick for psycholabeling consists primarily of a perceptual set, an expectation of illness rather than an appraisal of sanity or insanity based on hard evidence? In a restaurant customers who say they aren't hungry will be readily believed, but who believes a "mental patient" who claims to be sane?

The Rosenhan study shows that the perceptual set is so over-whelming, the initial diagnosis so powerful, that there is nothing one can do to overcome the label "mentally ill." The psychiatric label becomes the reality as perceived by the custodians of the cuckoo's nest. Once labeled *schizophrenic* by a trained professional, you are for all practical purposes schizophrenic despite exhibitions of normal, adaptive behavior—a classic illustration of the "is of identity" problem.

In fact, normal behavior is distorted to fit the mold of the diagnostic label. Notetaking by pseudopatients gathering data was perceived by staff members as an aspect of pathological behavior. Pacing the long hospital corridors from sheer boredom was interpreted as nervousness. One pseudopatient's personal family history was twisted into a shape more suitable to his diagnostic label. His history indicated a close relationship with his mother, but a remote relationship with his father during early childhood. During adolescence, however, he grew closer to his father but more remote from his mother. His relationship with his wife and children was close and warm. Aside from occasional angry exchanges, friction in the family was minimal. The children were rarely spanked. Yet his case summary prepared after his discharge twisted this history into a manifestation of a long period of pathology. The case summary reads in part:

> This white 39-year-old male . . . manifests a long history of considerable ambivalence in close relationships, which begins in early childhood. A warm relationship with his mother cools during his adolescence. A distant relationship to his father is described as becoming very intense. Affective stability is absent. His attempts to control emotionality with his wife and children are punctuated by angry outbursts and, in the case of the children, spanking. And while he says that he has several good friends, one senses considerable ambivalence embedded in those relationships also . . . [p. 253].

Korzybski's postulate "Whatever you say it is, it is not" gains real meaning in this context. Labels do not identify reality but merely reflect the perception of the labeler, but the attachment of the label to a person can shape our interpretation of that person's behavior to fit the label. This is reminiscent of the old joke about the psychiatric patient who, when arriving early for an appointment, is labeled *anxious,* when appearing late is called *hostile,* and when showing up on time is tagged *compulsive.*

Postman's criticism of the Rosenhan study seems even less valid when a companion experiment included in the same article by Rosenhan is considered. When the staff of a research and teaching hospital heard about the results of the study summarized above, they expressed doubts that such mislabeling of normal individuals could occur at their own institution. Rosenhan put their assertion to the test. The staff was informed that during a three-month period, one or more pseudopatients would attempt to gain entry into their hospital under false pretenses. This time the excuse that one would expect *only* sick people to seek help at a mental institution becomes irrelevant. In this instance, the staff was forewarned that they were being scrutinized and pseudopatients might be roaming about the premises. Each staff member was instructed to rate patients who came to the hospital according to the likelihood that they were pseudopatients. If sanity and insanity are distinguishable from each other, then staff members should be able to identify the pseudopatients from the genuinely sick individuals.

Of the 193 persons admitted for psychiatric treatment during this time period, forty-one persons were alleged "with high confidence" by at least one member of the staff to be imposters. Twenty-three were believed suspect by at least one psychiatrist, and nineteen were suspected by one psychiatrist and one other staff member. *No pseudopatients* were sent in by Rosenhan. So much for the illusion that trained professionals can recognize sanity from insanity.

Similar results were recorded in other studies as well. Langer and Abelson (1974) found that well-trained psychologists and psychiatrists rated an interviewee as reasonably well adjusted when told that the videotaped interview was a "job application," but more than moderately disturbed when led to believe the same videotaped interaction was a "psychiatric interview." Temerlin (1968) found that psychiatrists and clinical psychologists had their diagnoses of a professional actor acting out a script of a "mentally healthy" person significantly influenced by the "knowledge" that two prestigious psychiatrists had allegedly determined that the man was "psychotic." A layperson reading Temerlin's lengthy description of the script portrayed by the actor almost certainly would be struck by the lack of anything that could be called pathological in this man's behavior and demeanor. But then again, what do we know? As one psychiatrist influenced by the prestige suggestion put it, "Of course he looked healthy, but hell, most people are a little neurotic, and who can accept appearance at face value?"

Labels are not essences but merely approximations of reality. When clear empirically verifiable yardsticks for differentiating mental health from mental illness are missing, such labels as *schizophrenic, manic-depressive, psychotic,* and the rest of the psychiatric list of labels are quite literally *gross* approximations. The potential for abuse in this loose, pseudoscientific process of psychiatric diagnosis is monstrous because enormous stigma is attached to those wearing the badge of *social leper.* When trained professionals cannot accurately identify the mentally healthy from the mentally disturbed, psychiatric labels become more pejorative than diagnostic.

Diagnausea: It's Enough to Make You Sick

You would think that given the heavy stigma attached to psycholabels, and given the dubious accuracy of psycholabeling, great caution would be exercised before branding anyone "mentally ill." Actually, the opposite is true. It is as if the answer to the stigma problem were to be found in promulgating the notion that virtually everyone is mentally sick, some just more than others.

Karl Menninger (1963), the dean of American psychiatry, argued just such a proposition in his book *The Vital Balance.* A critic of psycholabeling, Menninger nevertheless claimed that "all people have mental illness of different degrees at different times, and sometimes some are much worse, or better" (p. 32). This was Menninger's attempt to persuade people that the "mentally ill" were just like you or me and thus undeserving of stigmatization.

The mass madness proposition, what I term *diagnausea* or the overzealous attribution of "mental sickness" labels, has become something of a mass movement. In the longitudinal study of mental health in New York City called the Midtown Manhattan Study (Srole, 1962), it was alleged that approximately 80 percent of adults showed some symptoms of "mental illness," whereas 25 percent were afflicted with psychological "disorders" and 50 percent of the lowest socio-economic class were so afflicted.

Researchers from the Midtown project concluded from an extensive analysis of the data collected, that twenty-two items on the interview questionnaire could provide a "close approximation" of the psychiatric diagnosis of mental disorders. When you consider that four affirmative answers on any of these twenty-two items was sufficient for such an evaluation it is surprising that an even greater percentage of the subjects weren't branded psychologically "sick." When you examine the questions on this twenty-two-item survey, it is positively astonishing. Among the items were:

"Are you the worrying type—you know, a worrier?"
"You sometimes can't help wondering if anything is worthwhile anymore?"
"Are you ever bothered by nervousness, that is, by being irritable, fidgety, or tense?"
"You have periods of such great restlessness that you cannot sit long in a chair?"
"You are bothered by acid or sour stomach several times a week?"
[Dohrenwend and Dohrenwend, 1969, pp. 61–68]

In another case of diagnausea, Dr. Milton Mazer (1972) analyzed residents of Martha's Vineyard in Massachusetts using "parapsychiatric events" as measures of "psychiatric disorders." His list of such "mental illness" indicators included fines, probation, jail, divorce, premarital pregnancy, single-car accident, and high school underachievement. Despite this broad list of alleged indicators of "psychiatric disorder," Mazer found only 22 percent of the resident population suffered such an event in a five-year period (a stable bunch, these Vineyard folks). Nevertheless, Mazer (1974) sees this figure as only the tip of the proverbial iceberg. You see, "psychiatric disorders" can contaminate an entire population, producing "sociocultural disintegration" of the community, which in turn increases the prevalence of disorders. Workers in the "mental health" field, according to Mazer, are like a man surrounded by snakes, forced to keep on killing the nasty little beasts in the hope that all the snakes will perish before he himself collapses.

The boundary between the mentally well and the mentally sick has been blurred. Normality (that is, "mental health") is that elusive goal Freud called an "ideal fiction." This belief in the "fiction" of normality was manifested in a claim by a psychologist for the National Institute of Mental Health that virtually no family in the United States is entirely without "mental disorders" (cited in Gross, 1978, p. 6). To be unhappy or anxious is to be "neurotic."

Diagnausea, however, received its biggest boost when the "psychosomatic illness" became a popular explanation for ailments with uncertain or unknown causes. The term "psychosomatic" means "imaginary" to many people, but the term as used by some in the medical field refers to illness which is strongly affected, even caused by human emotion. Most standard medical texts cite stress as a causative factor in anywhere from 50 to 80 percent of all human disease (Pelletier, 1977). The thesis is that the mind (emotions) cannot be separated from the body (the organism), which is an obvious truism. When we experience emotional stress our physical well-being is imperiled. Pelletier (1977) reviews a substantial body of research suggesting the deleterious effects of stress on the human body.

As Gross (1978) demonstrates, the field of psychology and psychiatry has seized upon the well-established "mind affects the body" thesis as a rationale for creating in effect a Therapeutic Society. The psychosomatic theory of disease has served as a springboard to a psychoanalytic theory of organic illness. Despite evidence to the contrary (Gross, 1978, pp. 85–92), "personality disorders" are trumpeted as causative factors of such organic diseases as heart attacks, ulcers, even cancer. The "coronary personality," for instance, is typically the stereotyped compulsive, slave-driving, excessively competitive, nervous individual with underlying aggression and resentment and inadequate sexual adjustment (Gross, 1978, p. 87). The Chicago Institute of Psychoanalysis claims asthma patients often fear losing their mothers and have trouble crying, duodenal ulcer patients allegedly suffer from a conflict over dependency needs, and neurodermatitis patients strongly crave physical closeness.

While there is truth in the claim that stress has deleterious effects on our physical well-being, research generally does not support the leap in logic required to accept "personality disorders" as causative agents of organic diseases.

Diagnausea, the tendency to see psychological illness in virtually everyone (which, come to think of it, makes diagnausea a good candidate for a new "psychological disorder"), is highly dangerous. First, when the lines of demarcation between mental health and mental illness are blurred, and normality is perceived as an "ideal fiction," anything that looks even slightly out of the ordinary becomes a potential "psychological disorder." Simple deviance or nonconformity to established societal norms can easily fit the rubber yardstick of the psycholabelers.

Some of the more embarrassing and controversial "deviance is disease" decrees of the past include *drapetomania* (the disease of slaves who continually tried to escape from bondage), *masturbatory insanity* (does it require an explanation?), *protest psychosis* (aimed primarily at black militants who reject white culture), and *homosexuality*.

The controversy within the ranks of the American Psychiatric Association over the status of homosexuality is a graphic illustration of how the "deviance is disease" psycholabeling process works.

First you must understand that diagnosis of "mental disorders" is inferential. Symptoms of the "disease" are mostly behavioral not organic. There is no direct observation of the "illness" such as an X-ray or lab test. The diagnostician must infer from clinical observation of behavior reported and observed what is going on inside the person.

It is consequently a highly subjective process which allows bias and one's own perception of what is "normal" and "healthy" to influence one's judgment of "mental sickness" or "health."

The list of official diseases catalogued in the *Diagnostic and Statistical Manual of Mental Disorders (DSM),* the bible of psychiatry, is decreed, not discovered. The psycholabels, the official nomenclature, are decided by majority vote of the members of the American Psychiatric Association. You might say it's a plebiscite on "pathology." As Lewis

(1978) points out, "the resulting nomenclature tends to reflect the moral and social views of the larger society [p. 177]."
Homosexuality was listed as a "mental disorder" until 1973. After heated argument the organization voted to excise homosexuality from the list of disorders. It was reclassified as a "sexual orientation disturbance," meaning the person was unhappy with his sexual orientation and wished to change it. Homosexuality per se, however, was no longer a disorder. According to the APA, people should not be labeled "sick" if they function effectively in society and do not consider themselves ill. To so label them is "cruel and irrational discrimination," so said the APA. As Lewis (1978), however, observes:

> Before the "gay" movement became a fashionable cause, the majority of psychiatrists did not appear to be especially concerned about the possibility that their system of classification might lead to "irrational discrimination." Their attitudinal change was clearly a product of changing moral views within the larger society not a result of new research data [p. 178].

There are numerous studies which validate the thrust of what Lewis claims, namely, that conformity to moral and social standards of society (and more specifically the APA) is the litmus test of "mental health."

The Broverman (1970) study previously cited showed that deviation from sex role expectations can result in the stigmatization of women as "mentally ill." Feinblatt and Gold (1976) and Israel and others (1978) found similar results, including attributions of "mental disturbance" for males exhibiting nonconformity to sex-role stereotypes. In addition, Abramowitz and others (1973) found that female clients described as left-wing political activists were labeled as more "maladjusted" by nonliberal clinicians than similarly bent males, and Katz (1974) discovered that conformity to a norm of social attractiveness (sociable and likeable) strongly influences the judgment of psychiatric staff concerning the "mental health" of mental hospital patients.

The danger of this "deviance is disease" point of view lies in the use of psychiatry for social control. Where that can lead is made clear in

Block and Reddaway's (1977) book *Psychiatric Terror*. It details the abuse of psychiatry in the Soviet Union. The situation in the U.S. is obviously not that extreme but the Russian experience should serve as a sober warning of what may lie ahead for us if we continue to travel in our present direction.

A second danger of diagnausea is misdiagnosis of organic disease. As the popularity of the psychosomatic illness point of view grows and psychiatrists and psychologists are more frequently looked to for "cures," there is an increasing likelihood that organic ailments that are difficult to diagnose or simply defy medical explanation because medical knowledge is limited, will be preemptively mislabeled hypochondriasis, personality disorder, and the like.

Physical illness can induce psychological symptoms. Pellagra, a vitamin-deficiency disease whose symptoms include depression, irrationality, and even hallucinations, was at one time treated as a "mental disease" and victims were committed to "lunatic asylums." Neurosyphilis and dystonia are other examples of illnesses labeled "mental" that were primarily organic.

Dr. Phillip Rossman (1963), a Los Angeles internist, did a study of 115 patients sent to psychiatrists by their doctors because they were allegedly "psychoneurotics." Every one of these 115 patients turned out to have a serious organic ailment. The patients were erroneously diagnosed. Of these 115 "neurotics," 31 died of organic illness—25 from cancer. Eight patients were given electroshock treatments for their "mental illness." Three of these 8 actually had hyperthyroidism, whereas the rest had undulant fever, drug intoxication, chronic pelvic inflammatory disease, tumor and aortic aneurysm. The premature psycholabeling of an individual and the easy acceptance of the mass madness thesis can lead to such human tragedies on a far greater scale.

The third danger of diagnausea is the creation of a Therapeutic Society, where even the most inconsequential afflictions, insecurities, and feelings of inadequacy become "neuroses" or "anxiety disorders." We have become so uptight about our mental well-being, as measured by an ever-elusive standard of "normality," that I believe we are heading towards creating a "sick society."

When standards of "normality" are elastic and overly exclusive, the distinction between psychological sickness and health becomes more a matter of persuasion and belief than science. Convinced that anxiety or self-doubt is abnormal, huge numbers of Americans seek therapy.

Schrag (1978) has marshalled an impressive array of evidence depicting the dimensions of the Therapeutic Society. Consider just a small sample of this evidence. The number of psychiatrists in America has mushroomed from barely 3000 just prior to World War II to roughly 30,000 in 1976, and the number is probably significantly higher now. There are more "mental health" workers in America than police officers. Depending on how restrictively you define it, from 7 to 40 million people receive "treatment" each year. Unable to provide psychoanalysis or psychotherapy for such an enormous number of people because of its time-consuming nature, doctors have prescribed psychoactive drugs. (A study by the American Psychiatric Association reported that 1000 hours of analysis are required to "cure" the typical patient of his or her "psychological disorder.") Thus, by 1975, American physicians wrote 240 million prescriptions for such mood altering drugs, enough to medicate every American for a month.

This mass medication of Americans, however, produces maintenance, not cures, of psychological ailments (Schrag, 1978, and Zimbardo and Ruch, 1977). Symptoms are kept under control by large doses of these drugs (called "chemical straitjackets" by critics), and although the drugs may produce better coping through chemistry, the "psychological disorder" is not eliminated; rather the symptoms are "in remission."

Although drug "therapy" provides maintenance, there is considerable evidence that psychoanalysis and psychotherapy may be similarly ineffectual in providing "cures" (Zimbardo and Ruch, 1977). Improvements in the psychological well-being of patients receiving such therapy may have more to do with the placebo effect than with the therapy.

Dr. Arthur Shapiro (cited in Gross, 1978) explains the placebo effect in psychological treatment. "Most psychological explanations are nonsense, but it is another way to get at the placebo effect. If the patient is told about his unconscious Oedipus complex, the understanding can act as a placebo even if the theory is not true, which it isn't" (p. 34). There is magic, then, in the psychiatric label called *diagnosis.*

Mendel (1964) demonstrated than even incorrect interpretations (mis-diagnosis) can have therapeutic effects. He concocted a set of all-purpose interpretations such as "You seem to live your life as though you were apologizing all the time." Patients agreed with twenty of the twenty-four vague intrepretations Mendel invented. The level of anxiety patients experienced decreased after they received such fortune-cookie "therapy." The perceptual set of patients, that the psychiatrist has the scientific answer to what ails us mentally, lends credence even to outright nonsense.

Aside from the placebo effect, what psychiatrists and psychologists do during "treatments" may have little or no influence on the amelioration of patients' ailments. Myerson (1939) observed many years ago what is still true today:

> The neuroses are "cured" by Christian Science, osteopathy, chiropractic, nux vomica and bromides, benzedrine sulfate, change of scene, a blow on the head, and psychoanalysis, which probably means that none of these has yet established its real worth in the matter . . . moreover since many neuroses are self-limited, anyone who spends two years with a patient gets credit for the operation of nature [p. 641].

The various therapists take credit for cures because patients improve after receiving therapy. In the absence of scientific evidence that it was the therapy and not something else (such as the mere passage of time) which *caused* the "cure," therapists are guilty of what is called a *post hoc* fallacy of reasoning. This means that we can't assume a cause–effect relationship simply because two things occur in sequence or simultaneously.

For instance, several years ago an associate pastor of a Baptist church in Tallahassee, Florida, launched a campaign to burn records by various rock stars. He reasoned that rock music "appealed to the flesh" and he cited as "evidence" an alleged study which showed that out of a group of 1,000 girls who became pregnant out of wedlock, 984 "committed fornication while rock music was being played." Assuming his statistics are valid (a preposterous suggestion), the simple fact that two phenomena occur simultaneously does not prove a causal connection. Therapy and psychological well-being may occur together but still be unrelated to each other.

Although millions of Americans may be wasting a good deal of time and money on therapy that has yet to be proven effective, many people would argue that even the placebo effect is worth an investment of time and money if the patient feels better. Despite my tightwad nature, even I could agree with such a viewpoint if it were not for the danger inherent in any psychological therapy. As there is no surgery that is completely safe, likewise there is no psychological therapy that is totally innocuous. There are risks intrinsic in any form of psychological treatment because many of us have highly fragile self-images.

Martin Gross (1978) in his book *The Psychological Society*, a penetrating critique of the "mental health" field, documents several potential harms of therapy. He points out that many patients may be persuaded that their minor anxieties are indicators of much deeper problems. Some patients may become worse not better while receiving treatment because of the intense nature of some therapies. Other patients may become therapy junkies, unable to break the habit of treatment.

Schrag (1978) notes similar problems with drug "treatments." The use of psychoactive drugs for "psychiatric disorders" is rarely specific, often indiscriminate, careless, and inappropriately prescribed, and subjects patients to dangerous side effects and possible addiction from massive dosages and prolonged usage. The eight pseudopatients in the Rosenhan (1973) study, for instance, during their twelve admissions to psychiatric hospitals for an average time of nineteen days apiece, were given nearly 2,100 doses of potent psychoactive drugs while having almost no contact with psychiatrists who prescribed the "treatments." Despite the fact that all pseudopatients presented identical symptoms and all but one were diagnosed "schizophrenic," a wide variety of drugs was administered. Thus, the jury is still out regarding the effectiveness of psychotherapy and drug treatments. What is known, however, is that both can be highly dangerous. This doesn't justify abolishing such "therapy," but it does argue for much tighter regulation and increased research into the effectiveness of such treatments and conditions for optimum success.

The dangers of diagnausea are therefore very real and give cause for alarm. Although psycholabels can be highly stigmatizing, the answer to such dehumanization does not lie in convincing a whole society that everybody is sick. The psycholabelers, in trying to achieve a noble purpose, namely, the amelioration of human suffering, have oversold their product. The great majority of those in the "helping professions" who deal with psychological problems are not shysters and proselytizers looking for converts to a psychiatric religion. Yet, in the absence of some major changes in the approach to "mental illness," and a more restricted definition of "psychological disorders," many dedicated, concerned professionals in the field of "mental health" will look very much like psychiatric evangelists.

The Therapeutic Society that will inevitably result from diagnausea transforms the treatment of illness into a method of social control of deviance. It increases the likelihood that any organic disease that is difficult to diagnose will be branded "psychosomatic"—meaning either imaginary (all in your head) or emotionally based and therefore the province of the psychiatric professional. Finally, "treatments" whose efficacy still must be proven, can manufacture psychological illness by stripping away the protective covering that shelters the self-esteem of individuals, exposing their vulnerabilities to the light of day. Although some may benefit from such soul searching, others may be devastated. Like drug "therapy" that can lead to addiction or other serious physical side effects, psychotherapy and psychoanalysis can be dangerous and should be proven effective for specific illnesses rather than used indiscriminately.

The New Semantics of Psychological Sickness

Given the problems associated with psycholabeling, it is tempting to suggest bookburning as a solution. Incinerate the psychiatric book of labels and eliminate the stigma by repudiating the whole psycholabeling process.

The behaviorist school of psychology advocates such a position. Behaviorists argue that we should concentrate on observable behaviors rather than on what goes on inside a person's head. It is not disease but "pathological behavior" which needs to be "extinguished" (eliminated). The symptom, not the cause, is the object of treatment (called behavior modification). The symptom *is* the disorder.

There is merit in the behaviorist viewpoint and approach. It is, however, a limited approach, one which has not proven either superior to psychotherapy (Shapiro, 1980) in the treatment of disorders for which both claim utility, or broad enough in application to handle all or even most disorders (Zimbardo and Ruch, 1977).

Although behaviorism eliminates the psycholabels, it does not eliminate the problems of psychological disorder. Deviance is also as likely to be called a *symptom* that must be "extinguished" (stamped out) in the behaviorist perspective as it is likely to be called *disease* in the psychiatric perspective.

Although there is stigma attached to psycholabels, a classification scheme of "mental disorders" can serve useful purposes. It can help us order our knowledge, revealing how much or how little we know. It can make possible greater precision in communication and research relevant to psychological disorders. It can also act as an overall blueprint, guiding research into the causes of such disorders and the effectiveness of various treatments under specific conditions.

The answer, then, to the problems of psycholabeling does not lie in abolishing the mental illness labels. What is required is an empirical approach to the whole issue of "mental illness." By this I mean any classification scheme used should be a product of research. Research, of course, can't tell us what classification system is best because that is a value judgment, but it can tell us which scheme will likely assist us in the achievement of the goals we deem worthwhile. Worthy goals, it seems to me, would include reduction of stigma attached to the psycholabeling process, greater reliability in diagnosing (consistency with which individuals are classified), and the elimination of diagnausea.

Gore (1980) provides our point of departure when he more narrowly and precisely defines "mental illness" than has generally been the case. He defines "mental illness" as

. . . a specific phenomenon involving personal discomfort (as indicated by distress, anxiety, depression, etc.), or mental disorganization (as indicated by confusion, thought blockage, motor retardation, and, in the more extreme cases, hallucinations and delusions); or a combination of both conditions, that is not caused by an organic or toxic condition [p. 347].

This definition provides a solid (albeit not perfect) foundation for achieving the goals I cited above.

First, it is a restrictive and precise definition of mental illness. It restricts mental illness to functional disorders (those which impair our ability to act), excluding those categories of disorder which have an organic cause or result from a toxic condition. Thus, the "organic brain syndrome," i.e., mental retardation, senile dementia, and so forth, are excluded and so are alcoholism and drug addiction.

Deviance in and of itself is also excluded from the definition of mental illness. "Personality disorders" and maladjustment to sex-role stereotypes are not functional disorders. They are violations of social norms.

Gore's definition of mental illness is an improvement for a second reason. It is grounded in research and it exhibits a philosophical consistency—meaning two distinct verbal maps (*deviance* and *disease*) are separated, not muddled together. Those disorders that are included under the rubric "mental illness" have similarity of symptomology; for example, severe distress is a symptom in all cases. They generally respond to the same general forms of therapy (though the placebo effect may account for much of this), and cross-cultural and historical evidence suggests that the concept of mental illness does not usually include categories of disorders excluded by Gore's definition. Thus, the importance of consistent, conventional usage of a verbal map to prevent misunderstanding and confusion is validated.

There is one weakness to Gore's definition, however. No levels are set for the amount of distress, anxiety, confusion, and so forth necessary for an attribution of mental illness. Unless we set these levels fairly high, we end up again with the diagnausea problem wherein mild anxiety, occasional depression, and periodic distress from living in a complicated world become disease.

This definition of mental illness gives us a model to work from, but other elements must also be present if the problems of psycholabeling are to be ameliorated. One significant element is the inclusion of operational definitions.

An operational definition points to a territory. It grounds a high level abstraction (categories of disorders) by setting the boundaries and specifying the content of the abstraction. Specific symptoms, duration or course of an illness, levels of severity of impairment, detailed descriptions of what a particular disorder looks like, even what it is not, are examples of operational definitions.

Research reveals conclusively that greater reliability and accuracy of diagnoses are achieved when operational definitions are provided (Spitzer and others, 1980). In the absence of operational criteria, the psycholabelers must use their own concept of the disorder in question, which can easily degenerate into diagnausea. The latest edition of the psychiatric book of labels (DSM-III) represents a significant improvement in regard to operational definitions from previous editions of the diagnostic manual.

DSM-III, the result of several years of research, is in general a better conceived, more empirically sound, useful system of psychiatric classification than DSM-I and II. The vague Freudian abstraction *neurosis,* for instance, has been replaced with *anxiety disorders.* This is important because *neurosis* was never anything more than a reification of a Freudian symbol. Neurosis was always considered abnormal and easily served as a source of diagnausea. Anxiety, on the other hand, is not always negative, in fact in moderate amounts it is quite normal and even constructive. Like the difference between *race* and *ethnic group,* *anxiety disorder* is not merely a different label for neurosis. It represents a different concrete reality.

DSM-III also repudiates the notion that social deviance is mental illness—certainly a step in the right direction. Unfortunately, such a disclaimer is not reflected in the list of diagnostic categories of disorders.

DSM-III has not shed the deviance is disease perspective. *Personality disorders, conduct disorders, substance use disorders* all reflect this point of view despite the statement that social deviance is not mental illness. Spitzer and others (1980), the architects of DSM-III, in explaining the various categories of disorders, clearly manifest a deviance-is-disease viewpoint. In their explanation of *conduct disorders,* they refer to "management" of "antisocial behavior." Included under *substance use disorders* is the justification that drug abuse "in almost all subcultures would be viewed as undesirable [p. 157]." It thus becomes a disorder if we exhibit antisocial behavior even in the absence of personal distress to the "patient." Again referring to *conduct disorders,* Spitzer and others (1980) define it as a "repetitive and persistent pattern of aggressive or nonaggressive conduct in which either the basic rights of others or major age-appropriate societal norms or rules are violated [p. 155]."

DSM-III consequently does not conform to Gore's definition of mental illness. It encourages diagnausea. In fact, DSM-III adds some new twists to the diagnausea problem. There is a "tobacco-use disorder" and "caffeinism" (too much coffee can make you crazy). Richard Proctor (cited in Goleman, 1978), a psychiatrist in Winston-Salem, North Carolina, facetiously commented on these two new "disorders": "I trust that . . . when the DSM-IV is compiled, missing a three-foot putt on the 18th hole will be classified as a psychiatric disorder. It would make about as much sense as the tobacco or caffeine classifications [p. 32]."

There are also other shortcomings to DSM-III. For example, is it appropriate to single out homosexuality as a "disorder" even though the new category "Ego-dystonic homosexuality" applies only when the homosexual is disturbed by, in conflict with, or wishes to alter his sexual orientation? By the same criteria, does masturbation become a "disorder" also? DSM-III also includes organic illnesses as "mental disorders," something Gore specifically excluded.

Gore's definition of mental illness and DSM-III minus the shortcomings just discussed can reduce inappropriate psycholabeling, thereby diminishing the problem of stigma. Greater reliability in diagnosing resulting from operational definitions can help with the mislabeling problem identified in the Rosenhan (1973) study. The more restricted classification system proposed here can diminish the problems of diagnausea.

There are additional barriers, however, to the amelioration of problems of psycholabeling. Although the classification scheme suggested by Gore is an improvement over previous attempts, basic attitudes of members of the mental health profession must coincide with the new scheme or nothing will really change. For instance, despite DSM-III, many psychiatrists may still believe homosexuality is itself a mental disease. If they continue to hold that viewpoint, deviance as disease will continue to be treated as pathological not social.

Second, psycholabeling is still inferential in nature no matter what scheme is used. As Temerlin (1968) discovered, psychiatrists and clinical psychologists easily confuse inferences (interpretations) and facts (descriptions). Asked to avoid inferences and report observations of behavior that supported their diagnosis of "psychosis" or "neurosis," the psycholabelers could not do it. Most of them either mixed inferences and descriptions or reported inferences exclusively. Some labeled their inferences as descriptive observations. Inability to separate inferences from facts can result in misdiagnosis. Psycholabelers must become more skilled in distinguishing the two. DSM-III with its operational criteria should assist those who are conscientious.

Third, much of the jargon of psychiatry can easily deteriorate into esoteric pseudoscientific mystification. This can become a serious problem when talking to lay persons about psychological disorders. It is critical that psycholabelers be able to explain the disorders and treatments in simple, understandable language which nonprofessionals can grasp.

Finally, a semantic lobotomy should be performed on the Freudian jargon of psychoanalysis, which some have called *psychobabble*. Freudian psychoanalysis is what Postman (1976) calls a "self-confirming system." There is no way to prove "penis envy," "Oedipus complex," "sibling rivalry," "anal fixation," and the rest of the Freudian gobbledygook that poses as science. If you're a woman, how do you prove that you aren't afflicted with penis envy? Try disproving you have an anal fixation. Watch out though! You're "repressing" if you protest too loudly and strongly. This whole esoteric jargon masquerades as science when science is powerless to test Freudian theory. It rests on the willy-nilly interpretations of the psycholabelers who can demonstrate the creative potential of the human mind with their phantasmagoric "explanations" of various "disorders," but they certainly don't demonstrate an intelligent approach to psychological afflictions.

SUMMARY

This brief analysis of the semantics of mental illness merely touches the major issues of a complex and controversial subject. The suggestions I've made concerning changes in the psycholabeling process are probes as well as solutions. I do not offer them as the final word on the subject; rather, I offer them as an agenda for further discussion, criticism, and research. The basic consideration is that psycholabels can severely stigmatize. While some psycholabeling seems necessary, it is vital that it be limited in scope, accurately applied, and constantly evaluated for its utility. We don't need to manufacture madness with sickness semantics. We need to learn how best to reduce psychological disorders. Careful, responsible, empirically based labeling practices are places to start.

EPILOGUE

I end this book with some trepidation. I worry that in recapitulating key points already developed, and grouping "solutions" to language misuse and malpractice into a few general categories, this may have the effect of diluting my entire work into a few simple recipes, a kind of cookbook approach to language. If you're looking for simple quick fix panaceas, then you've misread these seven chapters. If anything, you should be aware of the complexity of this problem of careless and irresponsible language practices. Each chapter analyzes the problem in detail and offers pragmatic alternatives throughout.

Nevertheless, I feel a need to tie this book together in at least a general way by isolating fundamental "solutions" alluded to earlier when analyzing sources of language misuse and malpractice.

Awareness that there is a problem in the first place is a prerequisite for language used in a scrupulous, conscientious fashion. Unless you understand that language is a powerful vehicle of communication and that reification and ignorance of the abstracting process and how it functions can produce very serious consequences, then little can be accomplished by detailing what we can do about language misuse and malpractice. You must appreciate—not intellectually, but emotionally—the seriousness of this subject and its relevance to humankind's well-being, even survival.

Basic "solutions" fall into three categories (by no means an exhaustive list). These are symbol reactions, extensionality, and language appropriateness.

Symbol reactions are the antithesis of signal reactions. Signal reactions, as already noted, are immediate (unreflective and automatic), conditioned (molded into a habit pattern), rigid, and inflexible, with little variability and thus great predictability. Symbol reactions, by comparison, are more delayed (reflective and thoughtful), flexible (weighing of alternatives), and not easily predicted. To paraphrase an old political slogan, symbol reactions offer a choice while signal reactions produce an echo.

The responsible and conscientious speaker of language searches for the meaning of a message in its context, not in the words themselves. Thus, taboo language will not invite violence and aggression from such a person unless upon reflection such language is clearly intended to provoke. Even then, there are other options to consider.

Lest I be accused of promoting a two-valued conception of language (either signal reactions or symbol reactions), let me explain that I am talking about a continuum, not discrete polarities without a middle. Korzybski argued that we are all "semantic reactors." A semantic reaction is the total response (mind–body) of the organism to a stimulus that produces meaning. The two ends of the semantic reaction continuum are signal and symbol reactions. We can exhibit greater or lesser degrees of either. In my opinion, the symbol reaction end of the continuum is a better place to be in most instances, for reasons already elaborated.

A second "solution" is the development of an extensional orientation. This requires a greater reliance on empirical evidence to validate what it is that we selectively perceive in the world around us. It calls for an emphasis on denotative meaning of words in order to avoid misunderstandings, and a consciousness of the problems associated with connotative meanings of words. Abstractions are carefully related to specific referents, grounded in the territory, not simply left as vague maps destined to lead us into a swamp of confusion. Inferences and judgments are not confused with facts. Words are not reified.

General Semantics offers several methods to become more extensionally oriented. The first method is a list of "extensional devices." They include the following:

1. *Etc.*—using *et cetera* reminds us that there is more to be said. It combats our penchant for allness statements, stereotyping, etc. Since the world is infinitely complex and our senses are finite, we can never say everything about anything, so we must remind ourselves of the limitations of our language to reflect our reality. Something is always left out of the picture.

2. *To me*—this device suggested by Wendell Johnson (1972) recognizes that the map and the mapmaker are inseparable. Our selective version of "reality" represents what we see through our semantic filters. When we say, "To me this is what reality or truth is," we are noting that my reality is not your reality. What we see is our personal vision of the cosmos, and it will never be identical to anyone else's vision. We can describe what that vision looks like, but it will never produce an identical image in another person's mind. "To me," "as I see it," "in my view," and other similar versions of this device emphasize that meanings of words are in the people using the words. These verbal maps, although often similar, are never identical.

3. *Dating and indexing*—these devices recognize change. Knowledge is not static but dynamic. Science^{1982} is not science^{1972} nor will it be science^{1992}. Black^1 is not Black person^2 anymore than Jew^1 is Jew^2. Mental illness^{1982} will not be mental illness^{1986}. Our enemies in 1982 are not our enemies of 1972 even though they may have the same names. Language can freeze our perceptions, camouflaging change and producing inaccurate evaluations. Dating and indexing combat stereotyping with its inaccurate verbal maps and fro-

zen evaluations. It highlights the non-identity principle that stipulates that no two things are identical and language does not identify immutable essences.

4. *Quotation marks*—these signal to others that a word is loaded and may trigger a signal reaction. Quotation marks also warn that a word is being used in an unconventional sense, has hidden assumptions, or has multiple, sometimes contradictory usages. The term "race" is an example of a word used in such ways.

It is often obtrusive and awkward to use such devices except on occasion for emphasis. It is useful to apply them, however, when we are thinking of, evaluating, and processing information. I am talking about developing an extensional *attitude*. These devices, although not panaceas, can help develop such an attitude.

A second method for developing an extensional orientation is the use of operational definitions. Einstein once said that "When you sit with a nice girl for two hours you think it's only a minute. But when you sit on a hot stove for a minute you think it's two hours. That's relativity." Although this is an overly simple explanation of his Theory of Relativity, Einstein has operationalized it to some degree for the layperson.

I spoke of operational definitions already when addressing problems of psycholabeling, so I won't elaborate much here. An operational definition explains a concept, grounds an abstraction by pointing to a territory. It says "for our purposes" an "A" student is anyone who scores 90 or above on the final exam, or "severe anxiety" is when a person cannot eat, think clearly, remember simple details, and sleep at night because of stress. It pins the verbal map to a specific territory.

A third method for developing an extensional orientation is use of the scientific method as operationalized by Wendell Johnson (1972). Johnson's conception of the scientific method reduces to three questions. They are:

What do you mean?
How do you know?
What then?

The first question makes certain that the way I understand the message is the way you intend it. It clarifies how the words are being used. The second question is a validity check. What is your evidence? How have you arrived at your conclusion? What yardstick are you using for measurement, and is it consistent and empirically based?

The final question asks us to look at the consequences of what we say and do. It is another way of asking, "So what?" If you misuse your language, what then? I hope that by now you realize the answer to that question.

These three questions, then, can expose our many hidden assumptions and the confusion created by vague language. What do we mean by "military superiority"? How do we know when we have achieved it? What are the consequences of striving to achieve it?

A third "solution" to language misuse and malpractice is language appropriateness (not to be confused with language etiquette). Postman (1976) explains language appropriateness very effectively. Put in a slightly different manner from the way Postman does in his book *Crazy Talk, Stupid Talk*, language appropriateness involves an analysis of the speaker (who), the audience (who), the purpose (why), the method (how), and the occasion (where and when) associated with the message (what) communicated. Postman refers to this as a semantic environment.

If meanings are not in the words themselves and if language is to function as a flexible tool of communication, then simple dictums such as "all dirty words are inappropriate" or "taboo words are never inappropriate" ignore any necessity for analysis of the semantic environment. As previously observed, taboo language must be considered in context (the *who, what, where, when, why,* and *how* questions). The normally racist term *nigger* is not always used in such a fashion. Black people sometimes call themselves "niggers" without the attachment of a racist message. Am I a "dirty talker" if I discuss taboo language in my college classes without using circumlocutions and expurgated forms of the offending words? I think not.

Postman notes that Korzybski insisted that the language of science, and no other, is the language of sanity, yet can we really accept only the detached tentative, objective, and sterile language of science for *all* occasions and purposes? As Postman aptly observes, such an impoverished conception of the human experience brands the language of religion, lovemaking and romance, and other human enterprises as insane. "How do I love thee, let me count the ways" was never intended to be a scientific exploration. Imagine a romantic conversation derailed by one party's insistence that the other person operationally define what he or she meant by the statement "My love for you is boundless and endless. We are as one." Don't be silly. Leave well enough alone and go with the flow.

Language is a flexible tool of communication that functions poorly in a restricted and stultifying environment. Religious language (such as "Amen, brother"), while appropriate in church because it helps fulfill a religious purpose of spiritual unity and togetherness, is inappropriate in a classroom because a purpose of that educational environment is not the development of blind and unquestioning acceptance but rather its opposite. Jargon and euphemisms are not always a misuse of language. They serve useful and constructive purposes in certain limited settings. If our purpose, however, is to foster honesty and clear communication, then they are frequently inappropriate. Analyze the whole semantic context; don't look for simplistic absolutes and ironclad rules.

What I am offering is a group of tentative "solutions." They work well in their proper context, but that may need alteration as our knowledge and insight on language grow.

There is more for you to learn than what appears in these pages. Search for it. In order for this book to be of any value to you, it must be put into actual practice. It serves little purpose to cognitively appreciate the importance of careful language usage but never to make an effort to change your own language behavior for the better.

Language is an instrument of communication that offers us a means of bridging the rivers of tears created by humankind's inhumanity and insensitivity. Used wisely and skillfully, language can aid us in developing better human understanding. Ultimately, we must learn to master our own invention, not become its slave. It is a challenge we all need to accept.

BIBLIOGRAPHY

BOOKS

ABRAHAMS, R.D. *Deep down in the jungle.* Hatboro, Pa.: Folklore Associates, 1964.

AUSTIN, L., FENDERSON, L., & NELSON, S. (Eds.). *The black man and the promise of America.* Glenview, Ill.: Scott, Foresman, 1970.

BALL-ROKEACH, S. The legitimation of violence. In J.F. Short and M.E. Wolfgang (Eds.), *Collective violence.* Chicago: Aldine Publishing Co., 1972.

BENEDICT, R. *Race: Science and politics.* New York: Viking Press, 1959.

BLAKESLEE, T.R. *The right brain: A new understanding of the unconscious mind and its creative powers.* Garden City, N.Y.: Anchor Press, 1980.

BLOCK, S., & REDDAWAY, P. *Psychiatric terror: How Soviet psychiatry is used to suppress dissent.* New York: Basic Books, 1977.

BLUMENTHAL, M.D. *et al. Justifying violence: Attitudes of American men.* Ann Arbor, Mich.: University of Michigan, 1972.

BLUMENTHAL, M.D. *et al. More about justifying violence: Methodological studies of attitudes and behavior.* Ann Arbor, Mich.: University of Michigan, 1975.

BOBRAKOV, YURI. War propaganda: A serious crime against humanity. In M.H. Prosser (Ed.), *Intercommunication among nations and people.* New York: Harper and Row, 1973.

BOIS, J.S. *The art of awareness.* Dubuque, Iowa: Wm. C. Brown, 1978.

BOSMAJIAN, H. *The language of oppression.* Washington, D.C.: Public Affairs Press, 1974.

BOSMAJIAN, H. Sexism in the language of legislatures and the courts. In A.P. Nilson (Ed.), *Sexism and language.* Urbana, Ill.: National Council of Teachers of English, 1977.

BOURNE, G.H. (Ed.). *Progress in ape research.* New York: Academic Press, 1977.

BOWERS, J.W., & OCHS, D.J. *The rhetoric of agitation and control.* Reading, Mass.: Addison-Wesley, 1971.

BOYER, W. *Education for annihilation.* Honolulu: Hogarth Press–Hawaii, 1972.

BREMBECK, W.L., & HOWELL, W.S. *Persuasion: A means of social influence.* Englewood Cliffs, N.J.: Prentice-Hall, 1976.

BURRESS, L. A brief report of the 1977 NCTE censorship survey. In J.E. Davis (Ed.), *Dealing with censorship.* Urbana, Ill.: National Council of Teachers of English, 1979.

CARPENTER, E. *Oh, what a blow that phantom gave me.* New York: Bantam, 1973.

CARROLL, J.B. (Ed.). *Language, thought, and reality: Selected writings of Benjamin Lee Whorf.* Cambridge, Mass.: M.I.T. Press, 1956.

CHAFETZ, J. *Masculine/feminine or human?* Itasca, Ill.: F.E. Peacock Publishers, Inc., 1974.

CHASE, S. *Power of Words.* New York: Harcourt Brace Jovanovich, 1954.

CHASE, S. *The tyranny of words.* New York: Harcourt Brace Jovanovich, 1938.

CLARK, D.G., & BLANKENBURG, W.B. *You and media: Mass communication and society.* San Francisco: Canfield Press, 1973.

CLARKE, R. *The science of war and peace.* New York: McGraw-Hill, 1972.

CONDON, J. *Semantics and communication.* New York: Macmillan, 1975.

COREA, G. *The hidden malpractice.* New York: Morrow, 1977.

DALE, P.S. *Language development: Structure and function.* Hinsdale, Ill.: The Dryden Press, 1972.

DE CROW, K. *Sexist justice.* New York: Random House, 1974.

DE VITO, J. *The psychology of speech and language: An introduction to psycholinguistics.* New York: Random House, 1970.

DOHRENWEND, B.P., & DOHRENWEND, B.S. *Social status and psychological disorder: A causal inquiry.* New York: John Wiley, 1969.

DONOVAN, J.A. *Militarism, U.S.A.* New York: Scribner's, 1970.

EDGERTON, R.B. *The cloak of competence: Stigma in the lives of the retarded.* Berkeley: University of California Press, 1967.

EHRLICH, P.R., & FELDMAN, S. *The race bomb.* New York: Quadrangle/The New York Times, 1977.

ERWIN, E. *Behavior therapy: Scientific, philosophical, and moral foundations.* Cambridge, England: Cambridge University Press, 1978.

FARB, P. *Humankind.* New York: Bantam, 1980.

FARB, P. *Word play: What happens when people talk.* New York: Bantam, 1973.

FARBEROW, N.L. (Ed.). *Taboo topics.* New York: Atherton Press, 1963.

FARMER, J.S., & HENLEY, W.E. *Slang and its analogues.* New York: Kraus Reprint Corp., 1965.

FISHMAN, J.A. *Sociolinguistics: A brief introduction.* Rowley, Mass.: Newbury House, 1972.

FRANK, J. *Persuasion and healing: A comparative study of psychotherapy.* Baltimore, Md.: Johns Hopkins University Press, 1973.

FRANK, J. *Sanity and survival: Psychological aspects of war and peace.* New York: Vintage, 1967.

FREUD, S. *Totem and taboo* (J. Strachey, Ed. and trans.). New York: Norton, 1950.

GAMBINO, R. Watergate lingo: A language of non-responsibility. In H. Rank (Ed.), *Language and public policy.* Urbana, Ill.: National Council of Teachers of English, 1974.

GLESSING, R.J. *The underground press in America.* Bloomington, Ind.: Indiana University Press, 1970.

GOFFMAN, E. *Stigma: Notes on the management of spoiled identity.* Englewood Cliffs, N.J.: Prentice-Hall, 1963.

GOLD, M. *Delinquent behavior in an American city.* Belmont, Calif.: Brooks/Cole, 1970.

GOLDBERG, I. *The wonder of words: An introduction for everyman.* New York: D. Appleton-Century, 1938.

GOODHEART, E. The rhetoric of violence. In R. Liedlich (Ed.), *Coming to terms with language.* New York: John Wiley, 1973.

GORMAN, M. *General semantics and contemporary Thomism.* Lincoln, Neb.: University of Nebraska Press, 1962.

GREBLER, L. *et al. The Mexican-American people: The nation's second largest minority.* New York: Free Press, 1970.

GROSS, M. *The psychological society.* New York: Random House, 1978.

GROSS, R. On language pollution. In R.D. Liedlich (Ed.), *Coming to terms with language: An anthology.* New York: John Wiley, 1973.

GRUNBERGER, R. *A social history of the Third Reich.* London: Weidenfeld and Nicolson, 1971.

HARTOGS, R. *Four-letter word games.* New York: Dell Pub. Co., Inc., 1967.

HAYAKAWA, S.I. *Language in thought and action.* New York: Harcourt Brace Jovanovich, 1972.

HERRIOT, J. *All things bright and beautiful.* New York: Bantam, 1973.

HITLER, A. *Mein Kampf.* New York: Stackpole Sons, 1939.

HOBBS, L. *Love and liberation.* New York: McGraw-Hill, 1970.

HOSOKAWA, B. *Nisei: The quiet Americans.* New York: Morrow, 1969.

JENKINSON, E.B. Dirty dictionaries, obscene nursery rhymes, and burned books. In J.E. Davis (Ed.), *Dealing with censorship.* Urbana, Ill.: National Council of Teachers of English, 1979.

JENSEN, A.R. *Bias in mental testing.* New York: Free Press, 1980.

JESPERSON, O. *The growth and structure of the English language.* New York: D. Appleton, 1923.

JESPERSON, O. *Language: Its nature, development and origin.* New York: Holt, Rinehart & Winston, 1922.

JOHNSON, D.W. & JOHNSON, F.P. *Joining together: Group therapy and group skills.* Englewood Cliffs, N.J.: Prentice-Hall, 1975.

JOHNSON, W. *People in quandaries.* New York: Harper, 1946.

JOHNSON, W., & MOELLER, D. *Living with change: The semantics of coping.* New York: Harper & Row, 1972.

KATZ, D., & BRALY, K.W. Verbal stereotype and social prejudice. In M. Fishbein (Ed.), *Readings in attitude theory and measurement.* New York: John Wiley, 1967.

KING, R.G. *Fundamentals of human communication.* New York: Macmillan, 1979.

KLUCKHOLN, C. *Mirror for man.* New York: McGraw-Hill, 1949.

KORZYBSKI, A. *Science and sanity: An introduction to non-Aristotelian systems and general semantics.* Lakeville, Conn.: The International Non-Aristotelian Library, 1933.

KROUT, J. *United States since 1865.* New York: Barnes & Noble, 1965.

LABOV, W. *Sociolinguistic patterns.* Philadelphia: University of Pennsylvania Press, 1972.

LEACH, E. Anthropological abuses of language: Animal categories and verbal abuse. In E. Lenneberg (Ed.), *New directions in the study of language.* Cambridge, Mass.: M.I.T. Press, 1964.

LEGAULT, A., & LINDSEY, G. *The dynamics of the nuclear balance.* Ithaca, N.Y.: Cornell University Press, 1976.

LEVY, G.E. *Ghetto school: Class warfare in an elementary school.* New York: Pegasus, 1970.

LIFTON, R.J. Existential evil. In N. Sanford *et al.* (Eds.), *Sanctions for evil: Sources of social destructiveness.* Boston: Beacon Press, 1971.

MACCOBY, E., & JACKLIN, C. *The psychology of sex differences.* Stanford, Calif.: Stanford University Press, 1974.

MANDELBAUM, D.G. (Ed.) *Selected writings of Edward Sapir.* Los Angeles: University of California Press, 1949.

MANN, J. *Changing human behavior.* New York: Scribner's, 1965.

MEIER, A., & RUDWICK, E. *From plantation to ghetto.* New York: Hill and Wang, 1966.

MENNINGER, K. *The vital balance: The life process in mental health and illness.* New York: Viking, 1963.

MERTON, T. War and the crisis of language. In R. Ginsberg (Ed.), *The critique of war.* Chicago: Henry Regnery, 1969.

MICHENER, J.A. *Kent State: What happened and why.* New York: Random House, 1971.

MILLER, C., & SWIFT, K. *Words and women: New language in new times.* New York: Anchor Press, 1977.

MONTAGU, A. *The anatomy of swearing.* New York: Macmillan, 1967.

MONTAGU, A. *Man's most dangerous myth: The fallacy of race.* New York: Oxford University Press, 1974.

MONTAGU, A. *The natural superiority of women.* New York: Macmillan, 1968.

MORAN, T.P. The language of education. In N. Postman *et al.* (Eds.), *Language in America.* New York: Pegasus, 1969.

MURRAY, R. *Red scare: A study of national hysteria, 1919–1920.* New York: McGraw-Hill, 1955.

NILSEN, A.P. Sexism as shown through the English vocabulary. In A.P. Nilsen, *et al.* (Eds.), *Sexism and language*. Urbana, Ill.: National Council of Teachers of English, 1977.

NUNNALLY, J. *Popular conceptions of mental health*. New York: Holt, Rinehart & Winston, 1961.

OGDEN, C.K., & RICHARDS, I.A. *The meaning of meaning: A study of the influence of language upon thought and of the science of symbolism*. New York: Harcourt Brace Jovanovich, 1923.

OHMANN, R. Grammar and meaning. *The American heritage dictionary of the English language*. New York: Houghton Mifflin, 1969, pp. xxxi–xxxiv.

OPTON, EDWARD M. It never happened and besides they deserved it. In N. Sanford (Ed.), *Sanctions for evil: Sources of social destructiveness*. Boston: Beacon, 1971.

OSGOOD, C.E., SUCI, G., & TANNENBAUM, P. *The measurment of meaning*. Urbana, Ill.: University of Illinois Press, 1957.

PELLETIER, K.R. *Mind as healer, mind as slayer*. New York: Dell Pub. Co., Inc., 1977.

POSTMAN, N. *Crazy talk, stupid talk*. New York: Dell Pub. Co., Inc., 1976.

President's Commission on Mental Health. *Task panel reports*, Vol. 1–4. Washington, D.C.: U.S. Government Printing Office, 1978.

PRESTON, I.L. *The great American blow-up: Puffery in advertising and selling*. Madison, Wis.: University of Wisconsin Press, 1975.

RANK, H. (Ed.), *Language and public policy*. Urbana, Ill.: National Council of Teachers of English, 1974.

RENNER, K.E. *What's wrong with the mental health movement?* Chicago: Nelson-Hall, 1975.

RESTAK, R.M. *The brain: The last frontier*. New York: Warner Books, Inc., 1979.

RIVERS, W.L., & SCHRAMM, W. *Responsibility in mass communication*. New York: Harper & Row, Pub., 1969.

ROSENTHAL, R., & JACOBSEN, L. *Pygmalion in the classroom: Teacher expectation and pupils' intellectual development*. New York: Holt, Rinehart & Winston, 1968.

RUBIN, S. *Crime and juvenile delinquency*. New York: Oceana, 1958.

SAGARIN, E. *The anatomy of dirty words*. New York: Lyle Stuart, 1962.

SARTRE, J-P. *Being and nothingness: An essay on phenomenological ontology* (H. Barnes, trans.). New York: Philosophical Library, 1956.

SCHEFF, T.J. *Labeling madness*. Englewood Cliffs, N.J.: Prentice-Hall, 1975.

SCHRAG, P. *Mind control*. New York: Dell Pub. Co., Inc., 1978.

SENDEN, M.V. *Raum und gestaltauffassung bei operierten blindgeborenen vor und nach operation*. Leipzig: Barth, 1932.

SIEGLER, M., & OSMOND, H. *Models of madness, models of medicine.* New York: Macmillan, 1974.

SILBERMAN, C.E. *Crisis in the classroom: The remaking of American education.* New York: Random House, 1970.

SLATER, J. Population defense reconsidered: Is the ABM really inconsistent with stability? In R. Harkavy and E.A. Kolodziej (Eds.), *American security policy and policy-making.* Lexington, Mass.: Lexington Books, 1980.

SROLE, L. *et al. Mental health in the metropolis: The midtown Manhattan study.* New York: McGraw-Hill, 1962.

STARK, R. Protest + police = riot. In J. McEvoy and A. Miller (Eds.), *Black power and student rebellion.* Belmont, Calif.: Wadsworth, 1969.

STOHL, M. *War and domestic violence: The American capacity for repression and reaction.* Beverly Hills, Calif.: Sage Publications, 1976.

SZASZ, T.S. *The manufacture of madness.* New York: Dell Pub. Co., Inc., 1970.

SZASZ, T.S. *The second sin.* New York: Doubleday, 1973.

TENENBAUM, F. *Over 55 is not illegal.* Boston: Houghton Mifflin, 1979.

THORNDIKE, R.L. Review of Rosenthal, R., & Jacobsen, L. *Pygmalion in the classroom. American Educational Research Journal,* 1968, *5,* 708–711.

THORNE, B., & HENLEY, N. *Language and sex: Difference and dominance.* Rowley, Mass.: Newbury House Publishers, Inc., 1975.

TOLSTOY, L. *On civil disobedience and non-violence.* New York: New American Library, 1968.

TORREY, E.F. *The death of psychiatry.* Radnor, Penn.: Chilton Book Co., 1974.

TURNBULL, C.M. *Tradition and change in African tribal life.* New York: Avon, 1966.

VERNON, P.E. *Intelligence: Heredity and environment.* San Francisco: W.H. Freeman and Company, 1979.

WALKER, D. *Rights in conflict.* New York: New American Library, 1968.

WALUM, L. *The dynamics of sex and gender: A sociological perspective.* Chicago: Rand McNally, 1977.

WELLS, D.A. *The war myth.* New York: Pegasus, 1967.

WESTING, A.H. The military impact on the human environment. In SIPRI Yearbook 1978, *World Armaments and Disarmament.* London: Taylor and Francis, 1978.

WESTLEY, W.A. *Violence and the police: A sociological study of law, custom, and morality.* Cambridge, Mass.: M.I.T. Press, 1970.

WHORF, B.L. *Collected papers on metalinguistics.* Washington, D.C.: Dept. of State, Foreign Service Institute, 1952.

WITKIN, H.A., *et al. Personality through perception.* New York: Harper & Row, 1954.

WOLFRAM, W., & FASOLD, R.W. *The study of social dialects in American English.* Englewood Cliffs, N.J.: Prentice-Hall, 1974.

WOOD, A.L. *Deviant behavior and control strategies.* Lexington, Mass.: Heath, 1974.

WOOD, B.S. *Children and communication: Verbal and nonverbal language development.* Englewood Cliffs, N.J.: Prentice-Hall, 1976.

YOUNG, W. *Eros denied.* New York: Grove Press, 1964.

ZIMBARDO, P., & RUCH, F. *Psychology and life.* Glenview, Ill.: Scott, Foresman, 1977.

PERIODICALS

ABRAMOWITZ, S.F., *et al.* The politics of clinical judgment: What nonliberal examiners infer about women who do not stifle themselves. *Journal of Consulting and Clinical Psychology,* 1973, *41,* 385–391.

BATE, B. Nonsexist language use in transition. *Journal of Communication,* 1978, *28* (1), 139–49.

BAUDHUIN, E.S. Obscene language and evaluative response: An empirical study. *Psychological Reports,* 1973, *32,* 399–402.

BEECHER, H.K. Generalization from pain of various types and diverse origins. *Science,* 1959, *130,* 267–268.

The bell tolls for a galloping ghost. *Newsweek,* September 25, 1967, pp. 27–28.

BEM, S.L. Theory and measurement of androgyny: A reply to the Pedhazur–Tetenbaum and Locksley–Colten critiques. *Journal of Personality and Social Psychology,* 1979, *37,* 1047–54.

BERKO, J. The child's learning of English morphology. *Word,* 1958, *14,* 150–177.

BERNSTEIN, B. Elaborated and restricted codes: An outline. *Sociological Inquiry,* 1966, *36,* 254–261.

BERNSTEIN, B.J. Roosevelt, Truman, and the atomic bomb, 1941–1945: A reinterpretation. *Political Science Quarterly,* 1975, *90,* 23–65.

BIRNBAUM, D.W., *et al.* Children's stereotypes about sex differences in emotionality. *Sex Roles,* 1980, *6,* 435–440.

BLAUBERGS, M.S. Changing the sexist language: The theory behind the practice. *Psychology of Women Quarterly*, 1978, *2*, 244–261.

BOSMAJIAN, H. Freedom of speech and the language of oppression. *Western Journal of Speech*, 1978, *42*, 209–221.

BOSTAIN, J.C. Wishing will not make it so: A linguist takes on the grammarians. *Today's Education*, April–May, 1981, pp. 28G–31G.

BOSTROM, R.N., BASEHEART, J.R., & ROSSITER, C.M. The effects of three types of profane language in persuasive messages. *Journal of Communication*, 1973, *23*, 461–475.

BREGGINS, P., & GREENBERG, D. Return of the lobotomy. *Congressional Record*, March 13, 1972, pp. 8167–8168.

BREGGINS, P. The return of lobotomy and psychosurgery. *Congressional Record*, February 24, 1972, pp. 5567–5577.

BRICKLIN, M. Things here and there. *Prevention*, 1977, pp. 80–86.

BRODEUR, D.W. The effects of stimulant and tranquilizer placebos on healthy subjects in a real life situation. *Psychopharmacologia*, 1965, *7*, 444–452.

BROPHY, J., & GOOD, T. Teachers' communication of differential expectations for children's performance. *Journal of Educational Psychology*, 1970, *61*, 365–374.

BROSS, I.D.J., *et al.* How information is carried in scientific sub-languages. *Science*, 1972, *176*, 1303–1307.

BROSS, I.D.J. Prisoners of jargon. *American Journal of Public Health and the Nation's Health*, 1964, *54*, 918–927.

BROVERMAN, I., *et al.* Sex-role stereotypes and clinical judgments of mental health. *Journal of Consulting and Clinical Psychology*, 1970, *34*, 1–7.

BROWN, R.W., & LENNEBERG, E.H. A study in language and cognition. *Journal of Abnormal and Social Psychology*, 1954, *49*, 454–462.

BUCKLEY, T. A voice of reason among the nuclear warriors. *Quest*, March, 1981, pp. 17–20.

CAMERON, P. Frequency and kinds of words in various social settings, or what the hell's going on? *Pacific Sociological Review*, 1969, *12*, 101–104.

CARMICHAEL, L., HOGAN, H.P., & WALTER, A.A. An experimental study of the effect of language on the representation of visually perceived form. *Journal of Experimental Psychology*, 1932, *15*, 73–86.

CHASE-MARSHALL, J. Drawing better with half a brain. *Us*, March 7, 1978, pp. 44–45.

CONKLIN, N.F. Toward a feminist analysis of linguistic behavior. *The University of Michigan papers in women's studies*, 1974, *1*, 51–73.

CONOVER, P.J., *et al.* Mirror images in Americans' perceptions of nations and leaders during the Iranian hostage crisis. *Journal of Peace Research,* 1980, *17,* 325–37.

COUGHLIN, W.J. The great mokusatsu mistake. *Harper's Magazine,* March, 1953.

CRUMPTON, E., *et al.* How patients and normals see the mental patient. *Journal of Clinical Psychology,* 1967, *23,* 46–49.

Cutting Words. *Time,* March 4, 1966, p. 56.

DEAN, J. Rituals of the herd. *Rolling Stone,* October 7, 1976, 38–58.

ELLIS, A. Should some people be labeled mentally ill? *Journal of Consulting Psychology,* 1967, *31,* 435–446.

FARINA, A., *et al.* Mental illness and the impact of believing others know about it. *Journal of Abnormal Psychology,* 1971, *77,* 1–5.

FARINA, A., *et al.* The role of stigma and set in interpersonal interaction. *Journal of Abnormal Psychology,* 1966, *71,* 421–428.

FARINA, A., & RING, K. The influence of perceived mental illness on interpersonal relations. *Journal of Abnormal Psychology,* 1965, *70,* 47–51.

FEINBLATT, J.A., & GOLD, A.R. Sex roles and the psychiatric referral process. *Sex Roles,* 1976, *2,* 109–122.

FILLENBAUM, S. Verbal satiation and the exploration of meaning relations. In K. Salzinger and S. Salzinger (Eds.), *Research in verbal behavior and some neurophysiological implications.* New York: Academic Press, 1967.

FISHMAN, J. A systematization of the Whorfian hypothesis. *Behavioral Science,* 1960, *5,* 323–339.

FLEMING, J.D. The state of the apes. *Psychology Today,* January, 1974. 31–38ff.

FRIEDMAN, C.T., *et al.* The role of expectation in treatment for psychotic patients. *American Journal of Psychotherapy,* 1980, *34,* 188–196.

FOREIT, K.G., *et al.* Sex bias in the newspaper treatment of male-centered and female-centered news stories. *Sex Roles,* 1980, *6,* 475–481.

GALTON, L. A serious threat to the elderly: Misdiagnosis of senility blights the last years of many with treatable ailments. *Parade,* November 4, 1979, pp. 7–11.

GAYLIN, J. How hints are transformed into facts. *Psychology Today,* April, 1976, p. 114.

GOLD, M., & WILLIAMS, J. National study of the aftermath of apprehension. *Prospectus,* 1969, *3,* 3–12.

GOLEMAN, D. Who's mentally ill? *Psychology Today,* January, 1978, pp. 34–41.

GOVE, W. Mental illness and psychiatric treatment among women. *Psychology of Women Quarterly,* 1980, *4,* 345–362.

GREENBERG, B.S. The effects of language intensity modification on perceived verbal aggressiveness. *Communication Monographs,* 1976, *43,* 130–139.

HARRISON, S.I., & HINSHAW, M.W. When children use obscene language. *Medical Aspects of Human Sexuality,* 1968, *2,* 6–11.

HASKETT, M.S. An investigation of the relationship between teacher expectancy and pupil achievement in the special education class. *Dissertation Abstracts,* 1969, *29,* 4348–4349.

HERMAN, D.T., LAWLESS, R.H., & MARSHALL, R.W. Variables in the effect of language on the reproduction of visually perceived forms. *Perceptual and Motor Skills,* 1957, *7,* 171–186.

HOIJER, H. Cultural implications of some Navaho linguistic categories. *Language,* 1951, *27,* 111–120.

HORNE, A. Verdun—The reason why. *The New York Times Magazine,* February 20, 1966, p. 42.

JONES, R.L. Labels and stigma in special education. *Exceptional Children,* 1972, *38,* 553–564.

KANFER, S. Sispeak: A msguided attempt to change herstory. *Time,* October 23, 1972, p. 79.

KARNOW, S. Vietnam: Legacy of desolation. *The New Republic,* March 16, 1974, pp. 18–19.

KATZ, D., & BRALY, K.W. Racial stereotypes of one hundred college students. *Journal of Abnormal and Social Psychology,* 1933, *28,* 280–90.

KELLEY, H.H. The warm–cold variable in first impressions of persons. *Journal of Personality,* 1950, *18,* 431–439.

KELMAN, H., & LAWRENCE, L. American response to the trial of Lt. William L. Calley. *Psychology Today,* 1972, pp. 41–45ff.

Killing laughter. *Time,* August 2, 1976, p. 58.

KNIGHT, J.A. Holistic health: No stranger to psychiatry. *Journal of Clinical Psychiatry,* 1980, *41,* 38–39.

KOCHMAN, T. "Rapping" in the black ghetto. *Trans-action,* 1969, *6,* 26–34.

KORSCH, B.M., & NEGRETE, V.F. Doctor–patient communication. *Scientific American,* 1972, *227,* 66–73.

LAMBERT, W.E., & JAKOBOVITS, L.A. Verbal satiation and changes in the intensity of meaning. *Journal of Experimental Psychology,* 1960, *60,* 376–383.

LANGER, E.J., & ABELSON, R.A. A patient by any other name. Clinician group differences in labeling bias. *Journal of Consulting and Clinical Psychology,* 1974, *42,* 4–9.

LANTZ, D.L., & STEFFLRE, V. Language and cognition revisited. *Journal of Abnormal and Social Psychology,* 1964, *49,* 454–462.

LARRABEE, E. The cultural context of sex censorship. *Law and Contemporary Problems,* 1955, *20,* 672–679.

LENNEBERG, E.H. Cognition in ethnolinguistics. *Language,* 1953, *29,* 463–471.

LENNEBERG, E.H. On explaining language. *Science,* 1969, *164,* 635–643.

LENNEBERG, E.H. A probabilistic approach to language learning. *Behavioral Science,* 1957, *2,* 1–12.

LEWALLEN, J. Ecocide: Clawmarks on the yellow face. *Earth,* April, 1972, 36–43.

LEWIS, T. The semantics of psychiatric labels. *Et cetera,* 1978, 175–183.

LIFTON, R.J. The "gook syndrome" and "numbed warfare." *Saturday Review,* November 18, 1972, pp. 66–71.

LONDON, I.D. A Russian report on the postoperative newly seeing. *American Journal of Psychology,* 1960, *73,* 478–482.

LUBORSKY, L., *et al.* Comparative studies of psychotherapies. *Archives of General Psychiatry,* 1975, *32,* 995–1008.

LUBORSKY, L. Research cannot yet influence clinical practice. *International Journal of Psychiatry,* 1969, *7,* 135–140.

LUMSDEN, M. The UN conference on inhumane weapons. *Journal of Peace Research,* 1979, *16,* 289–292.

MANSSON, H.H. Justifying the final solution. *Omega,* 1972, *3,* 79–87.

MAZER, M. Parapsychiatric events as expressions of psychiatric disorder. *Archives of General Psychiatry,* 1972, *27,* 270–273.

MENDEL, W.M. The phenomenon of interpretation. *American Journal of Psychoanalysis,* 1964, *24,* 184–190.

MERTON, R. The self-fulfilling prophecy. *Antioch Review,* 1948, *8,* 193–210.

MOORE, M.S. Some myths about "mental illness." *Archives of General Psychiatry,* 1975, *32,* 1483–1497.

MYERSON, A. The attitude of neurologists, psychiatrists, and psychologists toward psychoanalysis. *American Journal of Psychiatry,* 1939, *96,* 623–641.

OPTON, E.M., & DUCKLES, R. Mental gymnastics on Mylai. *The New Republic,* February 21, 1970, pp. 14–16.

Organic foods: Merchandizing Health. *Consumer Reports,* July, 1980, pp. 413–414.

OSGOOD, C.E. Cognitive dynamics in the conduct of human affairs. *Public Opinion Quarterly,* 1960, *24,* 365–371.

Patient's rights: What to ask of your doctor—and why. *Good Housekeeping,* September, 1978, pp. 253–254.

PATTERSON, F. Conversations with a gorilla. *National Geographic*, October 1978, 438–465.

Peace with honor. *The New Republic*, March 9, 1974, p. 4.

Physicians' plea: Ban the bomb. *Time*, January 12, 1981, p. 22.

Police: Under fire, fighting back. *U.S. News and World Report*, April 3, 1978, pp. 37–45.

POMERANTZ, H., & BRESLIN, S. Judicial humour—construction of a statute. *Criminal Law Quarterly*, 1965, *8*, 137–139.

PREMACK, D. The education of Sarah. *Psychology Today*, 1970, *4*, 54–58.

The public disillusioned. *Time*, May 20, 1974, pp. 20–22.

RAPPEPORT, J.E., & LASSEN, G. Dangerousness: Arrest rate comparison of discharged patients and the general population. *American Journal of Psychiatry*, 1965, *121*, 776–783.

READ, A.W. An obscenity symbol. *American Speech*, 1934, *9*, 264–278.

RICE, B. Can psychiatrists spot "dangerous" defendants? *Psychology Today*, December, 1977, p. 91.

ROSENHAN, D.L. On being sane in insane places. *Science*, 1973, *179*, 250–258.

ROSS, H.E. Patterns of swearing. *Discovery*, November, 1960, pp. 479–81.

ROSSMAN, P.L. Organic diseases simulating functional disorders. *GP*, August, 1963, pp. 78–83.

ROTHWELL, J.D. Verbal obscenity: Time for second thoughts. *Western Speech*, 1971, *35*, 231–242.

RUMBAUGH, D.M., *et al.* Reading and sentence completion by a chimpanzee. *Science*, 1973, *182*, 731–733.

RUTZICK, M.C. Offensive language and the evolution of First Amendment protection. *Harvard Civil Rights–Civil Liberties Law Review*, 1974, *9*, 1–28.

SAPIR, E. Conceptual categories in primitive languages. *Science*, 1931, *74*, 578.

SARBIN, T.R., & MANCUSO, J.C. Failure of a moral enterprise: Attitudes of the public toward mental illness. *Journal of Consulting and Clinical Psychology*, 1970, *35*, 159–173.

SCHELL, O. Pop me some dinks. *The New Republic*, January 3, 1970, pp. 19–21.

SCHULTZ, M.R. Rape is a four-letter word. *Etc.*, 1975, *32*, 65–69.

SCHWARTZ, A.E. Androgyny and the art of loving. *Psychotherapy: Theory, Research, and Practice*, 1979, *16*, 405–408.

SCHWARTZ, R.A. Psychiatry's drift away from medicine. *American Journal of Psychiatry*, 1974, *131*, 129–133.

SCHWARTZ, R.O., & SKOLNICK, J.K. Two studies of legal stigma. *Social Problems*, 1962, *10*, 133–142.

SECORD, P.F., BEVAN, W., & KATZ, B. The negro stereotype and perceptual accentuation. *Journal of Abnormal and Social Psychology*, 1956, *53*, 78–83.

SELIGMAN, D. A special kind of rebellion. *Fortune*, January, 1969, pp. 70–71ff.

SHAH, S.A. Dangerousness and civil commitment of the mentally ill: Some public policy considerations. *American Journal of Psychiatry*, 1975, *132*, 501–505.

SHAPIRO, A. Placebo effects in medicine, psychotherapy, and psychoanalysis. In A.E. Bergin and S.L. Garfield (Eds.), *Handbook of psychotherapy and behavior change: Empirical evidence*. New York: John Wiley, 1971.

SHAPIRO, D.A. Science and psychotherapy: The state of the art. *The British Journal of Medical Psychology*, 1980, *53*, 1–10.

SHEILS, M., *et al.* Searching for a strategy. *Newsweek*, June 8, 1981, pp. 30–39.

SIVARD, R.L. The arms race: What it costs. *The New Republic*, January 4, 1975, pp. 9–11.

SMITH, J. Ego-dystonic homosexuality. *Comprehensive Psychiatry*, 1980, *21*, 119–123.

SPENCE, J., *et al.* Ratings of self and peers on sex role attributes and their relation to self-esteem and conceptions of masculinity and femininity. *Journal of Personality and Social Psychology*, 1975, *32*, 29–39.

SPITZER, R.L., *et al.* Clinical criteria for psychiatric diagnosis and DSM-III *American Journal of Psychiatry*, 1975, *132*, 1187–1192.

SPITZER, R.L., *et al.* DSM-III: The major achievements and an overview. *American Journal of Psychiatry*, 1980, *137*, 151–164.

SPITZER, R.L., *et al.* Research diagnostic criteria: Rationale and reliability. *Archives of General Psychiatry*, 1978, *35*, 773–782.

SPITZER, R.L., & FLEISS, J.A. Re-analysis of the reliability of psychiatric diagnosis. *British Journal of Psychiatry*, 1974, *125*, 341–347.

STEADMAN, H.J. The psychiatrist as a conservative agent of social change. *Social Problems*, 1972, *20*, 263–271.

STEFFENSMEIER, D.J., & KRAMER, J.H. The differential impact of criminal stigmatization on male and female felons. *Sex Roles*, 1980, *6*, 1–8.

STONE, L. On the principal obscene word of the English language. *The International Journal of Psychoanalysis*, 1954, *35*, 435–482.

TEMERLIN, M.K. Suggestion effects in psychiatric diagnosis. *Journal of Nervous and Mental Disease*, 1968, *147*, 349–358.

TRINGO, J.L. The hierarchy of preference toward disability groups. *The Journal of Special Education*, 1970, *4*, 295–306.

TURNBULL, C.M. Some observations regarding the experiences and behavior of Bambuti pygmies. *American Journal of Psychology*, 1961, *74*, 304–308.

WESOLOWSKI, J.W. Obscene, indecent, or profane broadcast language as construed by the federal courts. *Journal of Broadcasting,* 203–219.

WHITE, R.K. Misperception in the Arab–Israeli conflict. *Journal of Social Issues,* 1977, *33,* 190–208.

ZELLMAN, G.L. Antidemocratic beliefs: A survey and some explanations. *Journal of Social Issues,* 1975, *31,* 31–53.

NEWSPAPER ARTICLES

Antishark dye fails test—They eat it. *The Oregonian,* October 5, 1976, p. A10.

Children labeled slow learners may be deaf instead. *Eugene Register-Guard,* May 20, 1978, p. 13C.

FCC allowed to ban words. *Eugene Register-Guard,* July 3, 1978, p. 1A.

The Gallup Poll, "Image of Red Powers." *The Santa Barbara News-Press,* June 26, 1966, p. 14.

Hatfield amplifies views on SALT II. *Eugene Register-Guard,* April 1, 1979, p. 27A.

HILLINGER, C. Stanford asks "taking gorillas," researcher to leave. *Eugene Register-Guard,* October 26, 1979, p. 11C.

NEWHALE, B.F. Perrier water is in good taste, but does it taste good? *The Herald,* August 19, 1980, p. 8A.

The new permanence. *Eugene Register-Guard,* August 30, 1975, p. 8A.

Papers cautious on quote. *Oregonian,* October 5, 1976, p. A4.

Some media delete undeleted expletives. *Oregonian,* July 10, 1974, p. 20.

Text of Nixon's address on war decisions. *Eugene Register-Guard,* May 9, 1972, p. 6A.

WICKER, T. Nuclear debate full of baloney. *Eugene Register-Guard,* August 12, 1980, p. 14A.

LEGAL CASES

Ginsberg v. *New York* 390 U.S. 707 (1968).

Grove Press, Inc. v. *Christenberry* 276 F. 2nd 433 (2nd Cir. 1960).

Grove Press, Inc. v. *Gerstein* 378 U.S. 577 (1964).

Hoyt v. *Florida* 368 U.S. 57 (1961).

In re *Lockwood,* 154 U.S. 116 (1898).

Jenkins v. *Georgia* 94 S. ct. 2750 (1974).

Memoirs v. *Massachusetts* 383 U.S. 413 (1966).

Miller v. *California* 413 U.S. 15 (1973).

Papish v. *the University of Missouri* 410 U.S. 667 (1973).

Roth v. *United States* 354 U.S. 476 (1957).

MISCELLANEOUS

BEM, S. *Psychology looks at sex roles: Where have all the androgynous people gone?* Paper presented at University of California—Los Angeles Symposium on Women, May 1972.

CARLSON, J.G., & WOOD, R.D. *Need the final solution be justified?* Unpublished manuscript, University of Hawaii, 1974.

HAAN, D.H. *Obscenity law since Miller: Another troublesome balancing formula.* Paper presented at the meeting of the Association for Education in Journalism, Seattle, August 1978.

HAZELTON, N., *et al. A survey and education plan around the issue of community care for the mentally ill: The Santa Clara County experience.* A monograph, Office of Communications, Health Education Section, California State Department of Health. July, 1975.

JONES, R.L. *New labels in old bags: Research on labeling blacks culturally disadvantaged, culturally deprived, and mentally retarded.* Paper presented at annual convention of Association of Black Psychologists, Miami Beach, September 1970.

KATZ, M.P. *The assessment and treatment of mental patients as a function of their attractiveness* (Ph.D. dissertation, Standard University, 1974).

LEWIS, J.J. *Reactions of the general public to obscenity at college demonstrations.* Paper presented at the meeting of the International Communication Association, Phoenix, April 1971.

LODLE, S.E. *Sexual and excretory vernacular: A delineative examination and empirical analysis of the nature, scope and function of taboo, exhibitory, euphemistic, and dysphemistic communication paradigms* (Master's Thesis, California State University, Long Beach, 1972).

MAZER, M. *Concepts of prevention in rural mental health services.* Paper presented at the meeting of the Summer Study Program in Rural Mental Health, University of Wisconsin Extension, Madison, June 3–7, 1974.

NILSEN, A.P. Grammatical gender and its relationship to the equal treatment of males and females in children's books. (Ph.D. dissertation, University of Iowa, 1973).

NYKODYM, D., & BOYD, A. *Expletive deleted: A study of language usage.* Paper presented at the meeting of the International Communication Association, Chicago, April 1975.

POWELL, J.V. *Saying the unspeakable: The euphemism.* Paper presented at the Western Conference on Linguistics, Eugene, Oregon, October 19–20, 1972.

PREMACK, D. *A function analysis of language.* Paper presented at the meeting of the American Psychological Association, Washington, D.C., 1969.

RABKIN, J.G. *Public attitudes about mental illness: Literature review and recommendations.* Unpublished paper prepared for the Task Panel on Public Attitudes and Use of the Media for Promotion of Mental Health, President's Commission on Mental Health; Epidemiology of Mental Disorders Research Unit, Psychiatric Institute, New York State Department of Mental Hygiene, July 1977.

ROSSITER, C.M., & BOSTROM, R. *Profanity, justification and source credibility.* Paper presented at the meeting of the National Society for the Study of Communications, San Francisco, April 1969.

ROTHWELL, J.D. *Verbal obscenity: Constructing and testing a theoretical model.* (Ph.D. dissertation, University of Oregon, 1977).

SCHNEIDER, J.W., & HACKER, S.L. *Sex role imagery and the use of the generic "man" in introductory texts: A case in the sociology of sociology.* Paper presented at the meeting of the American Sociological Association, New Orleans, August 1972.